Maria & The Devil

First published in 2013 by TheNeverPress
Second edition published 2021

A CIP record of this book is available from the British Library.

ISBN 9780956742216

Cover designed by Leighton Johns: *www.leightonjohns.co.uk*

@TheNeverPress

www.theneverpress.com

For my family

"There is no sadness greater than in misery
to rehearse memories of joy"

Dante Alighieri

Maria

&

The Devil

PART ONE
Dangerous Lovers

CHAPTER ONE

The Sumner Farm, Montana, 1877

The Sumner residence was a single-storey log cabin on a flat plain just a day's trek from Hell's Gate Village by the Clark Fork river, in between the Rattlesnake Mountains to the north and the Bitterroot Mountains to the south.

Daniel and Clara Sumner with their newborn son Conrad lived in tranquil peace, isolated enough to be able to walk around freely and near enough to civilisation to not be forgotten. Their modest log cabin held a functional kitchen, a sitting room by an open fire, a room to the back which was a nursery for Conrad and adjacent to that, Daniel and Clara's bedroom with its easterly facing window, which let in too much light in the morning for Daniel and not enough for Clara. The Sumners were early rising folk. Their bed was made come 5.30am no matter the season and they took great pleasure in serving the Lord peacefully by enjoying the bounteous resources of the land and giving praise to Him with prayers of thanks and in the love they gave each other. They held hands when in town, talking freely and openly about any topic they wished, and they cared not for raised eyebrows of the townsfolk. Daniel and Clara did not believe that praise of the Lord should be sombre and serious as the world was hard and tough enough already, instead they believed in life and laughter. The Sumner household was a perfect slice of the world and they felt truly blessed to be alive and free.

The winter had come in strong on the heels of autumn and the barn that Daniel had been constructing beside their home had yet to be finished. The structure had been erected and was secure, however the roof was missing and Daniel desperately wanted to break the back of the work before winter tightened its grip. It was a race against time and so he rose even earlier and worked even later each day.

On this day, the sky was cloudless and the air biting. Daniel worked in the doorway of the barn, sawing furiously at a large beam. Inside the house, Clara sat in her rocking chair breastfeeding Conrad and looking at her man outside braving the elements to construct a larger, safer home for them all. She rocked slowly, draped in two thick shawls with Conrad suckling neatly and the fire next to her crackling away.

Clara looked down at the baby, gently holding onto her breast as he fed and she fell in love with him all over again. Conrad, with his tiny hands and his tiny ears. She pulled the shawl over his head so that only his cheek and little nose were visible. She looked back out to her man and said quietly to God, "I don't want anything more."

Daniel's work was back-breaking but he took to his task with great vigour, spurred on by the vision of the spring months when the barn would be finished and when he and Clara could take their supper out under the stars and watch as Conrad tried to walk and tumble onto the soft ground. He thought about that vision of heaven and also about the reality he was in. He imagined, correctly, that Clara was watching him work while she rocked their son to sleep. He hoped that she would see how hard he toiled and how dedicated he was. He prayed to God to enlighten her and show her that above all else, their welfare was his only thought. And God spoke to him and told him that it was so; thus his muscles did not ache from the work, his fingers did not grow numb from the cold and his lungs did not burn from the sharp winter air. He was so enraptured with his life and his work that he did not see the rider approaching from far over the plain, emerging from the blinding white snow like a drop of ink on a blank page.

From inside the house, and through the dull window pane, Clara could not see the rider. She could not see beyond Daniel working away by the barn. She began to whisper a lullaby to Conrad who had finished feeding and was dozing in her arms.

When I was a little boy, I lived by myself,
And all the bread and cheese I got I put upon a shelf;
The rats and the mice, they made such a strife,
I was forced to go to London to buy me a wife.
The streets were so broad, and the lanes were so narrow,
I was forced to bring my wife home in a wheelbarrow;

The wheelbarrow broke, and my wife had a fall,
And down came the wheelbarrow, wife and all.

Clara finished a third repetition and kissed the baby softly enough to keep him asleep, but tender enough to filter into his dream world and tell him that he was safe. She looked up and, through the window she finally saw the figure approaching Daniel. Her contented smile fell away and she stopped rocking in her chair.

Daniel's blade finally cut through the beam and the two lumps fell heavily into the snow. He stood tall and stretched, releasing the tension in his muscles. He exhaled and wiped the sweat from his brow. When he took his eyes from the heavens and back to the horizon, he saw the dark rider approaching some fifty yards away. Daniel's expression changed. The furrow in his brow from exertion disappeared and his breathing slowed. His eyes became sad and still.

The rider approached, cloaked in a thick black bear skin and wearing a wide brimmed hat which obscured his face. It mattered not to Daniel. He knew exactly who the rider was. Somehow The Devil had found Daniel Sumner. He sighed and turned to look at the house. He saw that Clara had risen from her chair and was looking out at the two men. Daniel's smile was loaded with melancholy and sorrow and he hoped that his regret and love would carry over the distance between them.

Inside the house, Clara only saw Daniel turn and look at her, his expression mired by the murky window. She held the baby tight to her breast and watched as Daniel turned from her to face the stranger. She watched as they engaged in conversation for a few moments and watched as Daniel slowly placed the saw across the bench and put his hands behind his back. For a few seconds she believed her dread at the stranger's arrival to be ill-founded. She was wrong. The stranger, lightning fast, swung what looked like a large rifle from his waist and crashed the butt into Daniel's head, splitting it open and sending him slumping down into the snow. Clara screamed, awakening Conrad and causing him to scream too. She pulled the baby in tightly and tried to smother his cries by shushing him. She looked out to see the stranger dragging Daniel into the barn by his feet, all the while looking over to the house, directly at her. She had to hide.

Daniel's vision returned and he saw, in his delirium, the structure of the barn overhead swinging and whirling as The Devil dragged him by his ankle. He tried to shout and protest but the pain in his head and jaw prevented him. He blinked rapidly, trying to pull his world into focus and snap his consciousness back into place. He had almost orientated himself when he saw, overhead, a rope ascend into the rafters, swing over a beam and hang down above him. The Devil stopped dragging him and Daniel knew what was about to happen. He began to shake his head and murmur a prayer to God to spare him and his family. The Devil bent down and picked Daniel up by the lapels. He was staring The Devil in the face and he could not quite believe his eyes. The Devil was a boy of no more than fifteen years of age: soft pale skin, blue eyes, blonde hair. Daniel tried to speak, but The Devil shushed him by stroking his face with one hand, while wrapping the noose around his neck with the other. Daniel looked deep into the boy's eyes searching for reason, or salvation. He saw no sympathy and no remorse. If the boy had feelings of compassion, then they were not for mankind. Daniel began to mouth his prayer once more as The Devil pulled down on the rope as if ringing a bell in a cathedral. Daniel shot up ten feet into the air, swaying, gurgling, thrashing, eyes bulging and hands clawing at his neck and the knot. The Devil tied the rope off and walked out of the barn, making towards the house. Daniel kicked and thrashed harder, desperate to break free and go to his family's aid, but his life force depleted all the quicker for his protestations.

Clara tried to stifle her sobs, but her whimpering could not be trammelled. The warmth of her breast and the closeness at which she held Conrad had assuaged his earlier screams and he had fallen back to sleep. After seeing her dearest love struck down, Clara had sought to hide under the bed, as she used to do as a child to escape her brothers and sisters when they came searching for her during their games of hide-and-seek. There were better places to hide, but in her primal fear she had instinctively gone there, back to the safe and happy place of her youth.

Clara held the baby tightly and looked out from under the hanging cotton valance. She saw the front door open and a pair of boots she knew were not Daniel's step across the threshold. They halted in the doorway and she knew that the stranger was on the hunt for her. The left foot tapped pensively, the spur chiming elegantly. She slowly lifted a hand off of Conrad's head and cupped her own mouth to stifle further any treacherous whimpers that might escape. The boots left the doorway and walked away into the kitchen. Clara looked at the open doorway and the thick snow outside. She thought about crawling out from under the bed and running out into the wild. But to where? She needed to leave. Terror was gripping her, but her practical nature fought back. She looked from under the bed to see if she could reach for some nearby shoes to better serve her escape through the snow. She saw none to hand, but instead saw the butt of Daniel's shotgun resting against the dresser. She could fight. She gently rested Conrad onto the boards under the bed and prepared to crawl out towards the gun by the dresser. She angled herself and threw a last look back towards the open doorway at the end of the hall.

The stranger's boots were there. She froze in terror. The boots walked up to the bed.

———⊗⊗⊗———

Daniel's vision was fading and his legs no longer thrashed. His fingers were raw and bleeding from pulling and scratching at the coarse rope. He was in his final moments when he saw The Devil walk out of the house, mount his horse and ride off into the blinding white plain without caring to look back. A spark of life ignited inside Daniel and he kicked and struggled harder. Above him, the beam began to creak and move. He struggled on.

———⊗⊗⊗———

Clara's hands quivered as they reached out and gripped onto the edge of a floorboard. Her knuckles bent and her fingers contorted as she managed to drag herself along the floor by her fingertips alone. All colour had fallen from her vision and the walls seemed to twist and contort as she moved slowly across the room. She could not quite understand why her dress felt so wet when it hadn't been raining and why breathing was becoming more and more laboured. Ahead of her, the brightness of the doorway seemed to her to be the gateway into heaven and she assumed that to gain entrance, one must be penitent and arrive on one's belly. She pulled herself towards the light and towards heaven, all the while her life blood flowing from the large gash across her throat.

———✇———

The beam cracked and Daniel fell to the ground, landing awkwardly on his ankles and buckling in pain. He crawled across the ground, still unable to remove the noose from his neck. Like his wife, he assumed the light of the doorway to be the entrance to heaven and as his life faded, he crawled out of the barn and like Clara who had dragged herself out of the house and onto the porch, he found himself not in heaven, but in a hell of freezing snow. Their eyes grew accustomed to the light. Clara saw the barn and Daniel dragging himself across the ground. Daniel saw Clara gurgling and spluttering as she slithered down the porch steps and onto the snow. He could see the blood from her neck seeping out. There was to be no salvation for the two lovers. Clara managed to crawl a few feet towards Daniel before finally stopping and rolling onto her back. Daniel crawled towards her, but his will finally left him and he slumped down face first into the snow, arms outstretched and tantalisingly close, yet agonisingly far from the touch of Clara's bloodstained fingers. They lay there in the snow, together and apart, and they both closed their eyes.

Twenty-One Years Later

CHAPTER TWO

The House in the Clearing

Maria rested her cheek on the kitchen counter and watched as the hobo spider approached. She remained unblinking as it crawled over the dirty plates on the other side of the sink, stopping only to inspect the three-day old residue embedded upon the china. The cold springtime air filtered underneath the crude window frame and tickled Maria's face and she felt a lock of her tied-back hair glide over her ear and gently tickle her neck. The draught fell down further over the counter and wrapped itself around her bare feet. She did not move. She did not blink. The spider continued its inspection of the dinner plates before moving off and continuing on its journey along the counter.

The creature soon reached the edge of the sink, the white ceramic basin presenting it with a great obstacle. Should it cross the narrow sink edge and risk sliding down into the basin and to its doom, or should it turn back and refuse the challenge? Maria hoped it would brave the test, cross over the sink and continue on its journey. She happily imprinted her own emotional desires onto the spider. She wanted it to dare to cross the basin. The spider stood on the edge for a few seconds.

Maria watched as it tentatively began walking along the edge of the sink. The spider took its time, cautious and seemingly aware that one wrong movement could send it sliding down into the inescapable basin. Maria focused her large, unblinking brown eyes on the creature as it precariously walked over the edge, slipping a few times but always managing to right itself, always managing to preserve itself and keep going forward. She watched as it made it all the way across the sink and come to rest on the other side of the counter just two feet from her face.

Maria breathed out and watched as the spider reacted to the change in the air. She could see the hairs on its legs flutter as her breath caressed it. The spider seemed to dig in. Hunched down, sensing its surroundings. It had traversed the deadly sink-edge, what now lay ahead for it? What other trap waited to be sprung? The spider crept forward slowly. Maria held her breath.

It crept forward, now just six inches from her face. Maria, slowly, lifted her arm from her side. She was holding a large carving knife. Without taking her eyes off the arachnid, she brought the tip of the knife down and pierced its belly, skewering it to the counter top. She watched as the force of the point caused the creature's legs to crane upwards, contorting in pain. She twisted the point. The spider's body buckled and the legs twisted round, forming an odd, eight-legged spiral. Finally, Maria angled the knife and sliced downwards, cleaving the spider in two and extinguishing its life.

She pulled the knife out of its belly. It did not move. It did not do anything. She prodded it with the tip of the blade. It lolled a bit. A few parts stuck to the knife. She calmly wiped the blade clean across the edge of the counter.

The kitchen was in slight disrepair and she could not remember the last time she had bothered to clean it properly. Hours? Days? Months? She looked to the clock hanging above the stone mantle. The hands were moving. Time still passed it seemed but it held little currency. Maria turned from the sink and sat down at the rickety kitchen table.

She looked at the place settings. She had finished her breakfast, but the setting next to her remained untouched. She was not surprised. It was always like that. It had always been like that. He never ate. She looked at the plate piled high with hearty food and ran her hands over the rough grain of the table. He had made it. He had hewn the wood from the surrounding trees and fashioned the table where they 'ate'. He was a master with an axe.

Maria closed her eyes as her fingers ran over the tabletop, taking in every divot, groove and imperfection. She tried to recall the moments that gave meaning to the scrapes. Each mark was a document of a time spent living. A knife scrape from cutting vegetables, and a divot from an over eager cleaver-chop when preparing a joint. As she ran her fingers over them, she could not recall a single moment. Instead, she invented a life. She conjured a history, a happy, lively story which was documented by the table through all its knocks and scrapes.

Another breeze drifted under the window behind her and crept up her back. She opened her eyes. The place settings remained. Her plate empty, his plate full. She sighed. He never ate.

Maria stood up and gathered the plates. She turned to the bin by the sink and scraped his untouched food into it. She dumped both plates by the sink and took off her apron.

Maria's house was small, cosy and isolated – a simple, two-storey wooden abode with a nice porch and sturdy roof, secluded neatly in a clearing surrounded by woodland. Directly in front of the porch, around fifty yards ahead, there lay a straight ridge with a severe brow. From her front porch, if anyone were to approach the house, Maria would see them the moment they crested the ride and that was of great security to her. Indeed, anyone living in the wilds of Montana needed all the natural help they could get. The world was a dangerous place, but Maria had never once felt threatened in her little house. The woodland would protect her. Montana would protect her. The Devil would protect her and, of course, she would protect herself.

———————

The front door opened and Maria stepped out onto the porch and sat in her rocking chair. According to the sun, it was late morning. She looked out to the ridge and rocked, the cold air not bothering her in the slightest. She looked over to the rickety wooden fence that encircled her compound and her eyes fell to Azazel, her Montana mountain goat who remained, as always, tethered to his hitching post. She watched as he lay on his side and rubbed his body against the ground in an attempt to scrape off his moulting hair. Maria knew that she should untie him and let the goat wander over to the trees to find relief from the irritating scratch of his coat at the hard bark of the Douglas Firs. She thought about it for a few seconds before lethargy overcame her and she fell into a light springtime sleep.

❦

Late afternoon had come by the time Maria awoke from her sleep. Azazel had finished trying to shed his coat and had laid against the hitching post, no doubt dreaming of his best friend Cinereous, The Devil's horse who would, when home, spend all his time with Azazel. The goat bleated softly in the quiet afternoon and rested his chin on the ground, his breath kicking up a few grains of loose dirt. The birds did not sing and the trees did not sway.

Maria rocked her chair, looking at Azazel and waiting for the sun to begin to set and just clip the top of the trees, sending the first of her friends, the shadows, to come visit. She was approaching her thirtieth year but felt as though she had been alive for centuries. Often she felt at odds with the house and her surroundings, and would sit upon the porch and look out at the world and believe that, as time moved forward, she stayed the same. Oftentimes she would pace up and down the porch and contemplate the summers and the winters and the endless clouds that drifted overhead. Her apron, threaded and bare, remained tied around her throughout the day as she cleaned, as she ate, and as she paced. Her isolation never seemed to break upon her, but instead drifted around her waist as if she was standing alone in a melancholy lake surrounded by a lamenting mist. It was the minutes leading up to the arrival of the shadows that reminded Maria that time was still a factor in her life. She rocked in her chair, her head tilted to the side, and she waited and waited.

The sun clipped the tops of the trees and began to dip and Maria smiled as the shadows came, slowly, slowly across the ground as if cautiously walking out of the gloom of the treeline. She sat upright in her chair as soon as she saw them. Azazel, likewise comforted by the shadows, bleated and lifted his head up as the brightness of the day began to subtly ebb away. He looked over to Maria and snorted. Maria smiled at the goat and reached into her apron pocket. It was time for her pipe.

The night was coming and, as was her ritual, Maria filled her pipe and lit it. She had rationed her supply of tobacco but it was running out. She had enough for one, maybe two more weeks. After that, she might have to forgo her first pipe, smoked while lying alone in bed in the morning. If things got worse, she would have to forgo the afternoon pipe and then, at the end of all things, she would have to forgo her 'wildcard' pipe which she could smoke whenever she liked. Her wildcard pipe: to Maria, it was the most wondrous of pleasures. It was the only surprising element in her life. The wildcard pipe could strike at any time and it was that sudden impulse to smoke it, whenever it came, that gave her spirit some anima. That surprise visit almost felt like someone else lived with her, forever hiding in a cupboard or behind a door to leap out and ravage her.

Maria rocked on her chair and smoked her afternoon pipe, careful not to let her mind wander from the moment of enjoying that specific pipe and not onto the giddy expectation of when the wildcard pipe would arrive.

Maria finished smoking and tapped the pipe's contents out on the arm of the chair, not caring if the remnants fell onto the wooden floorboard or the seat of the chair. She stood up and looked to the sky. The night was closing in fast and the shadows were all around. Though the chill in the air forced her to pull her shawl around herself, the shadows comforted her and made her calm solitude serenely welcome. She looked down to her left and smiled at the long twisted shadow cast from the hoe resting against the porch beam. At that time of twilight, the tip of the shadow morphed with the one cast from the hanging watering can and rocking chair to create the impression of an ancient, stooped man with a large, bulbous nose and a walking stick. Maria stood for a few moments and, in her mind, shared a few kind words with it. To her right, the shadow from the broken barrel fell against the wall and hung underneath the living room window sill, making it appear as if a hanging basket loaded with blooms hung there. She nodded her hello and walked into the house.

The hallway was warm and inviting. She closed the door to the porch and made her way to the ground floor bedroom where she opened a wardrobe containing The Devil's clothes, left behind when he rode out all those months ago. The smell of the clothes and the dead air inside the wardrobe hit Maria like a bucket of cold water and she felt a renewed and acute sense of reality. The Devil was gone and she was alone. Maria took out The Devil's poncho and put it on, the smell of him still set deep within the fabric and caressing her longing memories of her lover. She took out his battered and worn boots and put them on. Next, she reached for his wide brimmed hat and put it on her head. Finally, dressed head to toe like The Devil she turned to the mirror and looked at herself. The darkness of the room hid her face and presented a dreadful absence where her head should have been. Instead, in the mirror, was only the outline of the dreaded and infamous outlaw The Devil. In fact, the only thing that reminded Maria that she was still herself and had not been assimilated into the corporeal idea of The Devil was her large, protruding belly forcing the poncho to rise up into a mound.

CHAPTER THREE
The Rider

Maria stroked her belly and sighed, allowing herself to fall into memory and, as was her ritual, she imbued her memories with a fully realised omnipotence whereby she could inhabit the body of her lover and see the way she hoped he saw and feel for her the way she dreamt he did. She closed her eyes and the nighttime fell away and the dawn came bringing with it The Devil. Her lover returned.

The morning sun glinted over the treetops and the rider sat upon his horse, silhouetted and motionless on the ridge. Maria, standing on the porch, rested against the wooded support and sighed as the relief at the sight of his return swept over her. He had come home. A heightened sense of her surroundings overcame her and she could almost hear the scratching of the rove beetle as it made its way across the porch. The zephyr made the tall grass up at the stable sigh like a choir, the branches of the trees flanking the house creaked restlessly and the light dappled her face, warming her intensely as she closed her eyes to soak it all in. The moment permeated her every sense.

⎯⎯⎯⎯∞⎯⎯⎯⎯

The rider, too, was attuned to the effect of his return. The wind on his neck gnawed against his skin and wove its chill fingers through his blonde shoulder-length hair. His rough beard captured the air and held it still to his face causing his cheeks to become flushed. His lips chapped, from riding hard and drinking little over the months outdoors, puckered reactively to each gentle gust. His joints no longer ached from the ride and the hardships endured. The weight of Leviathan, his customised Winchester rifle slung over his back, did not pull him down and Erebus and Lucifer, his Colt .44 sidearms, did not press into his sides, but sat well and comfortably. The rider's icy blue eyes squinted as the sun invaded the corner of his vision and forced his focus onto the house, causing a glowing iris to fall around it as if all else was superfluous except the sight of that house and that woman who stood upon the porch. The rider's vision began to flood with light as the sun crested the trees and the house below became too distorted to view. He lifted his gloved hand to his brow, shielding the light from his eyes. The house remained. It was no mirage. He tensed slightly, tightening his legs against the barrel of his horse as he exhaled, letting the fog from his breath warm the edges of his cracked lips before it dissipated into the crisp air.

The ash-coloured horse, still strong and breathing steadily despite the arduous journey home, did not crane his head to look down at the house, though he knew where he was, relieved to be home. He looked down and inspected the rough, uneven ground, knowing that the moment of reunion for his master and his lover was sacred to only them. Cinereous was a patient beast and knew that soon enough he would feel the woman's soft hand run over his muzzle and along the side of his cheek. The horse neighed quietly and the rider patted his neck, turning him to face the ridge. Cinereous obeyed and began to walk down towards the house.

Upon the porch, Maria breathed in excitedly as she saw the rider turn to face her and finish his journey home. Up until that point, she could not be certain if he would do so or instead turn away from her and ride out again. She would never dream of second guessing any man, let alone The Devil, and until she saw him make his approach, she resided purely in the realms of uncertainty and hopeful expectancy.

—∞—

The horse and rider entered the clearing proper and walked slowly through the open gate, stopping just a few yards from the porch and from Maria. The horse finally looked up and neighed, happy at seeing her once more. Maria smiled. The horse neighed again. She cast her eyes up to the rider's and her smile dropped. The rider's eyes, searing and bright behind the brim of his hat, shone out and bore right into her. He dismounted and stood by his horse, his arm resting on the saddle's horn. The Devil clenched his jaw and placed his left hand upon its usual resting place:

that of the grip of Erebus. Maria stepped off the porch and up to the horse, all the while keeping her large, brown eyes on the rider. She reached up to the horse's head and held out her hand. Cinereous happily lifted his head and rested it in the palm of her hand, breathing contentedly. With her other hand, Maria stroked his muzzle and ran her fingers along his cheek, much to his delight. Maria rested her cheek against the horse's head and leaned against it for support. The rider, now just a few feet from her, tipped up his hat, throwing off the shadow from his face. He smiled at her. Maria closed her eyes and smiled back, and they stood like that for a few moments until the rider broke the spell and spoke.

"Cinereous," was all he said.

The horse neighed in response to his name, nuzzled Maria's head gently, then walked over to the open stable and entered. Maria and The Devil looked at each other for a few seconds before he broke off his gaze and looked firstly to the sky and then to the trees all around, taking in the surroundings and breathing in the air deeply. When he returned his eyes to her, he found her turning away from him with her hand extended out, intending for him to take it and be led into the house. The rider bit the tip of his leather glove and pulled his hand free, exposing the soft, long and strangely delicate fingers to the crisp air. He took her hand and although he could not see her face as she led him into the house, he knew that she was smiling. The gentle squeeze of her grip and the way her thumb rubbed over his knuckles when their hands touched told him so. Into the house they went to rediscover each other and under the clear day, with the windows open, they made love and were unified once again.

Maria sat up in the bed and pulled the cover up around her chest. She sat back against the railings and took pleasure in the shuddering sensation of the cold metal against her flesh. Her hair fell haphazardly about her shoulders, her chest and cheeks were flushed and her breathing started to regain its regular pattern. She brought the pipe to her lips and rejoiced in its taste which had somehow become more sublime.

Her lover lay beside her, the beads of sweat running down the raised scar tissue that criss-crossed his back like great rivers. He slept soundly, one arm over her lap and the other on the chair next to the bed, his hand resting on the grip of Erebus, thumb over the hammer and holding it in a precarious position.

The Devil's breathing was so shallow that Maria had the feeling that he could be dead, or that he would suddenly die in their bed and she would have no clue until she had finished her pipe and tried to move him, only to find a lifeless corpse beside her. She smiled at the notion and exhaled. Nobody can kill The Devil. She looked over to the window and out into the darkness beyond. The clear night sky and bright moon cast its beams down through the woodland

and she could see Cinereous walking around. The horse was as free as she was and grazed openly, neighing quietly and contentedly in the moonlight. Next to him, yet still tethered to his post, sat Azazel the goat. Cinereous, as was his way when at home, did not stray too far from the goat and indeed, in the coldest nights when perhaps Maria had forgotten to untie Azazel, the horse would kick the post down and guide the goat towards the warmth of the stable. That night, however, while The Devil slept and Maria smoked her pipe, both Azazel and Cinereous were happy to be outside under the moonlight.

Maria felt calmed by their presence. She felt protected and safe knowing that the goat and the horse were nearby. She thanked them in her mind and turned her gaze back to the room. Across from the bed, her lover had draped his coat over the back of the resting chair and placed his hat upon the hook above it. In the moonlight, The Devil's items threw a great shadow across the wall beside the bed. Maria looked at it and smiled at what appeared to be the silhouette of a giant, broad shouldered man looming over her. Even the shadows it seemed were conspiring to keep her safe. And, of course, the shadows and the beasts outside were not the only forms of security. Erebus, in the hand of The Devil, lay waiting and so, across the room, did Lucifer and the Leviathan. Though Lucifer remained in the gun belt hanging off the wardrobe handle like a coiled snake, she knew that it was sleeping with one eye open, waiting for any sign of danger and longing for its master to unleash it. Similarly, propped against the wardrobe rested the Leviathan, loaded and cocked. She thought infrequently about the chaos The Devil brought whenever he rode out and she had trained herself to beat back any unnerving thoughts surrounding his deeds. She did not want to know and feared to open that Pandora's Box. His passion and love for her was fierce and deep, that much was obvious and she knew full well that men who love fiercely and unconditionally also fight fiercely and kill mercilessly.

'There ain't nothing so dangerous as lovers,' she thought as she finished her pipe. She tipped the remnants of the bowl onto a little plate on the bedside table by her pillow, so that its dying aromas could infiltrate her dreams when she lay down and finally went to sleep. Maria looked around the room once more, perfectly settled mentally, before sliding back down into the bed, pulling the covers over them both. She kissed The Devil on the nape of his neck three times and pulled him tightly into her chest, so that there was no part of her front that was not in contact with his back. Maria closed her eyes and fell into a dreamscape filled with calm seas and gentle breezes.

But that was many months ago and Maria, still dressed in The Devil's clothes and sat alone in the living room looking at his empty chair, awoke from her dream. He had returned, and he had also left. She was alone and pregnant. She was positioned, as always, in the little rocking chair in the corner of the room. Every time she rocked backwards, the chair hit against the wall. She didn't mind. It was soothing. From her corner, the fireplace was immediately to her left, to her right another chair. In front of her lay the rug, and beyond that sat his chair, backed against the window and with his guitar resting against the arm. She rocked and looked at the empty space. The window behind the chair had a yellowing lace curtain draped from a crude rail above it. The view from the window presented the woods surrounding the compound and, beyond, the ridge. As with the chair on the porch, this offered the same, needful view. Maria faced the ridge. Facing forwards. Waiting. She looked at his guitar lying against his empty chair and tried to feel sad for it. She tried to imprint her own loneliness upon the instrument and somehow connect with it, but she could not. It may as well have been a tree, or a cloud. She rocked back, hit the wall behind her and rocked forward, keeping time with the clock in the hallway. Waiting.

CHAPTER FOUR
Maria's Dream

Maria finally stopped rocking when her daydream of his return had fully faded and the reality of the warm and silent living room overcame her nostalgia. The fire was dying and the shadows in the room were shaking and faltering, soon to leave her for the night. It was nearly time for bed. She rubbed her belly, feeling the child inside, and slowly stood up. She walked over to the window by The Devil's chair and looked out, the silver moonlight draping over the flat ground before fading to nothingness by the dense treeline.

From the window, she could not see Azazel but she held little worry for him. It was warm enough outside for him and she knew that he would be quite happy to remain out under the stars keeping an eye out for the return of The Devil and his horse. Maria ran her hand over the cold glass window pane and wished the goat goodnight before turning away.

Maria's last ritual of the day was to walk around the house and stand in each room, dressed in The Devil's clothes, and try to assume his power. It was a desperate attempt on her part to try and trick each room and the shadows within into believing that he had returned and stood before them.

It was also the only way she could trick herself too. It was the moments before bed that were the most testing for Maria. When the day was done and night was about to take her, in between the push and pull of the two worlds was when Maria felt most divided and alone. She walked into the kitchen and sat in her lover's chair and looked across at her own seat, trying to assume his identity and to conjure an image of herself in the other chair. If she could be him for a few moments, maybe she could understand exactly why he had ridden out and left her. Maybe she could reach out through the spirit world and touch him in his sleep wherever he lay and plant the desire deep within him to come home to her. She sat there at the kitchen table for a few minutes and tried to picture the scene of the both of them at the table, enjoying a meal and smiling lovingly at each other in between mouthfuls of hearty food.

In the moments before bed she desperately needed the vision of a simple and happy life to materialise – just a few tantalising glimpses of the heaven that would be hers someday. She concentrated hard and looked around the room. Her attempt to project her desires did not work and the solitude of the house overcame her. She left the kitchen and walked to the empty side room, adjacent to the living room. Maria stood in the centre of the cold room and felt her belly once more. A sudden storm of despair raged through her and completely overthrew her defences. For the first time in months, perhaps years, Maria started to cry. She did not sink to the floor, nor bury her face in her hands, but simply stood in the centre of the empty room, dressed in the clothes of her lover, and sobbed loudly and desperately.

∽∽∽

The exhaustion caused from weeping had forced Maria to bed and into a deep sleep. It was in her dreamscape that The Devil came to her. She lay in bed, on her back with her arms over her bump and, as she regressed deeper through the stages of sleep, the bump fell away and her previous flat, taut stomach returned. Her few grey hairs disappeared and her crow's feet receded slightly. She was lying on her bed and the day was bright and hot. She was naked and covered in a slight coating of post-coital sweat. She breathed slowly and next to her, with his head propped on his hand, lay The Devil. It was in this memory-dream where Maria managed to leave herself, enter his mind and listen to his thoughts, all those months ago.

He looked at her for thirty minutes, acquainting himself with her crow's feet which had appeared since he last saw her. He reached out and gently stroked her soft cheekbones and her tiny ears. He marvelled at her. How had she come about? How was she alive and how had she survived the twenty eight years she'd been upon the earth? He knew nothing of her family, or of her desires and dreams of a life beyond him and she together. Simply, he knew her only as Maria, and their life together only as 'me and you, you and me.'

As he lay awake, head resting upon his hand, legs trapped under hers, he dared to ponder a life for Maria within which he did not exist. He dared to consider her aspirations and dreams, her thoughts and opinions, and he dared to imagine new lovers. The Devil studied Maria's hooked nose, that bent to the right at the end and was as uniquely signatory to her as was her own penmanship. He pondered her nose. Was it her father's? Her mother's? Had her family always had such a distinctive nose? Were they marked out by it? This thought triggered further, deeper channels of enquiry: her mother – was she a tyrant or a sweetheart? Did she love and dream, or did she walk through life with the same blank calmness that her daughter seemed to? Her father, what of him? Did he love his wife? Did he want to marry her? Did his legacy amount to anything more than producing the woman that lay across from him now? The Devil had no way of reconciling this galaxy of questions.

He looked down, first at her pert and inviting breasts rising and falling gently, then down to her belly and her hands resting upon it, inches up from her pelvis which led to the path down between her legs, to the well cared for sex that was as ensnaring and captivating as anything he could imagine. He ran his hands down over her body, this time taking care to press a little harder on her nipples and over her belly button to ensure that his gesture penetrated her dreamscape. Maria moaned slightly and her legs parted naturally. The Devil watched her knees rise and part, offering his hand an unhindered route to its prize. He cast away thoughts of her past and focused only on their coexistence in that moment.

Maria awoke from her dream flustered and confused. Her recollection of that memory clung to her fiercely and though the springtime air was brisker than the summer breeze in her dream, she could not quite be sure if she was dreaming now, and if her previous dream was reality. She looked over to the door handle and did not see his gun belt resting upon it. She looked to the pillow next to her which did not bear the imprint of his head. Finally, she looked down at her belly to see not the taut stomach of her youth, but the huge belly of a pregnant woman. She fell back into bed and looked up at the ceiling knowing that it had been a dream and that she was still alone. Without looking, she reached over to her bedside table and grabbed her pipe. She sat up, stuffed and lit it. The dream, though cruel, fortified her defences somewhat, and she did not cry as she had the night before but instead felt a twinge of shame for having done so. However, as she recalled the dream, and the unique perspective of being inside an approximation of her lover's mind, she felt a warming calm come over her and the tobacco scent agreed with the feeling. He did truly love her. As she remembered this, she understood that he could easily be in the house in body and she would still feel the same.

The morning routine saw Maria wash and inspect her belly, trying to muster a feeling of maternal care for the unborn child. She found it nearly impossible to do so. As time itself held little meaning to her in that house and in that environment, Maria felt it increasingly hard to track the growth of the baby, or even remember a time outside of dreams where it was not there. Of course, the kicks from inside her did, when they came, temporarily spark an excitement that pulled at her heart. But her longing for the lover was far greater than her desire to see the child. She had not even prepared the empty room that she had initially earmarked as a nursery. When she had realised that she was pregnant, just two weeks after The Devil had last ridden out, she had thrown out the dressing table, cabinet and chest of drawers that were in the room and burnt them in the yard out of panic, joy and rage.

It was her intention thereafter to turn the empty room into a nursery. She would fashion a little cot, perhaps journey into the nearest town to buy some pretty cloth to sew dolls and generally prepare for the arrival. It did not take but a further two weeks for that feeling to fade, falling from her heart as the morning sickness eschewed the waste from her body. The joy of pregnancy soon washed away and the burden of discomfort, pain and trepidation for the arrival of the child grew as her belly did. She knew that when it came, she would be doubly alone. Maria hated the child already as not only did it preclude her from a life of freedom, it also precluded her from death. Many times, in the early months of pregnancy, Maria had considered walking out into the dense forest, giving up her life to the fate of the wilderness and dying of exposure. But with each passing day, the burden of responsibility for the unborn child slowly killed that most elusive of freeing dreams: that of death by one's own control. No, she was stuck – alone and without hope of appearing as he had known her, should he return home.

Maria felt around her belly, prodding and rubbing here and there in a clinical and dispassionate way. Over the last week, she had begun to experience new and disturbing pains and twinges, shortness of breath and an awful creeping sensation of expectation. The baby was due to arrive soon and though she felt no true maternal feelings for it, she was gifted with the good sense to listen and understand her biological intuition. She knew that soon she would need to hole up in the house and have no need to venture outside. She needed to gather the remaining wood from the stable and bring it into the living room. She had enough food stored away and could, while she had some mobility left, corral a few chickens into the house, keep them in the spare room and slaughter them when she needed to. She knew that it was time to retreat her borders from treeline to porch and stay inside, thus shrinking her world and enhancing her solitude that much more. She had no choice.

Maria retired to her bedroom and dressed herself in her own clothes, taking great care to return The Devil's boots, poncho and hat to the cupboard where they belonged. Movement was laboured and slow, but soon she was dressed and ready for her morning's work: gathering the wood.

THE DEVIL'S SIDEARM:
'Lucifer'

The inscription along the barrel is taken from
Dante's The Divine Comedy and reads:

'Per me si va ne la città dolente,
Per me si va ne l'etterno dolore,
Per me si va tra la perduta gente'

'Through me you pass into the city of woe,
 Through me you pass into eternal pain,
 Through me among the people lost for aye'

CHAPTER FIVE

The Axe

Maria left the house and made her way over to Azazel who was grazing peacefully by his hitching post. The morning was fresh and the sky cloudless.

Maria, barefoot as was her morning way, took pleasure in the touch of grass under foot as she made her way towards the goat. She reached him and, cradling her belly, bent down as best she could to stroke the animal. The goat bleated happily and nuzzled her. Maria felt the full weight of the large goat's head press into her hand as he moved around to rub his body against her leg. Maria had to steady herself against the surprising power of the animal as he rubbed away, trying to shed some of his moulting coat. Maria laughed and scratched the goats back vigorously, pulling great clumps of soft white fur from him.

Maria pulled a clump of hair from Azazel's body and inspected it, rubbing the strands between her fingers and finding the texture pleasing. A striking thought came to her; the softness of the coat would make a good lining for something, perhaps a doll; perhaps a doll for the baby. Perhaps she should harvest some more and, perhaps later that day, begin sewing together a little doll for the child. The child would like it and would need some sort of comfort in the night when it couldn't be near its mother. It was the first time she had considered not the physical welfare of the child, but its emotional wellbeing.

A galaxy of thoughts and ideas birthed in her mind. The child suddenly had a sex, a selection of possible names and even shades of personality she hoped to discover. As Maria scratched and pulled the coat off of Azazel, she felt like an expectant mother in the truest sense. It was a sea changing moment.

As Maria fondled Azazel's moulting coat, she looked over to the hitching post and the thump of nostalgia rose up inside her. There, resting against the fence post was her axe. Her scratching slowed down as her eyes clouded over and a memory returned. Maria remembered the axe and its importance to her survival.

The Devil handed the axe to Maria and stood back as she felt its weight and power. In her hands it felt alien and ugly. She did not want to hold it and could sense clearly that the axe did not want to be held by her. It was eleven-thirty in the morning and Maria was uncomfortable with the situation. Only five minutes previously, she had been in a blissful state of serenity. The sun had risen fully, the dew had gone and the air was warm and still. Maria had been sitting upon the porch, smoking freely from the new tobacco supply her lover had brought her while watching him chop wood with mechanical efficiency a few yards away.

She had no intention of working that day, but instead wanted only to recline in the luxury of simply being alive and free in her perfect little scrap of land. She was beginning to drift into a light sleep, the sounds of The Devil's axe striking upon the chopping block a hypnotic lullaby.

Maria was denied the final push into her dream world by the cessation of his work. She opened her eyes and looked over to him. He was standing by the block, axe by his side, looking at her. Behind him, Cinereous looked out to the edge of the woodland while Azazel grazed at his hoof. A twinge of discomfort ran through Maria. She lifted her hand to shield her eyes from the sun and looked at him. He did not move.

"Maria," The Devil finally called in a flat, yet warm tone. He beckoned her over.

Maria smiled at his voice, the first time she had heard it since he had come home, and the first time she had heard it in months since he left. At first the sound of another human voice in the little clearing in which she lived was a strange sensation which almost ignited a debate as to whether she was dreaming or not. But as the words fell into her ears and filtered through her mind, the sprig of remembrance grew and she recalled his voice and the deepness of it. How it always remained steady and assured and carried a gravelled tone from years of exposure to the elements and his constant smoking. His voice was a wonderful tonic.

Once the words had dissipated in the air and filtered through her psyche, she slowly stood up and walked from the porch towards her lover. She stood by the chopping block and looked at her man, tired, sweating and breathing heavily in the sun. She knew that he had called her over to make love and she stood there awaiting his welcome gesture to remove her clothes.

She was wrong. The Devil did not reach for her clothes and did not remove his own but instead handed her the axe and stood back.

Maria crinkled her brow and looked quizzically down to the tool she was holding. The blade head was worn but still deadly, the handle beaten and weathered. She counted eighteen notches down the left hand side and a large, deep scarred arrangement upon the flat of the left blade that resembled a deep valley. The object was purposeful and simple and Maria regarded it with equal measures of fear and disdain, and the axe felt it. It did not want to be held by her.

Maria did not offer it back, nor hold it close, but kept it in the purgatory of space between them. She looked at her lover with confused eyes. He smiled reassuringly and gestured to the chopping block with a little nod of his head. Maria looked down and saw three rough logs waiting to be cleaved in two. She bent down and tried to pick one up. She could not. The weight of the axe in one hand combined with the size of the log made it impossible for her. She looked up at The Devil for some assistance. He folded his arms.

Maria rested the axe against the chopping block, spat on her hands, picked up the log and dumped it down upon the flat of the block. She picked up the axe and stepped back, lining the blade up with the centre of the log. She raised it above her, the weight of its head surprisingly powerful and pulling her backwards and slightly off balance. To overcome the sudden pull, Maria hurriedly brought the head back down and unleashed it upon the log.

Her form was poor and the fact that she struck to counter the axe's natural movement and not in a motion of smoothness, both parties complicit in their union, caused the axe blade to rebel slightly and she managed only a glancing blow across the log. The blade bounced off and slid down the chopping log, pitching Maria forward and causing her to twist and receive the butt of the handle into her stomach, winding her.

She hunched over and looked up once again to see The Devil. Maria wheezed at him and he looked down at her with an expressionless gaze. Maria saw nothing behind his eyes and for a split second, she knew his true self.

The wind returned to her and she stood up, refusing to be outdone by the axe and the log and refusing to let The Devil's steeled gaze take away her fire. Maria raised the axe one more time and, more assuredly than before, brought it down upon the log, this time striking true but with diminished power. The blade embedded itself into the log. Maria tried to pull the blade from the stump but to no avail. She pulled with all her might until the sweat from her hands overcame her purchase and she fell backwards onto the dusty floor.

Her rage overcame her and she got to her feet, stamping and glowering at The Devil. He smiled at her, his left eye glinting in the sun which sent her rage into a volcanic explosion. Maria bent down and picked up a stone to throw at him. She flung her arm back in preparation and was about to launch it when Azazel innocently bleated from the edge of the compound behind her. Maria instantly diverted her rage towards the beast, spun on her heel, screamed and threw the stone across the way. It was a true throw and the stone stuck the hind leg of the animal, causing him to bleat in pain and buckle which, in turn caused Cinereous to rear up half in surprise and half in anger at seeing Azazel mistreated.

Maria's rage was instantly beaten back by her shame. The animals both turned to her and made their disappointment clear by bleating and neighing respectively before turning their backs on her and facing out towards the treeline and the western mountains.

Maria lowered her head and turned back to The Devil to see him standing over the stump. In one easy motion, he heaved the axe out of the log and stepped over the block and up to Maria, his eyes calm with a gentle, reassuring smile on his face. She took the axe from him and stepped up to the chopping block once more, this time with a confidence and commitment swelling deep within her. His proximity calmed her greatly as it always did.

She stopped by the log she was about to cleave and he stood beside her, brushing her hair away from her face, his rough fingers gliding smoothly over her large, soft cheeks. She turned to him.

"This axe is your life, Maria," he whispered. "The axe is everything out here. He is your master, and your protector. You must learn to use him well, and use him true. If you cannot chop wood, you cannot keep warm or cook and you cannot survive. This simple tool is more powerful than any steam locomotive, more vital than any medicine and more deadly than any pistol. If you take care of it, use it well and love it, it will keep you alive, warm and safe. If you mistreat it, or ignore it, then it will not save you. The axe is your life Maria. Do you understand?"

Maria nodded. Up until then, the axe had resided in the wood barn unused. Before he left some months before, he had amassed a great stockpile of wood and Maria had wisely rationed the logs. Only now, upon hearing his words and understanding the importance of the simple tool, did she appreciate just how alone she was when he was not around. The axe really was her life. When she realised that, she also realised an awful truth that came with it: *'If he is teaching me to use this, then he will not be around for long.'* She was right.

The Devil knew he would be leaving again soon and he knew that he would be gone for longer than the season. He knew it, and so did Maria. The Devil looked to the floor in that moment of shared understanding. Maria looked at the log. She moved her feet apart and brought her chest around so that it was parallel to the log. Slowly, she brought up the axe and slid one hand down the handle until it found the end, the grain of the wood and the need of the axe to drive home true seemingly guiding her. She moved her other hand towards the head of the handle, gripping it tightly and wringing it. Her heart rate dropped and she began to breathe calmly and steadily. The warm air tickled her neck and she felt a bead of sweat slide under her blouse and down her shoulder blades. A length of hair fell to the side of her face and brushed her cheek and she softly blew it aside, keeping her vision clear and focused on the log before her. She blinked slowly, calmly, ready.

Maria dug her heels into the ground and kept them firmly planted, anchoring her centre of gravity. She twisted at the waist slightly to the right as she brought the axe up and above her shoulder in a controlled motion. She felt unified with the tool. As the axe rose up, her right hand slid down from the head of the handle to the bottom as she brought it back down again decisively onto the log with immense force.

She exhaled as the blade wedged into its target and drove itself all the way through until it embedded into the chopping block underneath. The log was hewn into two equal pieces that fell either side of the block. She looked down at the two pieces that were once united, and now lay broken. Maria knew full well what it meant and understood the symbolic nature of the activity. She looked over to The Devil and he looked into her eyes, not with a vacant expression as before, but now with a deep sadness and regret for where he was going, where he had been and who he was.

Maria felt tears rising and, though she wanted to let them fall, her deep resolve held true. She clenched her jaw and her fortress of lashes held true. She sighed, pulled the axe clear of the block, placed another log down and repeated the motion, cleaving the log in two with a clear, meaningful motion. As she did so The Devil noticed her jaw clenched in exertion, but her eyes vacant to the act.

CHAPTER SIX
Dinner Alone

Maria had neglected the axe and, as such, neglected her existence. She cursed herself for letting her solitude and laziness overcome her drive to live. She had been extremely lucky to have the moment of realisation at that time. What if she had forgotten about the axe completely and, come winter, found herself snowed in with no wood? What if she did not make it through the season, leaving only a corpse full of maggots and regret for her lover to find upon his return? What if she had not realised that she had a child inside her that needed love and affection?

Maria pulled some more hair from Azazel and stuffed the bundle into her apron pocket before kissing the animal in thanks for his lesson, and leaving to fetch the axe. As soon as she picked up the tool, her muscle memory recalled its power and weight and she felt even greater shame at having abandoned the instrument of her survival to the elements.

She ran her hand over the weathered handle and up to the dirty, blunt blade. Maria spat on the blade and rubbed the saliva into the metal with her thumb, clearing away the months of collected dirt. She was relieved to discover that, under the grime, the axe head was salvageable. She decided that later on in the evening, after her final pipe and before bed, she would spend a good few hours cleaning the blade and oiling the handle. She was sure that the axe would forgive her for her negligence and be happy to be inside in the warm and at hand for the rest of the seasons.

Maria held the axe tightly against her chest as if it was a child, and walked slowly towards the stable. She pulled open the rickety wooden door and stood in the large, open entrance. The four stalls, of which only one had ever been used, had a little bed of sad straw and the smell in the air was the same as outside, which disheartened Maria somewhat. Even though she knew it was impossible, as she approached the door she fantasised that when she flung it open, she would be greeted by that strong and pungent smell of a stable in use – of fresh straw, mud, horses and the warmth of their great bodies. She even dared to recall the times when Cinereous would be in there to welcome and to nuzzle her, and let her run her hands all over him, feeling his coarse ashen hair. Instead, it was an empty, clear and fresh smelling wooden structure.

Over in the far left corner, in a disused stall, she saw the remaining logs for the fire. She calculated that, if she were careful, there would be just enough to see her through the next month or two. Perhaps just long enough for her to give birth and recover her strength and agility enough to come back outside and chop some more. She put the melancholy thoughts regarding the emptiness of the building to the back of her mind and went over to the pile of logs. By

the wall rested a barrow. Maria laid the axe to one side
and, cradling her belly, bent down to pick up a single log
and dropped it into the barrow. It was going to be a long,
arduous task of ferrying the logs, four maybe five at a time
to the house, however the revelation of rediscovering the
axe lit a fire in her heart; Maria toiled without rest and
without complaining for the rest of the morning until
the remaining useable logs had been taken from the barn
and stored in the empty spare room. But that was not her
only task. After that, she untied Azazel and together they
managed to corral some chickens together and had herded
them into the spare room.

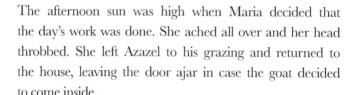

The afternoon sun was high when Maria decided that
the day's work was done. She ached all over and her head
throbbed. She left Azazel to his grazing and returned to
the house, leaving the door ajar in case the goat decided
to come inside.

Maria drank five glasses of water in quick succession and
forced herself to eat some hard bread, letting the water in
her mouth soften it so it did not get lodged in her throat.
Though she was thirsty, but not hungry, she knew that the
baby would not share her indifference to the need for food.
She needed to look after the child for it was soon coming
into the world and it would be Maria and Maria alone who

could ensure its survival. After nine months of indifference towards it, she felt now that it was time to become serious.

She looked out at the rear of the compound and drank, her large brown eyes not so much focusing on the world outside but the world inside and the future she was facing. Then, without consciously thinking about it, and barely looking at what she was doing, Maria began to prepare a large meal of boiled corn, bread and salted cured beef.

The automatic nature of her industry extended to clearing and setting the table for two, cleaning the dirty crockery to the side of the sink that she had neglected for three days. She had even ground some coffee for after dinner. By the time she had finished and come back to her senses, the kitchen looked impeccable and the house was filled with warmth and the inviting fragrance of food about to be served.

Maria put a plate of beef on the centre of the table and sat down, still wearing her apron. She looked at the empty plate across from her, then to the empty space where her lover should have been sitting. Where normally she would eat in sad silence and look at the space, today she felt that he should be there. She put down her knife and fork and left the table.

<hr>

Maria returned to the kitchen ten minutes later dressed completely in her lover's clothes. She sat down in his seat and began helping herself to the food. She had not only put on his poncho, but his trousers, chaps, shirt and waistcoat. She had found a long disused belt and tied it loosely around her waist in the fashion of her lover's gunbelt that held Lucifer and Erebus. She had even retrieved the axe and laid it across the table, in the same uncouth manner he used to lay his huge rifle, Leviathan.

As she ate, sat in his clothes and surrounded by pathetic props designed to conjure his appearance, a great rage began to boil inside her. She began to eat faster, stuffing more food into her mouth than she could chew, gagging as she swallowed great lumps of beef. She bit into the stale bread and pulled it free with her hands, throwing the crusts down on her plate and staring in anger at the empty seat across from her.

Maria chewed her cured beef and looked down at the full plate opposite her. The clock in the hallway ticked louder than it should have been permitted to do. She gritted her teeth, pulled a tough sinew from her mouth and wiped it over the table. She looked at her glass of murky, half purified river water. The clock ticked louder. She chewed on. Suddenly she bit into her lip and winced in pain, dropping her knife and fork. She grabbed the edge of the table and stamped her feet, not daring to let out a scream. She could feel the warm blood well up inside her mouth. She swallowed the food and inspected her lip. The crimson blood pooled over her finger. She held it up to the candlelight. It glistened hypnotically at her. Without blinking, Maria reached over and wiped her bloodied finger over the untouched corn on the plate opposite. She touched her lip and pooled some more blood onto her finger. This time, after inspection, she licked her finger clean. She tried to discern the copper taste from the taste of the salty beef. She could not. Maria looked down at her plate and picked up another strand of cured meat. She chewed on without emotion, as if she were chewing cud. Her rage fell away and she looked down at herself, ashamed of her anger and also acutely embarrassed at the sudden realisation of what she was doing; sitting there, dressed like him and eating like him.

Maria rubbed her belly tenderly and felt three kicks within which calmed her greatly. Slowly, she stood up and took off The Devil's clothes. The kitchen was warm enough for her to strip naked and so she did. She carried the clothes back to his cupboard and packed them away, hopeful that the sad yet compelling need to dress in his clothes was quelled for good.

She turned and looked at the mirror. The shadows in the room calmed her and the glow from the fire in the living room adjacent seeped in and bathed her in a soft glow. She looked at her naked, pregnant form and was struck for the first time by the immeasurable femininity she bore. She stood sideways and ran her hands over her belly. She cupped her large breasts and found them to be tender and engorged. She looked at her arms, still slender and strong, and finally she looked closely at her face. The warm glow softened her cheeks and erased her crow's feet and the furrows in her brow that the months of solitude had carved in. She felt female, desirable and comfortable in her own skin and so she decided not to redress, but return to the kitchen naked and clear away the plates.

Maria had scraped the plates clean, piling the remnants onto one large plate which she left on the porch for Azazel should he wish to eat. She stacked the plates and washed them as best she could, then she sat at her place at the table and poured herself a coffee. She watched the steam ebb from the cup and held her chin over it, feeling the wetness grow on the underside of her face.

Though she had cleared away the crockery and the axe from the table, she had left her pipe and tobacco and, as a reward for her hard work and as an act of self forgiveness, she decided to have two pipes in a row, and perhaps another wildcard before bed. Despite her solitude, she felt calm, far calmer than she had in months. Where before she considered herself to have been serene in her loneliness, only now, sat naked at the table and rubbing her belly, did she know that earlier she had been in utter turmoil and now she was truly at peace. The baby would be born soon. She smiled broadly and stuffed her pipe. As she did so, she noticed that the pile of tobacco had fallen out onto the table and collected in a little heap like an island. A memory sparked.

Maria tilted her head and looked at the heap. The spark of memory became a flame. She stood up from the table, fetched a large knife from the drawer and sat back down. She lit her pipe and leaned into the pile, pulling it apart and reshaping it. She picked up the knife and with its tip, she began scraping and chipping away at the surface of the table, carving around the island of tobacco and outwards, chipping and scraping as the memory rebuilt itself in her mind.

She smoked and worked well into the night, feverish at the wonderful and intoxicating memory that was reclaiming her heart. She was utterly alive.

CHAPTER SEVEN
The Dark Rider

Jeb Garret's farm was five generations old and stood two hundred miles north of Maria's. It was here that the wind blew fiercer and the seasons stamped down harder on the populous. Jeb, a forty-eight year old ex-soldier with a limp and a scar down his left cheek, worked his meagre land alongside his nine year old son Jeb Junior who was already growing up to be a strong, forceful young man, easily capable of riding out on his own and managing the day's round trip to Barston, the nearest settlement, for supplies. Jeb Sr sometimes ventured out, but since his last Great Adventure with The Devil some years prior, he had found no desire to and so entrusted the duties of manual labour to his young son.

His wife Maggie had died of the winter chill when Jeb Jr was a baby; Jeb Jr had been raised by his father, which was no simple task, given The Devil's predilection for turning up and summoning him to ride out. But that had not happened in years, and though he was old and his joints ached twice as much in winter, Jeb Sr was happy in his life, and so was Jeb Jr. They had shelter in their home, warmth in their many bear-skin layers and an almost unlimited supply of food. They had trout from the nearby lake; they had deer they could hunt and countless rabbits and hares to trap. Father and son were both keen hunters, Jeb Sr through his war experience and subsequent outlawing, Jeb Jr through his father's teachings. On this night, as was their way, the two men sat together and played cards.

Jeb Sr poured himself a large glass of whisky and looked over to his son who was looking curiously at the bottle. Jeb Sr moved the bottle closer to his son, but kept his hand on it. The son went to grab it, but his father moved it six inches out of his reach. The son giggled and leaned in further. The father moved the bottle to the left. The boy screwed up his face and went to grab the bottle again. The father went to move it out of the way, but the boy feigned with his left hand, and shot his right arm out, tricking his father and grabbing the bottle. He tried to pull it from his father's hands, but his grip was too tight.

"Think you're big enough for a drink?"

"Yes sir," said Jeb Jr. "I'm big enough! I'm nearly ten."

"Yes, yes you are… well, in that case, I guess you are man enough for a man's drink."

The boy smiled, released his grip from the bottle and pushed his tin cup across the table. Jeb Sr smiled, poured a little dram of whisky and watched as the boy gulped it down and nearly coughed his guts out. Jeb Sr laughed heartily. Jeb Jr coughed and thumped his chest before thrusting his cup across the table for another drink.

"Good man," said his father and poured him a larger drink, which Jeb Jr sipped carefully and managed to swallow without convulsing. His father ruffled his hair and dealt the cards once more.

Such was their contentment that they didn't see the four riders appear in the darkness and wait fifty yards across from their little farm. They did not see three of them dismount and approach the farm and they did not see the moonlight glinting off their drawn pistol barrels.

The fourth rider remained on his horse, watching as his men crept toward the farmhouse. The moonlight could not reveal his face. It tried, but the darkness of the rider's soul permeated his physical world and beat back even the night. The only things that did manage to catch the light were the fierce, determined pupils that scanned the farmhouse and the surrounding environment. Judging, assessing, and scheming. The horse remained motionless, calm in the night time. The three other men reached the house and waited by the porch.

Jeb Jr beat his father at cards and forced his old man to collect a mean trick. Jeb Sr ruffled his son's hair again and laughed just as the front door was kicked open and the three men burst into their home. The sudden intrusion took the Garrets by surprise and they fell backwards from their table, spilling cards, water, bread and crockery all over the floor. The three men, clad in warm and weathered leather trench coats, wide brimmed hats and handkerchiefs over their faces, loomed in over the father and son, guns trained on their heads. Jeb Sr had no time to reach for his pistol, which had spun across the floor in the confusion. One of the men, a fiercely intense looking man with arched eyebrows and a furrowed forehead, grabbed Jeb Sr. by the collar and, with surprising strength, dragged him out of the house and into the darkness as if the Angel of Death himself had come to collect a soul.

Young Jeb shouted for his father, scrambled to his feet and grabbed his assailant around the waist. The second intruder, brown eyes and thick eyebrows only visible betwixt hat brim and handkerchief, backhanded the boy around the jaw, sending him sprawling to the ground. The boy grabbed his hot face and fought back his tears as he stood back up and went back in for more. This time the third man stepped in his way, held out his pistol until it was point blank on the boy's forehead and pulled back the hammer. The boy stopped in his tracks. The man looked down at the boy with emotionless, young green eyes. The boy looked at him and though he could still hear the screams of his dad as he was dragged off into the night, he knew that it was no good arguing with this man. The second intruder left the house and the third pressed the barrel of his gun into the boy's head. Jeb Jr clenched his jaw and clamped his eyes shut, awaiting the bullet to be sent into his skull. The gunslinger lifted the gun away and pushed the boy out of the house and out towards his papa.

───✺───

Upon a ridge, fifty yards from the house, the fourth rider remained on his horse, their profile silhouetted in the night by the bright stars. His first accomplice arrived, dragging Jeb behind him. He threw the man down by the horse's feet. The second accomplice arrived and stood over Jeb Sr, each man with a gun trained on him. Finally, young Jeb Jr arrived, tearful and scared, with the third intruder behind him.

"What the hell do you want?" spat old Jeb to the mounted rider. The accomplice to his left clubbed the old man with his gun, sending him down to the earth. His son started crying. Old Jeb rolled onto his back and spat blood out onto his own face. The second gunslinger placed his boot on Jeb's chest and cocked his gun at the man's head.

"Where's The Devil?" he said through his handkerchief in a surprisingly elegant tone.

"Who?"

The accomplice who had dragged Jeb out kicked him in the ribs.

"Where's The Devil? You have ridden with him. You're Jeb Garrett. You held up the Maynetown Stage, you shot Two Hole Treacher; you raided the Ploughkeep bordello, shot up the lawmen in Spike Rock City. You're Jeb Garrett and you have ridden with The Devil."

"He ain't here," yelled out the terrified son.

"Quiet boy," snapped his father. "Ain't nothing to worry about!"

Jeb Sr got to his feet and stood up to face the mounted rider as best he could.

"I ain't ridden with The Devil since my wife was taken. Ain't seen him in near ten years. Devil took just about everything from me, what you gonna take?"

The mounted rider, still in profile, looked out and away to the treeline, still assessing the environment.

"Well, you can give him a message," said the gunslinger to his left.

"I told you, he don't come around here no more."

"You tell him that the Chill boys is a runnin' him down," said the other.

"Who?"

"You tell him when you see him in hell," said the first.

"You don't sc… "

Jeb Sr did not finish his sentence. The mounted rider, without looking and quicker than thought, drew his side arm and sent a bullet through the old man's head. His son, standing ten feet behind him, received his father's brains all over his face. His father's body slumped down and the rider slowly turned to look at the boy, the creak of his leather coat and saddle like thunder. The boy, in shock at having seen and felt his father's demise, did not wail or scream but let his tears fall slowly.

The mounted rider lit a cigarette, the flame from his match offering up tiny clues to his identity. The boy saw, in his terror, bright, oval eyes, a thin slender nose and high cheekbones. Then the flash of light was gone. The silhouette of the rider motioned for the third accomplice to step away from behind the boy. He did so. The rider motioned for the boy to put his hands up. He did so, his hands quivering, his lip wobbling and his eyes wide in terror. Then the mounted rider spoke.

"Where is The Devil?" he said in an awful, croaking voice that sounded more like a twisted demon or a stuck pig than a human. There was a terrifying and sickening vibrato to it that filled all who heard it with utter dread. The young boy lost control of his bladder. The rider inhaled the smoke from his cigarette and the light from the end picked out the pin pricks in his pupils; glinting out from large, deep eyes.

"I don't know sir," quivered the boy.

The rider inspected his gloved hands and then looked up at the sky.

"How old are you, boy?" he croaked.

"Nine, sir. Almost ten."

"Almost ten? Almost a man, wouldn't you say?"

The boy looked around at the other gunslingers, his terror overwhelming him.

"Yes sir," he quivered.

"And a man, a real man, doesn't lie, does he?"

"No sir."

"Where is The Devil?"

"I don't know sir, I don't."

The rider turned to the boy, the moonlight still not penetrating the shadow cast by the brim of his hat.

"Very well, I believe you. You are telling the truth."

"Will you let me go, sir?"

"I will," hissed the rider, "but you will have to earn your freedom. Can you do that?"

"Yes sir!" cried the boy, still in terror but now sensing his salvation.

"You must deliver a message for me. Can you do that?"

"Yes sir."

"Good man," said the rider, and he shot the boy in the gut, sending him tumbling backwards and gurgling helplessly. The other gunslingers looked away, trying to hide their shock. The dark rider dismounted, walked over and looked down at the dying boy, looming over him like the true Devil. The boy, with his faltering strength, tried to push himself on his back, away from his executioner. The dark rider watched the boy struggle a few inches before stepping on his ankle and halting his attempt at escape. The rider then leaned in close to the boy, the amber cigarette illuminating the rider's sharp, yet slender cheeks and his deep, almond shaped eyes.

"Before The Devil finds you dead," croaked the rider, "tell him that I am coming."

And with that, he took off his hat, letting his blond hair cascade down around his shoulders, leaned in close to the boy and whispered into his ear. The boy's eyes widened in shocked confusion and the last thing he saw, before dying, was the cigarette's glow illuminating the dark rider's white collar. He was a Preacher.

CHAPTER EIGHT
Wild Goose Island

Maria had smoked three pipes in succession and still she chipped and scraped away at the table. Now she had moved away from the island of tobacco and carved out the beginnings of a mountain range, stretching up to the edges of the table. She worked, furious and naked, possessed by the rapture of memory regained. As the knife dug in and carved away splinters of wood, her mind fell wholly into the memory and back to the same warm day in the yard with The Devil and the axe.

Maria had spent the rest of the morning and the early afternoon chopping wood relentlessly and without any encouragement from her lover. As she mechanically placed a log on the block, she raised the axe and swung low, The Devil had cantered Cinereous around the wooden fence of their home, all the while looking at her and gazing in love and admiration at the way she worked so tirelessly. He thought about the state of the house when he found it, with logs piled haphazardly in the woodshed, the axe upon the naked floor, neglected. He thought about the three-day old pile of dishes he had discovered and he wondered if she truly was lazy or if, in fact, during all the days and weeks on her own, she had become detuned to time itself and had been walking around in a daze unsure of what was real and what was a dream. The truth lay halfway between the two eventualities. Her solitude had invaded her somewhat and she had no real concept of time outside of her routine, but she was also lazy and could not be bothered with the grind of housekeeping. She was alone, and nobody was coming for her, so what difference if the crockery was dirty or not?

The Devil cantered around the house, passed the barn, woodshed and outhouse, out to the far end of the compound and up the slight incline towards the dark treeline that was so thick that the bright Montana sun was in constant battle to penetrate it. The rider and horse cantered along the line, and back around the clearing towards the front of the house to where, just to the left, Maria was chopping her wood. He pulled up Cinereous who neighed and shook his head, the exercise doing him good. The Devil patted his neck and dismounted, leaving the horse to freely go about his business.

The Devil hitched himself over the fence and sat upon it. He rolled a cigarette and looked at the worker toiling hard and well, but yet maintaining a delicate femininity that sparked a curiosity in him. He knew it was only a matter of time before he would have to ride out once more and now, seeing her work tirelessly, he was struck with the strange idea that perhaps he could take her with him? He lit the cigarette and inhaled. As he did so, and as if the smoke had brought them with it, he was filled with fantasies and visions of riding out with her. Perhaps she could use her ways to gain entry into banks, or expensive parties? Perhaps her hard work and quiet nature would ingratiate her with simple folk. It was in this thought that his idea began to blossom, for The Devil liked nothing more than to visit himself upon simple folk. They were his quarry and prey and, wonderfully, simple folk abounded Montana. He imagined the acts he would wring upon them, riding into a town with Lucifer and Erebus screaming from his hips and Maria walking beside, laying waste to all with Leviathan. He was sure she could take the power of that rifle and was sure she would not rest until the gun itself screamed, "Enough, enough, enough!" The Devil and Maria, he mused, they would over-run Montana and America herself.

He smiled and flicked the cigarette onto the floor. He had an idea.

Maria split the last log and the moment the two pieces fell down either side of the chopping block she knew her work was over, fatigue hijacked her senses. Her back screamed, her arms were on fire and sweat was pouring from her. The axe fell from her hands. She bent down to try and pick up the two pieces of log and take them to the pile in one last action of duty, but her hands refused to obey. They were locked in the shape of the axe handle. Maria's vision began to blur slightly as now, after the burning muscular pains and the sweat, her organs cried out for fuel. She needed water, and food. She stood up and looked around, the sunshine refracting off the sweat in her eyes. She wiped her brow with her arm, wincing as she did so to see The Devil walking towards her, smiling. She tried to smile back but instead found herself slumping down onto the chopping block looking over to him and gasping for air. Her lover walked over and picked her up.

"You have worked well, my love," he whispered, "but you should not work so hard in the sun without food or shade. I would have told you, but you should learn for yourself. I do not like to see you suffer."

Maria, held against his chest, craned her neck up and tried to look into his eyes, but the brim of his wide hat threw a dark shadow over his face and she could see only a void. She closed her eyes and quickly fell asleep. The Devil pulled her into his chest and kissed her forehead, a gesture which penetrated deep into her dream state and made its presence known. Maria murmured a little and tucked further into his chest. The Devil whistled quietly for Cinereous who trotted over.

The Devil, showing remarkable strength and gentleness, lifted Maria over the horse, before he himself climbed upon the great beast. Once upon him, The Devil carefully picked Maria up and sat her properly, so that she was in front of him and facing forward. She slept on but The Devil held her tightly and nudged Cinereous to move out. The horse obliged, but not before neighing to Azazel who bleated back before returning to graze on his scrubby patch of grass.

Maria awoke just after four in the afternoon when the sun had started to clip the tops of the trees. At first her eyes slowly began to open, but as soon as she got the first hint that she was not on her land, they snapped open and she sat bolt upright. Her mouth fell open and she stood up to take in the vista.

She was standing on the shore of a great lake; behind and above her the Rocky Mountain Douglas Fir trees shaded her with an all encompassing canopy that swept around the vast lake and raked up the sides of the flanking mountains. At the far end of the lake, she saw the great Rocky range stretch on, on, on to perhaps the end of the world. The sighing clouds of light were painted ochre by the setting sun and this in turn was mirrored by the silent, cool water that lapped at the shore by her feet, enticing her in. She bent down to the water's edge and touched the cool water, scoping some up and tasting it. It was fresh and beyond any other drink she had tried before in terms of its instant rejuvenating qualities.

"Do you see the island?" floated The Devil's voice from behind Maria. She turned to see her lover standing at the treeline, half covered in shadow and leaning on a trunk. He was rolling a cigarette. He gestured to her to look back out. She turned and looked out to the small island that stood alone in the middle of the lake.

"It's called Wild Goose Island. Do you know why?"

Maria, without turning shook her head. Behind her, she could sense The Devil smiling.

"Some generations back, there used to be two tribes who lived on either side of the lake. They didn't war with each other, they didn't mix or socialise. They just kept themselves to themselves like good simple folk."

Maria wrapped her shawl around herself a little tighter as a gentle and not too intrusive breeze drifted across the lake.

"Then, one day," her lover continued, "a great warrior from one tribe saw a beautiful woman from the other swimming out to the island. He watched her as she swam through the lake, alive, young and free. He fell instantly in love and forgetting about his duty to his tribe, he dived into the lake and swam out to meet her. He was right to do so, because as soon as he came up to the little island, the woman did see him and she, as he had, fell instantly in love. He climbed ashore and instead of making love, they simply exchanged names and talked and talked until the morning light whereupon they knew that a great connection had been made."

Maria sat down and dipped her feet into the lake, basking in the onslaught of sound and vision that was overcoming her senses.

"They agreed to meet again on the island the next day and together they would escape their lives and live as lovers wherever their destiny took them. Under the Promising Moon, they exchanged their vows, kissed and swam back to their respective tribes. But they were not welcomed home. Someone had seen their meeting and alerted the tribe leaders. However the lovers, knowing each belonged to the other, broke free of their bondage and, in the dead of night, escaped and swam back to the island to meet once more. Come morning, they were discovered missing and the outrage spread fast through both tribes; two opposing hunting parties were dispatched to retrieve the two runaways and deal with them appropriately."

Maria hunched up her legs close to her chest and looked at the island, The Devil's words painting in her imagination the scene so vividly she could almost feel the heat from the hunter's torches as they searched around for the missing lovers. The Devil smiled as he saw Maria hold herself tightly, knowing that his words were having their desired effect.

"But," he continued, "the Great Spirit was watching as always and in a moment of mercy, took pity on the lovers and turned them into geese. When the hunters reached the island, they found not two runaway lovers but a pair of wild birds. Upon seeing the intruders on their island, it is said that the two geese rubbed their necks together tenderly, turned and took flight never to return, to always be together, as geese mate for life. That's why it is called Wild Goose Island."

Maria shed a tear and smiled as, in her mind's eye, she saw the two geese take flight from the island and fly off into the sunset. The Devil stepped from the treeline and went to sit down next to Maria. When he did so, she rested against him. He put his arm around her shoulder and they both looked out at the grandeur of St Mary's Lake and Wild Goose Island.

———⊗⊗⊗———

The Devil waited until the sun had set behind the Rocky Mountains and the need for warmth was greater before he turned to Maria and stroked her neck and face. She turned to him, framed wonderfully by the mountains and illuminated by the last rays of light pulsing off the water.

The Devil leaned in and kissed her as she needed to be kissed, deeply, longingly and with the weight of truth that only those in love have. He finally broke off and brushed her hair away to reveal her large brown eyes. Maria looked at her lover and saw perhaps a thousand different people behind his eyes. She slowly lifted his hat off his head and let his tousled blonde hair fall down to his shoulders. The Devil took hold of both her cheeks and pulled her in close once more.

"We must never be apart," he whispered before laying her down on her back and making love to her by the shore of St Mary's Lake.

———⊗⊗⊗———

By the time the memory had transformed into dream, Maria lay face down on the kitchen table fast asleep. The knife lay by her side and the tabletop now presented a fully realised vista of St Mary's Lake with the Rocky Mountains behind, and where Maria's hand lay on the table her fingers were outstretched, just brushing against the shore of Wild Goose Island.

CHAPTER NINE

Burn It

The three accomplices dragged the two bodies into the house and lay them on their respective beds. Such was the size of the boy that he was easily carried, slung unceremoniously over the shoulder of the heavyset man who had dragged his father out into the courtyard. The other two carried Jeb Sr and tried their best not to let the contents of his head spill out over the floorboards. Once laid out upon their beds, and with coins placed over their eyes for the boatman, they took off their hats and waited for the fourth rider to enter.

The Preacher walked into the house and looked around the meagre living room. He inspected the walls and the shelves, looking over the few pictures that rested there and the few remaining trinkets that hadn't been sold for more food. The house was liveable, but the sustainability was in decline. The dark rider could assess that in two seasons, the occupants probably would have frozen or starved once the winter came in. As he looked around, he wondered why Jeb Sr had not prepared better for it. The food on the floor was portioned generously, the fire burned with an abundance of fuel. It seemed as though Jeb Sr didn't plan on making it through the next few seasons.

After looking around the living room, the rider walked into the bedroom and over to the bodies. He took off his hat, and in the warm glow of the room his features were revealed. He had a slender, small nose, high cheeks and large round eyes. His skin, though dirty, was fair and smooth. The dark rider looked over the bodies, the father with the back of his head blown off and his brain matter smeared over the dusty ground, the porch and the bed sheets, and his son, hands holding his gut, tongue lolling.

He crossed the arms of the corpses, took a small, battered bible out of his pocket and administered the last rites. The three gunslingers looked to the floor solemnly as the Preacher performed his duty. The Preacher made the sign of the cross over the bodies and gestured for his accomplices to wait outside. They stepped out in the night air and shared some tobacco.

The Preacher pocketed the bible, sat on the edge of the son's bed and looked over his corpse. He removed the coins from his eyes and tilted his head so that the boy was looking at his murderer.

"It was The Devil. Forgive me," he tried to whisper, though because of his cracked voice, it held little sincerity. He replaced the coins over the boy's eyes and kissed his cold forehead, the tears filling his icy grey eyes. He rested the boy back down and turned his attention to the father. He looked over the body and as he did so, he called forth in his mind all the men, women and children he had killed along his way. Each name and face was etched into his mind, but his mission and his will to finish it drove him on.

"Damn you," he cracked, "you should have given him up. But you didn't. Damn you."

The Preacher looked out of the window to see his accomplices milling about by their horses and smoking so, knowing he wouldn't be disturbed, he removed his glove, took his bowie knife and sliced into his lean, hairless arm, carving a mark next to a line of others that extended up into his sleeve and out of view. He stood up and let the blood trickle slowly down over the two bodies for a few moments before wrapping a tawdry rag around his arm, sheathing his knife, re-gloving his hand and leaving the house.

He walked out with his normal long and powerful stride, passed his men and mounted his great black steed. The men looked up at him, awaiting further instruction.

"Burn it," he said.

The men tipped their hats and walked back over to the farm house.

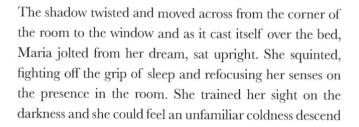

The shadow twisted and moved across from the corner of the room to the window and as it cast itself over the bed, Maria jolted from her dream, sat upright. She squinted, fighting off the grip of sleep and refocusing her senses on the presence in the room. She trained her sight on the darkness and she could feel an unfamiliar coldness descend upon the room. Her breath became visible. Maria squinted to see the shadow gliding across the room to the window, seeping under the frame and out into the night, up high into the air and dissipating into smoke.

The chill in the room fell away and the sharpness finally returned to Maria's vision. She sat back against the frame, the cold of the metal not bothering her, and considered the meaning of the departing shadow. She believed in omens and signs, it was what kept her alert and alive though she could not decipher the exact meaning of this. All she could deduce was that something was coming. She looked over at the space where her lover should have been sleeping and motioned to brush the hair from his face. But he was not there and the gesture was meaningless. Maria looked over to her pipe, resting on the plate of ash that still scented the room slightly. She slid back into bed, held her lover tightly in her heart and fell asleep to dream of avenging angels.

The torches had barely been introduced to the house before it was aflame. The three men had thrown them in and darted back to their horses in time to see it spring into fire and burst into flames, the great plume belching up into the black night. The four horsemen watched as it burned, each one warming themselves in preparation for a long night ahead and each one taking the few moments to gaze into the inferno and see into themselves.

One saw his wife in the flames, another saw his dead sister and the third saw the mother he never knew. The Dark Rider's vision was more complete than his accomplices' such was the ferocity of his mind and the absolute necessity to keep that particular image front and centre of consciousness. In his mind he saw a baby, hidden in a filthy crate under a bed in a farmhouse. He saw thick snow outside and vast tundra spreading outwards to the very limits of his memory. He moved from the house and drifted out of the door, towards a body lying in the snow. It was a beautiful woman, grey eyes faltering, breathing staggered. She was clutching her throat which gushed blood from a slash that reached deeply from her ear, down over her throat to her collarbone.

As the rider looked into the flames of the burning Garret abode, he recalled the frosty breath and the steam rising from the hot blood seeping from that woman's wound, and he saw The Devil on that ashen white horse of his riding off into the tundra.

The inferno raged harder, as if propelled by the angst and the pain that the four men had thrown onto it. The heat intensified; the horses became too uncomfortable and of their own volition, began to back up. Finally, the three gunslingers turned their horses around and rode off into the woods, leaving the dark rider to spend a few more moments staring into the bowels of the inferno and replenishing any conviction that might have been sapped from him to complete his mission and fulfil his destiny.

Finally, when his horse could bear no more, the Preacher turned around and went to join the others.

They had ridden deep into the forest and into the night before fatigue had finally caught up with them and they made camp. The men were so entrenched in the belly of the dense woodland that they held little fear of any renegade Crow raiding parties. They had tethered their horses and seen to them, unrolled their blankets and heated some tinned beans, and were sitting around the campfire. The three gunslingers sat in a semi-circle around the modest fire while their leader sat away from them, in profile to the fire, keeping one eye and one ear on them and their conversations, and the other eye and ear on his mission and his destiny.

Revenge is an all-consuming concept and one does not partake of it lightly. If one chooses that path, one must forgo any luxury or comfort and dedicate every moment, awake or in dream, to the mission and the goal. One must be ready to overturn heaven and hell to right the wrong, and the rider had made that commitment long ago. As soon as he had set foot upon that path, his old personality and identity had been discarded and he had risen anew: an avenging angel. And so it was that in times of quiet, all he would do was both reflect and look forward. He was a man of singular focus.

As the night wore on, the food eaten and the drink finished, the conversation turned as it always did, to current affairs and for the group of riders, there was only one affair – that of tracking down The Devil.

"I ain't seen woods like it, 'cept maybe south," said the gunslinger that had dragged old Jeb out of the farmhouse. He was a heavy-set man with a flat, twisted nose and equally flattened knuckles from his prize fighting days which were, quite clearly, far behind him. His name was Hobson Whitney and he made mention of the near impassable environment in a clear attempt to divert the conversation onto the one pressing matter: their next move.

"We ain't getting out of it for a good few weeks, you can be sure of that; boss, we gotta keep movin', right?" chirped Fraser, the second gunslinger who was sat next to Hobson.

Fraser Whitney, Hobson's younger and somewhat slower brother, was a fast and accurate sharpshooter but could not apply that skill and acumen to intellectual pursuits. Some people called him slow, but those that did usually fell foul of Hobson who hit like a locomotive.

"But where to? Garret farm was the last lead, last one to have seen The Devil. We're just walking into nothing. I knows it. God damn I'm hungry," said Hobson as he poked and prodded the fire.

"We're all hungry, Hobs, but we gotta trust in the boss. He knows," said the third gunslinger, Conrad, the right hand man of the Preacher. He was fierce, diligent and blindly loyal as those with faith were.

"Well we ain't got much choice. Draggin' us all out here. I tell you, killing them Garretts – bad idea. Now we ain't got shit." spat Hobson.

"You talk too much. You talk too loud," cracked their leader.

"Sorry boss, just hacked off with this god damned forest."

"Get some sleep," said the rider. "We ride out in three hours."

"Where to? Where we going?"

"Bel."

The mood in the camp dropped.

"You shittin' us boss?" said Hobson.

"You shittin' us boss?" parroted Fraser.

"Boss knows what he's doing," Conrad said diplomatically.

"I ain't ridi… "

The Dark Rider was already over the fire, pinning Hobson down and holding a knife to his jugular before the prize-fighter could react. Fraser got to his feet and reached for his gun. He halted when he looked over to see Conrad standing, covering their leader with his pistol aimed at Fraser.

Slowly their leader released his grip and stood back up, the fire catching his expression of utter conviction. Hobson got to his feet and dusted himself off. Fraser sat back down and Conrad holstered his firearm.

"Bel… that place is fucking crazy," said Hobson.

"Get some sleep," said Conrad as their leader turned away and walked into the darkness, to sleep alone and away from them all.

"We ain't getting out of that place alive," whispered Hobson to his brother as they lay down and pulled their blankets over themselves. "Rickman Chill, fearless leader, is gonna get us all killed for sure."

Conrad watched them as the brothers rolled away from him and went to sleep. He placed his gun to his side and looked at the darkness into which his leader, Rickman Chill, had walked. He broke up some twigs and threw them into the fire knowing that the town of Bel, and the mythical, twisted bastard known only as The Nameless who ruled the town was next on their trail and that none of them would survive. '*Damn you,*' he dared to think before tilting his hat down over his face and falling asleep with one eye on the Whitney brothers and one hand on his revolver.

THE DEVIL'S SIDEARM:
'Erebus'

The inscription across the barrel taken from
John Milton's Paradise Lost and reads:

'With impetuous recoil and jarring sound
Th' infernal doors, and on their hinges grate
Harsh thunder, that the lowest bottom shook
Of Erebus.'

CHAPTER TEN

The Devil's Lie

Despite waking in the night to the unerring feeling of dread in her house, Maria had managed to sleep well for the few hours left until dawn. The unborn child did not torment her as it used to and she slept comfortably, with her arms over her belly and her fingers interlinked.

She had awoken refreshed, and the gentle breeze tickled her face as it squeezed through the cracks in the window pane and cascaded over her. She sat up, prepared her pipe and thought on the day ahead. Normally, when she smoked in the morning, she did not think of tasks or chores and she did not plan for anything except perhaps her afternoon pipe on the porch. She used to sit there and smoke, adrift in melancholia. The last couple of days, however, had changed her. She now thought feverishly of the plans and preparations that needed to be done. The baby was coming and soon she would not be able to leave the house. She had to make sure everything was ready.

She finished her pipe, threw off the covers, and stepped out of bed onto the rough wooden floor. There was work to be done.

After washing and dressing, Maria tidied the kitchen and prepared a hearty breakfast for herself and the baby.

The portion was generous and as she sat and ate, she looked across to find to her astonishment that she had not set a place for The Devil. She stopped chewing and held the food in her mouth. She had been so focused on the day ahead that she had not thought about him. Had she forgotten her lover? Or had she found some sort of joy in the work she was doing that had temporarily occupied her mind? She remembered the last time she had compelled to attend to the practicalities of living. It was the morning after the day they had spent at St Mary's Lake. Maria chewed her food more slowly and recalled that morning in all its searing detail.

The Devil had awoken to find, much to his surprise, that he was alone in bed. The air was fresh and he could smell coffee, which did much to allay any suspicions that might have arisen. He stretched and climbed out of bed.

Maria had been up for hours. She had risen unusually early, climbed quietly over her lover and gone about a morning's work that, on any normal day, would not have commenced until at least eleven o'clock. She had gone to the wood store and collected enough wood for the day, checked on the stock pile to see that it was dry, and she had paid some attention to the axe, ensuring that it was oiled. She had seen to Cinereous and Azazel, bringing the goat some water and leading the horse to his trough. After brushing down the horse, she had opened the gate and let him loose to walk freely around the land. After seeing to the animals, she washed herself by splashing cold water from the covered barrel over her face and arm pits, doused her sex with a damp flannel and then went into the kitchen to clean and prepare breakfast.

The work of someone housebound tickled Maria slightly and she felt quite happy to attend to all manner of tasks that she normally would have forgone. She didn't once stop to question why she had had the sudden change of personality, instinctively attributing it to being happy to have her lover so close by.

By the time he came downstairs, she was sat at the breakfast table with a plate of eggs and some salted meat for herself and a double-sized portion for him. He smiled at her as he sat groggily down for breakfast. They ate in silence, and Maria found it hard to suppress a smile every time she put food in her mouth and looked over to see the food on the other plate diminishing. How rare a sight it was for her, as she always prepared his plate and it always went uneaten. The little vision was overwhelming her. The Devil finished his meal, pushed the plate aside and pulled out his tobacco pouch. He began to stuff a cigarette while Maria continued to enjoy her small portion of food.

"You should eat more," he said.

Maria shrugged as she cut up a piece of meat.

"You will have to. You will have to keep your strength up for when I'm… " The Devil halted his words as Maria stopped chewing and looked at him. He looked down at his tobacco and began to roll his cigarette.

"Don't look at me like that," he said, not wanting to make eye contact. "This is just temporary."

He finally looked up at Maria to see her staring fiercely at him, food still half chewed in her mouth. He looked back down at the table.

"You should eat more," he said again.

Maria stood up quickly, the chair scraping loudly across the floor, and she flung the plate across the room, obliterating it. She spat the food out of her mouth and stormed out of the house.

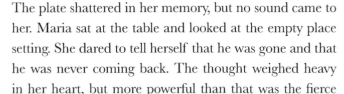

The plate shattered in her memory, but no sound came to her. Maria sat at the table and looked at the empty place setting. She dared to tell herself that he was gone and that he was never coming back. The thought weighed heavy in her heart, but more powerful than that was the fierce riposte her sense of self-preservation offered: *'Good'* it simply said.

Maria finished her large breakfast, sat back in the chair and looked at the single plate setting. She rubbed and stroked her belly tenderly and as she did so, she noticed a pair of hobo spiders making their way across the table. Maria studied them as they scuttled along, navigating the dips and divots of the Wild Goose Island carving. Maria clenched her jaw and bit her lip before leaning forward and trapping the spiders underneath two upturned cups and thrusting them into a prison of blackness. She stood up and moved the cups to opposite ends of the table, separating the two hobo spiders and leaving them to die alone in their black oubliettes. She then went about her day.

The dreams of men on the hunt are not fanciful, but purposeful. Their dreamscapes are lands filled with anxieties, questions and ideas birthed by their quest, and the strain that has placed upon their psyches. Men in pursuit know this and so, when asleep, they investigate their dreams and they remember the clues and omens presented to them by their subconscious. For men in pursuit of The Devil, the only thing more powerful in their dreamscapes than the clues and omens are the thunderous reasons of their drive. With their engine of revenge fuelled by that reason they set out to do what it is they need to do. And so, as the flames in the burning house of Garrett revealed to them their motivations, their dreamscapes made them temporally real. None of the men slept well, but instead rose early and alert. Rickman was already awake and watching over them. He kicked the boots of Hobson and Fraser to hurry them out of their slumber. The brothers sat up.

"Ten minutes," cracked the Preacher.

"I gotta shit," yawned Hobson.

Fraser was falling back to sleep, still sitting up, and received a reviving cuff around the head from his brother. The leader beckoned Conrad, who was already up, to go with him. Conrad obliged and the two men stepped away from the campsite while the other two sorted themselves out.

Conrad and Rickman walked to a break in the woodland. They were high upon a ridge, overlooking a valley, the Rocky Mountains in the distance and lower mountains all around.

"It's a week's ride to Bel and The Nameless, maybe more," said the leader as the two men stood above the world looking out at it all. "Deep into the heartland, deep into the darkness."

"We'll make it," said Conrad convincingly.

Rickman smiled.

"Why do you say that?" he tested.

"Because we have to."

"And The Nameless?"

"He has it coming. They have it coming. There is a whirlwind coming their way."

Rickman turned to Conrad and smiled at him. The young man was twenty one, though looked younger. He had green eyes, a thin wispy beard and straggly hair. He was fair, innocent looking and anyone could tell that he was decent at heart. But Rickman knew Conrad better than anyone else and he knew him to be fierce, with a stomach full of rocks. Conrad smiled at the Preacher.

"We'll make it through. We'll make it outta there alive, and with our minds. We'll go on to get to that son of a bitch."

"The residents of Bel," cracked Rickman. "They're gonna hold onto their lives dearly. You know that, don't you?"

"Well, there ain't nobody can hold onto nothing tight enough so as Rickman Chill can't take it away from them."

And with that, Conrad looked out at the great vista in front of him before turning back to join the brothers in disassembling the camp.

Rickman Chill, the dark rider, looked out at the world, and hatred and rage boiled behind his grey eyes.

"I am the whirlwind," he said to the landscape.

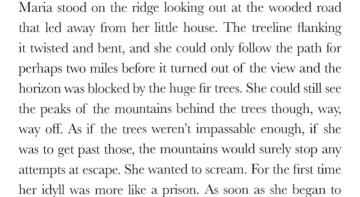

Maria stood on the ridge looking out at the wooded road that led away from her little house. The treeline flanking it twisted and bent, and she could only follow the path for perhaps two miles before it turned out of the view and the horizon was blocked by the huge fir trees. She could still see the peaks of the mountains behind the trees though, way, way off. As if the trees weren't impassable enough, if she was to get past those, the mountains would surely stop any attempts at escape. She wanted to scream. For the first time her idyll was more like a prison. As soon as she began to resent her world, the clouds came over and a chill wind fell down upon her. She could see, along the path, the leaves whip up as if the wind travelled up to her. She wrapped her shawl around her shoulders and faced the wind, defiant that she should be trapped and resentful of everything that denied her happiness. The Devil walked up and stood next to her.

"Storm is coming in, Maria. Come inside."

Maria clenched her jaw and looked out at the forest. The Devil put his arm around her but she shrugged out of it.

"Maria, please."

She stood defiantly.

"I am leaving," he said.

She shrugged.

"I can't stay here forever."

Maria gestured for him to go, ride out, leave now, head for the mountains and never return, for she didn't care. It was a definitive gesture.

The Devil looked to the floor and sighed in resignation. The wind was picking up and the clouds were coming in unnaturally fast. As if the lifecycle of a day had sped up, the clouds began to merge and an overwhelming darkness, like evening, descended all around. The Devil decided to ask her.

He looked up to her. She still looked away toward the oncoming storm.

"Come with me," he said.

Maria squinted in suspicion as his suggestion broke down her battlements and found its way into her mind.

That tiny flinch told him that she was not so angry. He smiled.

"Come away with me. We'll ride out together."

She turned and her eyes warned him that he had better be serious. He put his hands on her shoulders; the wind blew her hair across her face.

"Ride out with me, out there. You and me, me and you."

Maria thought for a few moments about the proposition. She made up her mind and, without giving away a hint of her decision, she took her lover by the hand and led him back into the house and into the bedroom.

———⊗⊗⊗———

The day was nearly over and as Maria smoked her afternoon pipe on the porch, the storm clouds from her memory filtered into the real world and a wind whipped around the compound. Azazel, still by the fence, moved around his hitching post, agitated by the oncoming chaos. Maria finished her pipe and stood up, wrapping her shawl around herself as she had done that day the storm had come and The Devil had lied to her. The wind grew stronger as she held her belly and walked over to Azazel. The goat was bleating loudly and stamping his hooves. The animal did not calm when he saw her, but stamped his hooves harder to spur her on. The dark clouds gathered and the air grew heavy with dread. Maria reached Azazel, untangled his tether from the hitching post, and together they hurried back to the house.

Maria picked up her pipe and tobacco from the seat of her rocking chair and closed the door to the house just as the first heavy drops of rain began to fall.

CHAPTER ELEVEN

The Visitor from the Storm

The storm battered Maria's house and she could not see more than ten feet out of the window. Inside, Azazel had gone into the side room which now housed some chickens and the stockpile of wood. The animals had understood that they were safe and warm from the elements and so co-habited the room peacefully. Maria had prepared the fire and the house was tranquil and calm. She cleared away the plates from her lunch and released the trapped spiders on the table after feeling ashamed at her earlier actions. She sat down at the kitchen table and looked over her carving of the Wild Goose Island and remembered lying naked by the lake's shore, entwined in her lover's arms, as free as the spirits around them. She resisted falling into her memory at that point and instead, as it was cosy and peaceful in the house, decided to wear The Devil's poncho and hat. She convinced herself that it was not an action born out of sadness or desperation but in fact a bittersweet gesture, like reading an old love letter and feeling only the embrace of nostalgia.

And so, as the storm thrashed around her tiny piece of the earth, Maria put on her lover's poncho and hat and retired to the living room. As she passed the spare room, her shadow spilled inside and for a few moments, Azazel was tricked into believing that his master had returned. The silhouette passed around the room and the goat watched head up and alert until the shadow snapped into the shape of Maria, unmistakable with her large belly. Azazel bleated quietly when he saw her walk past the doorway and into the living room to sit by the fire. Azazel was not so sad to see her instead of his master because, as she sat in the rocking chair, The Devil's shadow was thrown back into the spare room and rested upon the wall by the goat. Azazel shuffled to the wall and rested against it, imagining that his weight was against the legs of his master.

The Chill gang had only been travelling for a few hours when the storm clouds gathered overhead. The neighing horses, sensing the oncoming chaos, began rearing up as the air grew thick and oppressive. The riders held onto their hats and looked up through the swaying canopy of trees to the angry heavens.

"Goddamn, we got a helluva beatin' coming," called out Hobson as he struggled to maintain control of his circling horse.

"What we do boss?" shouted Fraser as his horse backed into Hobson's. Conrad looked over at the dark rider who sat motionless on his horse, looking out into the distance seemingly unaware of the madness around.

"Hey boss!" shouted Hobson as a crack of thunder rocked the landscape.

Conrad looked around and through the gloom of the trees he made out a safe spot – a cave entrance about fifty yards to the right.

"There!" he shouted, pointing towards the cave. "In there!"

The two brothers did not need telling a third time, and kicked their horses into action. The thunder cracked again and large, heavy droplets began to fall from the heavens, battering the two riders still outside.

Conrad geed his brave horse over to Rickman's and grabbed the rider by the hand. As soon as Conrad touched him, the dark rider was snapped out of his trance and Conrad suddenly felt the touch of steel under his chin. Rickman's large eyes were burning with unfocused rage.

"We gotta go, come on!" shouted Conrad over the din, and he backed his horse away. "Come on let's go!"

Rickman, who for a moment looked as if in a dream, snapped awake and spurred his horse to follow.

The cave was a dank abyss. The horses feared to enter and so stayed by the entrance, just covered enough for comfort. The men ventured into the blackness.

Maria rocked in her chair, the fire beside her popping and crackling as it hungrily burnt the logs she had prepared earlier that day. She smoked her pipe and rocked gently whilst the rain patted the window pane hypnotically. Maria could not resist any further and looked over to her lover's empty chair, projecting his image upon it.

The last time such a storm had come, he was there and together they felt like the immovable eye of it: tranquillity in the tempest. Maria looked over to her lover who sat by the window playing his guitar. He was exceptionally skilled and he improvised a soft and melancholic tune that twisted and danced around the room, holding Maria in that divine place between sleep and dream where elements from each state waltz together.

She looked at his fingers tenderly gliding over the fret board and to his boot softly tapping the rhythm upon the floorboards. She rocked back and forth, rested her head upon the back of the chair and looked at him, listening to his music spinning through her.

Unlike the storm that raged around her house in reality, cutting her off from the world, the storm that raged in her memory had brought the borders of the world that much closer to the compound and brought her pocket of Montana that much more tightly into its grasp; for that, she loved her world. Everything now was far more intimate.

The storm had forced The Devil to stay and so, in that house, they made love when they wanted and they made do with their meagre rations. What they did have tasted sweeter and the portions felt bigger because they were weathering the storm together.

On the seventh night she rocked on her chair by the fire, completely naked, her hair undone and falling over her shoulders, her pipe in her hand, the smoke rising up from it. Across from her The Devil sat, also naked, in his chair with his guitar across his lap. He was staring dreamily into the fire and Maria fantasised that he was dreaming about their future together.

In actual fact, he was dreaming of home and of his past. The places he had been and the things he had done. Where the borders of the universe had closed in on the house and felt wonderful to Maria, for The Devil it was another level of confinement which forced him to remain rooted for too long and when he did that, his past deeds would always come back and abound in his mind. The only thing that kept him in the house was Maria and the way she loved him. She was the only soul he had met that had dared to rail against his desire for chaos and freedom. She was the only thing that provided a contrast in his world and the woman continually surprised him.

He looked over to her; she smiled and lifted her leg up and rested it over the long, curved arm of the rocking chair, exposing her sex and inviting him in. The Devil placed the guitar to the side and went over to her.

Maria rocked in her chair, and as the ghost of The Devil set his guitar aside and came over to her, she angled her poncho to the side and awkwardly attempted to slide her hands under her swollen belly and between her legs to find some pleasure. The size of her belly and the awkwardness of her position made her body and her sex feel like an alien landscape to her hands and she derived no satisfaction despite a valiant and defiant attempt to try different routes to gratification. Eventually she conceded defeat and replaced the poncho back over her lap and rubbed her belly.

She looked over to her lover's chair which remained unoccupied. The guitar lay as it had done for many months, resting against the wall. The ghost had gone and the storm remained. Maria sighed and continued to rock in her chair, rubbing her belly and thinking about 'Ricochet' Stanley Spring, the boy who took her lover away.

The Devil and Maria had just made love in the living room and were still basking in love's afterglow when his senses twitched. He sat bolt upright and grabbed Erebus from his holster. Maria sat up and, on cue from a stern look from her lover, hurriedly got dressed. She pulled on her skirt and fixed her hair; by the time she had done so and looked around, The Devil had vanished. Then there was a knock at the door.

Maria stood up and edged towards the front door. Another knock came which made her jump slightly and pull her shawl together.

"It's alright," came the whisper from her lover. Maria looked around to see the barrel of Erebus lined up with the wall, The Devil, half in shadow and still naked, standing flat against the wall. Another knock came.

"Open it," he whispered. Maria, more confident now that she knew he was there, opened the door a crack.

"Good day ma'am," came the voice from outside in an accent she could not place. "I'm looking for someone. I mean you no harm ma'am. I'm looking for a man. Can I come in? Storm's a-fierce out here!"

Maria shook her head. The man stepped closer. "Speak English ma'am?" Maria did not respond. "You hear me ma'am?" Maria did not respond but instead looked cautiously over to The Devil. All that the darkness would reveal was the pin pricks of light in his eyes. She turned back to the door.

"Are you Maria, ma'am? My name's Stan, Stanley Spring, from Barston. May I come in? It's hell outside ma'am."

Maria looked over to the pin pricks of light. They twinkled which she read as a 'yes'. She stepped back and opened the door. Stanley Spring rushed in and closed it behind him, stamping his feet and shaking.

"Yu-hu-weee ma'am, it is hell on earth out there!" he said in a jovial, relieved tone. He threw his hat back, which hung around the back of his neck via a cord, wiped his thick black hair slickly over his head and looked at her. He was neither ugly nor handsome but pleasing enough with a round face, brown, vaguely stupid eyes and a well-kept beard that did not have the maturity to link moustache to jaw. He smiled a broad smile, showing a remarkable set of clean teeth.

"I tell you, I have been ridin' ridin' ridin'. You must be Maria. I can tell because you don't say much. People told me you don't say much. They say its coz Crow took your tongue. They told me Crow stuck a branding iron in your mouth and took your tongue! Is that true ma'am? Is it true?"

Maria, struck by the man's genuine enthusiasm and strange happiness, furrowed her brow. This, however, did not assuage him as she thought it might and he still stood there with a goofy, child-like grin, wringing his hands and rocking slightly from one foot to the next. Maria poked her tongue out at him, showing it to be plump, pink and completely unblemished. Stanley Spring gasped.

"I knew it! God dammit I knew it! That jackass Dumbleton bet me a quarter that Crow took your tongue! I knew it!" His demeanour changed, "but I bet him a dollar that you talk… but I guess you don't."

Maria folded her arms. Stanley Spring took the hint and went to take something out from his pocket. As he brushed his hand over his coat, he revealed to her a set of pearl handled six shooters attached to his belt. He had hardly moved when he heard the click of cocking hammer by his ear. He froze.

"No harm. Don't shoot!" he said quietly.

"Turn around," whispered The Devil. Stanley Spring obliged, slowly.

The Devil stepped into the light and lowered his gun.

"You're looking for me," he said with a wry smile as the candlelight flickered across his eyes.

CHAPTER TWELVE
The Aged Lovers

The storm had not abated for seven days and for the Chill gang life was hell. They had stayed in the dark cave for the night, but could not linger come morning and it was agreed, under a rare democratic decision, to push on through the day's rain and seek shelter come sundown. They calculated that they could come across a house or a reservation within two days of arduous trekking.

They were wrong, and by the night of the sixth day, the rain had penetrated into their psyches. Even Rickman Chill's internal landscape had become drenched in water and when he revisited places and events from his past, they were under torrential rain. The horses, as was their way, looked down at the ground as they trudged along and thought only '*press on*', '*press on*', '*press on.*'

The men had found shelter where they could: in small caves, under fallen trees, wedged between boulders with their coats draped over them like canopies, and yet still they pressed on. Nature is fierce stubborn and determined, but so is man, and none more so than Rickman Chill. Though the water seeped into his mind and flooded his memories, he refused to let it melt the tundra in his one driving memory – that of the woman lying on the freezing snow, blood draining from her neck as The Devil rode away. There was no element or force of nature that could soothe the power of that memory and so it held fast in his mind, the water from the storm washing through it like a flash flood, but never washing it away. He trudged onwards and behind him his crew followed.

On the seventh day of wind, rain and trekking, the Chill gang crested a ridge and saw below, some one hundred final yards farther, a small farmhouse. They halted on the ridge and took in the surroundings, Rickman calculating in his mind the potential dangers that might lie ahead. Conrad sidled next to him and scanned also, trying to see what the dark rider saw and hoping to pick out the one detail that separated the leader from the infantry man. Conrad saw only a house and a beacon of light inside, but he looked again nevertheless.

The Whitney brothers just looked at each other and hunched their shoulders up, praying that Rickman would deem the house safe and get them out of the damn elements.

Finally, their leader looked to them and nodded. The others, relieved that shelter was but a few moments away, knew what to do; all four cantered down towards the farm house in a calculated, unthreatening manner. They were ready for anything, of course, but they understood that they stood more of a chance of gaining entry to the shelter if they appeared desperate and not dangerous. They entered the compound and dismounted, leading their horses up to the porch but stopping short of the front door by a few yards.

Fraser stepped up onto the porch while the other men huddled behind him, their hats over their faces, their collars up and shivering to accentuate their plight.

Fraser knocked and waited. After a few minutes, the door opened a crack and an old pair of eyes peered out.

"Please mister," said Fraser in his soft, adolescent voice, "Has you a barn we can shelter in for the night? We'll pay, mister."

"Two days ride to Barston," hissed the old man.

"Yes sir, two days," said Fraser with sad eyes.

"More like two months, in this weather!" called out Hobson from the back of the line. The old man squinted at him. Rickman began to cough.

"Sir," he said, coughing to try and mask his terrifying voice, "we mean no trouble, just travelling on to deliver the good Lord's message."

The old man squinted harder. Rickman, from behind Fraser, coughed again and opened his coat slightly to reveal his Preacher's collar. The rest of the gang took that as their cue to take off their hats and look as angelic as possible.

"Barn's got no roof." said the old man.

"That's alright," said Rickman, coughing again. "This inn is full. Come on boys, the Lord intends for us to not seek the kindness of strangers. Thank you, sir and good day to you."

The boys nodded, put their hats on and began to shuffle off the porch and back out into the driving wind and rain. The old man relented.

"You can tie your horses on the porch," he said, still with the door held ajar. "They should be safe. You can sleep inside." and at that he left the door and disappeared into his house.

The Chill gang looked at each other. Rickman nodded, which told them to go on and do it, but keep their guard up nonetheless. The boys walked the horses onto the porch and tethered them to the beam. They walked into the house.

Inside was quaint and warm. The entrance led straight to the kitchen and to the side there was a staircase leading up to the bedrooms on the landing. The open space on the other side of the staircase was the living room, which housed a trunk with a blanket over it, two chairs and an open fire which licked and crackled pleasantly. Upon the mantelpiece there sat four faded pictures. Other than that, the room was bare. The men stayed in the hallway, removed their coats and laid them outside on the porch so as not to get water in the house.

The old man returned holding a large shotgun, the barrel shaking as his arms strained under the weight. Rickman stepped forward.

"Don't go making any sudden moves, you hear?" said the old man, his eyes revealing that he was more scared than he wanted to show. Rickman stepped forward and held his hands up.

"We are no danger, old timer, no danger at all," he said as softly as he could. The old man winced at the sound of his horrendous voice.

"It's alright, just a bed, just warmth." His eyes were hypnotically grey and calm. Rickman, with his hands up, slowly stepped into the line of fire.

"Just a bed, old man, just warmth."

The old man, lulled by the strange voice and the grey eyes, lowered his weapon just enough for Rickman, displaying lightning fast reactions, to whip the shotgun out of his hands and jab the butt into the old man's forehead, knocking him cold. Rickman slung the gun under his arm and turned to his men.

"Take him upstairs, find some food, and make yourselves warm. We ride out early, rain or not."

"Yes boss," they said, and Hobson and Conrad lifted the man and carried him upstairs.

"Fraser," said Rickman, as he began to walk into the kitchen, "bring our stuff in. Clean the guns, dry our clothes."

"Yes, Mr Chill," replied Fraser as he went back outside.

Rickman took the few moments of solitude to look around the house from the hallway. The living room was bare, the cushion on one chair old and threadbare, the cushion on the other chair in relatively good condition. Both chairs faced the fire, but were not angled towards each other. The two people who lived there liked to share the warmth, but not each other's company it seemed. He looked to the kitchen to see a tin of coffee still steaming fresh, and next to it a dirty cup and a single plate. On the table sat a place setting with no food upon it and the chair still tucked into the table.

Rickman was about to enter the kitchen and inspect his surroundings when Fraser pushed open the door, letting the wind and rain bluster into the house, obliterating Rickman's state of pensive calm. Fraser nodded at Rickman as he hauled the first load of their belongings into the living room. He had in his arms Rickman's saddle and saddle bags.

"Wait," said his leader. Fraser stopped by the doorway. Rickman walked up to him, unclasped one of the saddle bags and slung it over his shoulder, turned from him and walked up the stairs. Fraser went back to his duties.

The men had bedded down for the night and Rickman Chill had seen that the old man was sleeping soundly before leaving him alone. Rickman walked out of the room and locked the door from the outside, lest the old timer wake in the night and tried to shoot them all in their sleep. Rickman planned to talk to him in the morning in a more civilised manner.

The dark rider walked along the corridor to the room at the far end and opened the door. It was dark, but he managed to fumble around, find an oil lamp, and light it.

He was in a shrine. Cobwebs and dust everywhere. Pictures faded, paint peeling. The air was thick and stale.

Rickman moved the lamp around the room, inspected the
dresser, and the threadbare hairbrushes and cracked hand
mirror thereon. He opened a drawer to find some dusty
parchments; the ink was so faint he could only make out
certain words, but those words where enough: they were
love letters. One set penned by a Tobias H. Bowen, and
the corresponding set by Ellie Brush. He placed the lamp
on the dresser, pulled a rickety chair out and sat down. He
tried to decipher the faded and weathered letters and did
indeed discover a long and painful history of two lovers
who had been separated by not only class, but also great
distance. The oldest letters were filled with the hope and
conviction of youth and, as the letters continued in date,
that conviction was slowly replaced with the sadness and
longing that only the aged possess. The final letter however,
recaptured the spirit of their youth as it detailed their
reunion. Rickman made out the place, date and time of
a train to arrive in Barston that carried one of the lovers
to the other. He smiled at the seemingly happy-ever-after
ending to the story of the lovers. The date on the letter was
forty years earlier.

Rickman stood up, placed the letters back in the drawer
and moved the lamp around the room. He studied the
cracked and faded paper pasted onto the wall many years
before. He looked over the window ledge and out through
the glass to the storm outside. He lifted his lamp to the
window and squinted out to try and see what it was the
lovers used to see when they looked out of the window.

He could see only darkness. He drew the curtain and turned around towards the bed.

He almost dropped the lamp in shock. Upon the bed lay the corpse of a woman who had clearly been dead for many, many years. She had been laid out with arms crossed over her chest in a respectful pose. Rickman looked over the corpse of the dead lover and saw no gunshot or knife wound, no signs of distress or physical harm. The woman had died of natural causes, by God's hand.

Her face was near skeletal and putrefaction had long since passed. She had only one coin over her eye socket. The other, he deduced, had been placed with love and sadness when she had died, but had been retrieved at some point later when the old man had nothing left to buy bread with. Rickman wondered how the old man felt when he realised he would have to take back the coin. Did he cry? Did he pray for forgiveness, or did he take the coin with a hope that God and his lover's spirit would understand his actions and want him to buy another piece of bread? He could not know for sure, but he was certain that the old man missed his lover greatly and needed her with him, even if it meant denying her body the grace and dignity of a burial.

Rickman reached into his pocket and pulled out a handful of coins. He placed one over her eye, smiled and gently kissed her skeletal hand.

Rickman then went over to the door, shifted a dresser across to bar it, and returned to the bed. It was there on the floor, beside the corpse of the old man's lover, where Rickman Chill undressed and lay down naked, placing two coins over his eyes lest he die in his sleep and not be able to pay the ferryman. He crossed his arms and fell into a deep, contented sleep.

CHAPTER THIRTEEN

The Devil and Stanley Spring

S tanley Spring sat in Maria's seat at the kitchen table and wolfed down some broth, slurping and spilling it as he gabbled endlessly about the weather. The Devil, now dressed in a simple white shirt, black waistcoat and trousers sat opposite, arm stretched over the back of the adjacent chair and relaxed. He had a curious look on his face as if looking upon a child for the first time, enraptured with the joy and madness that it brought.

Stanley Spring, head still in the bowl and words directed more to the lumps of meat and vegetables than to his audience, began spinning a wild and difficult to decipher tale-within-a-tale. It concerned his father, Stephen Spring, who robbed his first stagecoach when he was fourteen and who only did that because Stanley's grandfather Sebastian Spring had lost the farm to cards. His grandfather blamed this on his own mother Stephanie Spring, a misery being who sent her son out to work even though he had the pox. But the stagecoach Stephen Spring robbed had no strong box inside, but instead three guards and a stockpile of bullets. The fourteen year old Stephen Spring shot them down in a hail of bullets, stole the horses, sold them, gambled the profits and won big, then bought a suit and charmed his way onto a river boat and won a fortune at cards. He then lost it all to a crooked lawman who drew on him when his back was turned. He only managed to escape by leaping overboard, swimming to the bank and living a life on the run; six years later he met a woman who lived with her dying father. He stole her heart and together they put the father out of his misery, lived in his house and fathered Stanley. Stanley grew up strong and soon left the home to seek his fortune and glory by tracking down The Devil and riding with him to hijack the Missoula express.

He paused for breath and was about to continue when The Devil laughed loudly and began clapping enthusiastically. Stanley Spring stopped eating and looked up at The Devil. He smiled a gormless smile. The Devil reached behind him, retrieved a bottle of whisky from the counter and poured two cups, sliding one to his guest. Stanley Spring gulped it down in one go and found his cup replenished instantly.

Maria stood in the doorway to the kitchen, arms folded, and scowling at the two men who seemed to be ignoring her very existence. Stanley was sitting in her seat, laughing and joking with her lover, eliciting a laugh from him that she had not heard before and making him sit in a posture she had not seen. Who was this stranger and what black magic had he cast upon him? Who was he that tricked his way into her home and ate at her table? A rage began to boil inside her.

The wind outside Maria's house had changed from a constant onslaught to more gentle waves, bringing hypnotic tides of rain to the window. The breaking waves upon the glass had lulled Maria into a deep sleep where she recalled the coming of Stanley Spring into her house. As the shadows in the room moved around, twisting and contorting as conducted by the flames in the crackling fireplace, the images of her dreamscape seemed to be projected outwards. Azazel, in the other room, watched curiously as the silhouette of The Devil was cast across the wall and was joined by the smaller silhouettes of Maria and a stranger whom it could barely recall from memory. The goat lay on his side peacefully and watched the shadow theatre perform around the room.

Maria, unaware of the shadows' dance, murmured and fidgeted in her chair as the anxiety of her memory overcame her dreamscape. Her hands fell off her belly and her leg began to jitter.

The men laughed loudly and The Devil thumped the table. They appeared as old friends reunited. Maria shrank from the doorway slightly, the shadows from the empty room to her left spilling out and masking half of her features. The two men turned to her slowly, strangely, laughing madly. The walls twisted slightly and a dull green hue fell about the house turning everything into a living illness. Maria's rage turned to fear and she felt rooted to the spot as the two men laughed at her before returning to their conversation.

Maria's mind was split. She knew that the stranger was about to convince her lover to leave. She knew that he would agree and that she would be left alone. She clenched the hem of her apron so tightly her knuckles turned white and she prayed to God that she was dreaming. He was going to leave her and there was nothing she could do.

The anger inside her turned to nausea and she had to grip the edge of the doorway, yet still she could not leave the spot where she stood. The men's laughter fell away and they both leaned into each other and began to whisper conspiratorially. Maria could not hear what was being said, but it mattered not to her. He was going to leave and this stranger was going to steal everything from her. She clenched her jaw and dug deep inside herself. A conviction rose up and a decision was made in her heart. As soon as it was, the nausea subsided and her feet were freed from the floor. She took a step backwards from the conspiring men and disappeared into the shadows.

Azazel rolled from his side onto his front and backed up to the corner of the room as the firelight shadows began to twist and deform. The pleasing dance that had calmed him was now a mad circus as the shadows loomed up over the walls, across the ceiling, dove down on the other side of the room and across the floor. The goat was in a nightmarish wheel of shadow and dread, so he backed up as far as he could and wedged himself into a little gap between the wall and the pile of logs, terrified of the maelstrom of shadows in the room.

Maria in her chair was moaning loudly and her leg was jittering. The calming waves of wind and rain swapped back to the constant battering of the anguished storm and its intensity had magnified, rattling the window pane and causing the trees outside to groan and twist. Maria's arms began to twitch and judder as a sweat broke out over her brow.

Maria backed out of the house and into the storm. The wind whipped around her and the rain drenched her instantly but, in her nightmare, she felt nothing but the conviction inside. She slowly walked backwards away from the house as, above her, a vast swirling black cloud began to form. The magnitude of the swell stretched out to the very edge of her imagination and it churned with a slow yet powerful volition.

Maria moved away from the house and into the barn where Cinereous stood, represented in her dream as a marble statue. She did not look to him and did not reach out to touch him as she always did, but instead walked passed, always keeping her eyes on the entrance of the barn and onward to the porch of her house. She backed up farther until she bumped into the rear wall. She reached down to her side and felt the handle of her axe brush against her fingers. She did not smile when she touched it. She did not even blink. But she knew beyond all doubt that the stranger was asking The Devil to leave her and that The Devil would say 'Yes'. Maria gripped the handle of the axe and stepped forward.

The Devil and Stanley Spring were no longer talking in hushed tones but had reclined in their chairs and were conversing in a more relaxed tone. Stanley was no longer gabbling, nor slurping his broth, but instead rolled a cigarette and talking slowly and calmly. The Devil had resumed his relaxed position, with his arm over the chair beside him. He was smiling at Stanley, clearly happy to have male company in the house. Stanley finished rolling the cigarette and handed it over to The Devil who took it, struck a match across the table and lit it. Neither man noticed that the storm outside had calmed, or that Maria left the house and returned. She was now standing in the hallway looking at them.

Stanley reached into his pocket, pulled out a ragged piece of paper and laid it across the table. The Devil leaned forward and, using cups and a candle, pinned the edges down. It was a crude map covering an unspecified region and drawn to no discernible scale. All that could truly be deciphered was a long snake-like set of parallel track lines running diagonally across it. A childlike 'X' had been scrawled in the centre spot of the map where the tracks appeared to twist through a narrow ravine. Stanley rolled a cigarette, lit it and tapped the 'X'.

The Devil rubbed his chin and nodded. Stanley Spring smiled and sat back in his chair.

Maria, from the hallway, held the axe at waist height and calmly entered the kitchen. The floorboards did not creak and the candles did not flutter as she stepped through the doorway and raised the axe.

Stanley turned in shock to see Maria's calm face looking not at him, but at The Devil, the axe raised high above her head. He was about to shout out when he noticed that The Devil was looking blankly at him.

The axe came down sharply and thundered into Stanley's chest, the inertia carrying through and thrusting him backwards off the chair and against the kitchen wall. Maria continued to look at The Devil and The Devil continued to look at Stanley Spring. Maria yanked the axe out of his chest, sending hot blood across the room, spattering the table. Maria swung the axe back, flicking blood onto the ceiling. She brought the axe back down again, this time into the side of his rib cage. Stanley slumped to the side and fell onto the floor. Maria, convinced that he still might take The Devil away from her, raised the axe a third time and, with all her might, swung it down and brought the blade diagonally across his face, cleaving right across his cheek, nose, left eye socket and above the ear.

She let go of the axe and staggered backwards, the handle still stuck in the air. She was breathing hard and soaked in blood and sweat.

The Devil peered over the table and looked down at the corpse of Stanley Spring, then turned to Maria. She could see in his eyes that her wonderful act of love had worked. He would never leave her. The Devil pushed the table aside, and stepped over to kiss Maria. He grabbed her by her blood soaked and matted hair and brought his lips close to hers.

Azazel was cowering between the logs and the wall when the shadows converged upon him, darting and twisting about the room. He instinctively bleated and thrust himself backwards, farther into the gap. His back leg kicked out to make more room, causing the logs to tumble to the ground.

At the sound of the logs crashing to the floor, Maria jolted from her nightmare just as The Devil was about to kiss her. She was breathing hard, covered in sweat and her left hand felt numb. She was sitting on it. She yanked her left hand free and, with her right, placed it back on her belly and looked around the room, caught in the flux of delirium between the dream world and reality. Her breathing calmed down. It had been a nightmare. She was not a murderer, but she was alone. The storm was over and dawn was breaking, the sunbeams beginning to penetrate the trees for the first time in a week. She was alone.

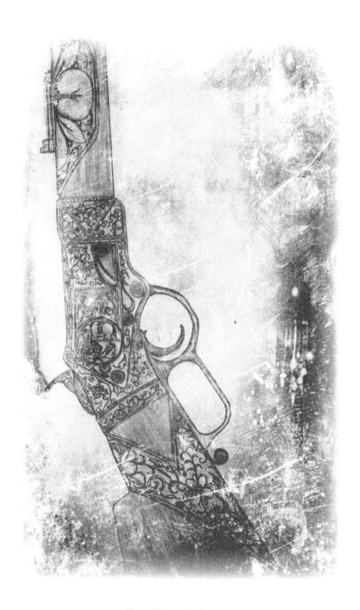

THE DEVIL'S RIFLE:
'Leviathan'

ENGRAVED DETAILING ON THE DEVIL'S RIFLE:
A rendering of William Blake's Behemoth and Leviathan

Chapter Fourteen
Conrad

The old man awoke just as the final throes of the storm were thrust against the house. He was lying on his back and staring up at the cracked ceiling. His head throbbed and he could not remember why he was there. Upon waking, there were usually only two sights that greeted him. The fireplace if he had slept in his chair. Or the skeleton of his wife if, in a lapse of deathly melancholia he had gone upstairs, climbed into their bed and slept next to her. He never slept in his own bedroom. He struggled to reconcile the pain in his head with the alien vision that greeted him. He remembered the rain, he remembered the wind and he remembered the knock on his door. He sat bolt upright and touched his wound. He knew that there were intruders in his house and that they had taken his gun. He knew instantly that they had no doubt found his lover's body. He also knew that it was a fool who kept only one shotgun in the house. He rolled onto his side, reached under the bed and felt around for the bolt clip that held his secondary shotgun in place. He unclipped it and pulled out the weapon, checked that it was loaded and looked to the door. He cocked the weapon and sat on the bed, waiting for the right moment to attack.

Conrad had not slept for a moment all night, despite the haven that had been provided. The men had found some food in the pantry, and some coffee beans which they had ground down to make a warming drink. They had dried and smoked their tobacco, and they had cleaned their weapons. In all respects, in the short time they had been in the house they had worked well and their bodies deserved some sleep. Yet Conrad could not bring himself to lie down next to the fire and sleep. He sat in a rocking chair which had the least threadbare cushion and rocked back and forth in time with the clock. He stared into the fire. In his mind he had regressed back to his youth.

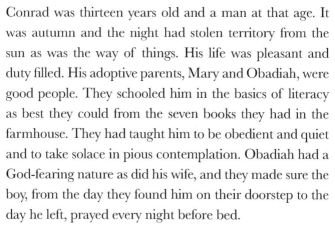

Conrad was thirteen years old and a man at that age. It was autumn and the night had stolen territory from the sun as was the way of things. His life was pleasant and duty filled. His adoptive parents, Mary and Obadiah, were good people. They schooled him in the basics of literacy as best they could from the seven books they had in the farmhouse. They had taught him to be obedient and quiet and to take solace in pious contemplation. Obadiah had a God-fearing nature as did his wife, and they made sure the boy, from the day they found him on their doorstep to the day he left, prayed every night before bed.

Conrad had been an abandoned child, left on the doorstep of a couple who could not bear children. They had tried relentlessly but God had failed to hear their prayers. Though they each harboured secret fears that the other of them was at fault, they never mentioned it, deciding instead to blame themselves for their own barren states.

The child had been found on a spring morning on their doorstep wrapped in a pretty, embroidered sheet and sleeping in a basket. The only sign of identification was sewn on the hem of the child's little bonnet. The blue lettering simply said "Conrad" and there was not a single moment when thoughts of turning the baby over to the authorities had crossed their minds. To Obadiah and Mary, the infant had not been abandoned, but delivered. He was a miracle. They took him in, partly to shield him from the evils of the world, and partly because they harboured a fear of him being recognised, they kept young Conrad close to their hearts and home, schooling him as best they could from their meagre resources. They put him to work around the farm. He was a good child.

However, on that autumn day when the nighttime descended far sooner than was natural, Conrad found himself not lying in bed and looking at the ceiling as was his way at night, but kneeling on his bed and looking out of the window to the dark and stormy night. He was lost in his thoughts. Since he had started to find surprising new strength in his muscles, strange new hairs on his body, and confusing and powerful new thoughts, Conrad had retreated more from conversation with his parents. They had assumed, rightly, that he was becoming a man and traversing a dangerous and tumultuous road. However, what they did not understand was Conrad's growing sense of anger and agitation. There was something deep inside him, something primal that made him restless at night. He felt constantly that there was an unknown injustice wrought upon him. It had been simmering inside him and was threatening to consume him. As he looked out over the dark and stormy plains from his window he noticed on the horizon a solitary rider approaching.

Conrad saw the rider enter the family compound. He did not dismount his horse until virtually at the porch and even then the horse did not stop. The rider simply swung his leg over as the horse was trotting, skipped down onto the ground and walked under the porch covering and out of sight without even breaking stride.

The young man jumped off his bed and went to his door, pressing his ear against it and listening. There was a strange and innate mixture of calm and expectancy swirling around inside him: calm because he felt that this interloper would not harm him, and anticipation for what the stranger might have brought into their lives. He pressed his ear against the door and listened. His hearing was keen and he could make out the voices of the stranger and his parents; however their tones were so quiet he could not decipher the exact conversation.

He stepped away from the door when he heard the talking come to an end and the creaking of the floorboards signal that someone was coming to his room. He had spent enough time in that room and in the company of his parents to be able to identify their footsteps. He knew his mother was approaching. He backed away from the door and sat on his bed waiting for her.

Mary knocked on the door and without waiting for permission to enter she did so, as was her way. Conrad saw that she was wringing her hands. He did not understand her innate sadness as a thirteen year old boy, but as a twenty-one year old man, and in that prison of memory, his mother in that doorway was the definition of despair.

Mary stepped from the doorway and offered the open passage to the boy. Conrad stood up and slowly walked passed her, not thinking to grace her with the reassuring touch of his hand that she wanted and needed, and that his older self remonstrated his younger self for not giving. He walked down over the landing and towards the staircase.

As he descended he saw the open-plan living room and kitchen and he saw the large table where he and his parents sat and ate every meal. Before, in his youth, running down those stairs to eat was as welcoming as the womb. On this day, in the clarity of his nostalgia, he felt loaded with dread and expectation. As he descended slowly, he saw his father sitting away from the table and facing the wall, his head in his hands. Conrad wanted to call out and ask if there was anything wrong, but his mouth stayed shut and his legs continued to carry him down the stairs, seemingly of their own volition. He stopped before he reached the bottom.

Many things in his past had been lost to Conrad throughout his hard formative years. Many feelings, incidents and passages had become mired with the pain and hardship of his time on earth. But one image burned brightly throughout all. One image held itself up as a beacon. When Conrad stepped off the staircase and faced the table he saw, before him, the dark figure of the Preacher in the wide brimmed hat; the sharp cheeks, gentle nose and deep, encapsulating eyes, and he knew his destiny had come for him. He had ridden out with Rickman that night, after hearing what the stranger had to say, and did not look back to wave goodbye to his adoptive parents.

Conrad looked over to the sleeping Hobson and Fraser and remembered recruiting them in Dunstan three years previously. The two drunken brothers had staged a heist with The Devil, only to be betrayed and left for dead until Rickman had found them. He wanted to help them on their way to the afterlife, but Conrad had convinced Rickman to let them ride along and help hunt down The Devil. It was an astute move as the Whitney brothers had proved invaluable in tricky situations.

Although Conrad did feel tired, he knew that he would not be able to sleep, so he put aside his history with Rickman and the two brothers and thought about his dead wife. It was torturous for him to think of Liza, with her red hair and porcelain skin. His guilt clouded everything concerning her and she stalked his subconscious, infiltrating his dream space, his thought processes and his decision making. He missed her so much and, as always, delved into a secure memory of her.

Conrad had met Liza in a backwater town called Red Springs when he was seventeen. He had been riding with Rickman for four years and had killed and maimed men, women and children on their blood-soaked streak of revenge. Up until Red Springs, Rickman Chill was his master, his mentor and his God. Nothing could have altered that; nothing except the shock of Liza's red hair and her spitfire heart, which ensnared him instantly.

They had stopped in the town to rest after a two week trek across the open plains, sleeping without shelter. They were low on supplies, mainly bullets, and they needed to re-shoe themselves and the horses.

They left their horses with the blacksmith and walked to the saloon across the boardwalk. Their reputation preceded them; people tipped their hats and gave a respectful berth to the dark avengers. As soon as he entered the saloon, Conrad saw her and his ideology shifted completely. Liza was the most beautiful woman he had ever seen, with a full set of teeth and a spirit of youth that had not yet been drained by the hardships of life. She was a miracle.

Rickman Chill, as was his way, had declined all offers of service and slept in an empty room. But the teenage Conrad wanted only Liza and, after a night within her embrace, he knew she felt the same way. He knew the things she said to him, no woman would say to just any man she just met. He knew that she meant every word of her pillow talk and that, despite her ten-year age advantage, she was the one for him. He loved her instantly. Liza did eventually grow to love him also.

CHAPTER FIFTEEN

Second Shotgun

T he sun was rising and Conrad continued to look into the fire, rubbing the knuckles on his right hand. He looked down as he did so, caressing and massaging each knuckle. Conrad's thoughts began to sail from that blissful first night in Liza's arms and towards the tragedy of his marriage, when Fraser tapped him on the shoulder. Conrad snapped out of his melancholia and pulled out his gun.

"Whoa, whoa! Conrad it's me! Just dumb ol' Fraser! Sorry, didn't mean to sneak up on yous. Here, you want some Joe?"

Fraser handed Conrad a tin cup of lukewarm and bitter coffee. Conrad sighed and holstered his gun.

"You ain't dumb, Fraser. You ain't," he said as he took the coffee and sipped. "It's good," he said, turning back to the fire and packing away his melancholia.

Fraser smiled and placed another cup by his still sleeping brother's head.

"What you up for?" asked Conrad, still looking into the dying fire, the tiredness finally affecting him. Fraser looked down to the plate he was holding, which had a few leftovers from his meal.

"Thought the old timer would be hungry. Being old 'n' all."

Conrad smiled and stood up. He kicked Hobson who growled and turned over, pulling his blanket over him. Conrad turned to talk to Fraser but saw that he was already half way up the stairs and approaching the old man's door. Conrad went to shout out to stop, but his cry was drowned out by the thunderous blast of the old man's shotgun as it blew the door off its hinges and tore a hole through Fraser's midriff, sending him flying over the banister and crashing down onto the floor below.

Rickman Chill had awoken a split second before the gun was discharged. So attuned was he and so intrinsically married were his dream world and his waking world, that the cocking of the gun had sounded like a mining explosion in his dream. He was already on his feet when the gun fired but unlike his crew, his thoughts were not on instinctively going for his guns, but going for his clothes. Above all things, he could not be discovered naked at any time and certainly could not die so. He heard the sound of the old timer stepping out onto the landing. He knew the old man would be coming straight for this room, to protect his shrine.

Rickman pulled on his trousers and reached for his shirt. From downstairs he heard the scream of Conrad followed by the scream of Hobson, followed by the cacophony of gunfire as the boys opened up on the landing.

The old man, still with bells ringing in his ears from the shotgun blast and the wound he had sustained the night before, ducked. He fell back into the room and rolled under his bed as Conrad and Hobson sent bullet after bullet after him. The dresser was reduced to kindling, the picture frames on the wall shattered and the window at the far end of the room was blown out. The old man lay in a foetal position as the debris and feathers from his bedding fell all around him. The ringing in his ears magnified and his teeth rattled.

Hobson fired, reloaded and fired again at a furious rate, screaming and hollering like a man possessed as he side-stepped across the living room and out to the reception room by the door where his brother lay. He looked down at him to see the light in his eyes fading away. Hobson fired his gun empty but, with his eyes still locked on his brother's, kept pulling the trigger. Fraser, his skin turning grey and his lips blue, turned to look up at his distraught brother and tried to speak. He opened his mouth and gurgled up some hot blood. He uttered some words that were unintelligible. He tried again but the light in his eyes extinguished before he could do so. His head lolled to the side.

Hobson stared down at him, his eyes bewildered and his arm still extended out, pointing the pistol back up at the landing and pulling the trigger slowly, the chamber clicking over like a clock. Conrad stepped over to Hobson and looked down at the body of his friend Fraser.

The old man, burning the last of his life's adrenaline, rolled out from under the bed, stepped out onto the landing, and raised his shotgun. Below him, Conrad sensed his movement and before he could think, he shoved Hobson forward, causing him to trip over Fraser's body. He himself dived backwards just as the old man fired.

The old man was panicked and did not have time to aim properly, shooting a hole in the wall next to Hobson, the buckshot blasting half of the man's face clean off. Hobson fell to the floor screaming. The old man looked over to the stunned Conrad, who had miraculously evaded the buckshot. Both men locked eyes on each other before they raced to reload their guns. They finished reloading at the same time and pointed their guns at each other.

Hobson lay on the floor next to his brother, gurgling pathetically and trying to stop his face falling off completely. He tried to scrabble around to get his gun, but the pain and confusion was too intense and he fumbled the gun and knocked it away.

Rickman was dressed and leaned against the dresser that he had pressed against the door the night before. He had both guns out and they were cocked. He could hear the old man walking slowly across the landing towards his room. Rickman backed away from the dresser and stood facing the door with both guns pointed at the lock.

"Conrad!" he called out in his twisted voice.

"Yeah?" his man called back.

"Holster 'em."

"But… "

"Do it!"

He heard the sound of the guns going back into their homes.

"Tobias? Tobias, can you hear me?"

Outside the room, Tobias's mouth dropped open slightly at the sound of his own name.

"Tobias?" came the awful voice from within the sacred room.

"My man ain't gonna shoot you. You have my word. Now, you can take your shot. I ain't gonna stop you and neither is he. I promise."

Inside the room, Rickman stood with his guns still trained on the door. He could, if he wanted to, shoot through the door and cut down the old man but something inside stopped him. The old man had no allegiance with The Devil. He was just an old man who lived in his own hell and killing him was not part of the plan. He deserved his shot.

"I'm going to count to three, and then we'll both shoot. Fair?"

"Fair," agreed the old man's voice.

Outside the room, Conrad's hands hovered over his holstered guns.

"One… Two… Three!"

Rickman fired one shot into the ceiling of the room. Tobias discharged his shotgun. The blast punched a six inch hole in the door, just above the dresser, and the buckshot peppered the room.

Conrad instantly drew his guns, ready, if Rickman was shot, to cut down the old man.

"Boss?" cried Conrad. The old man dropped the rifle onto the floor, ready for the hail of bullets that were about to come.

There was a scraping from inside the room and the door, freed from its barricade, swung open slowly. Rickman stood in the room. The old man rushed as best he could into his shrine and over to his dead wife, throwing himself over her.

"Leave her! Leave her! She's sleeping, leave her!" he garbled through manic sobs. Rickman backed away slowly, his hands in the air.

"Leave, leave her!" old Tobias continued to cry.

Conrad ascended the staircase, relieved to see Rickman alive and miraculously unharmed. He looked in astonishment at Rickman before peering into the room to see what he was looking at. As soon as he saw the old man cradling the ancient corpse of his lover he put his hand to his mouth and turned away.

The old man's sobs died down and he stood up to face the Preacher. Rickman reached into his pocket, pulled out a handkerchief and handed it to the old man, who took it and wiped away his tears.

"What you gonna do now? Shoot an old man? Send him away? Shoot an old man who got nothing?"

Rickman shook his head. The old man's eyes welled up again.

"You gonna shoot an old man?"

Rickman remained motionless.

"Please. Please shoot me. I'm tired. My head hurts." He backed up to sit on the edge of the bed.

Rickman shook his head.

"Please."

Nothing.

The old man looked at his wife and noticed the coin that had been replaced over her eye. He turned back and looked quizzically up at Rickman

"Are you The Devil?" he whispered.

Conrad looked over at the Preacher. Rickman said nothing but simply shook his head and tried to remain calm, even though inside, the suggestion that he was in fact The Devil caused revulsion to rise up. Had he gone too far? Was he lost? He tried to think of a memory that would quickly disprove the notion. He had only one: that of blood seeping into snow.

"What now, Boss?" whispered Conrad, noticing that look in his leader's eyes that said he was lost in introspective conflict. Rickman snapped out of his pensive state and looked at Conrad.

"We bury her," he said before walking out of the room. The old man turned back to his wife, climbed onto the bed, lay down next to her body and closed his eyes, the pain in his head still throbbing.

Rickman walked down the staircase to inspect the bodies of the Whitney brothers. Hobson's gurgles were shallow and his movements were slow. Rickman looked over him and felt a great conflict rise up. Hobson was now useless to the mission. Deadweight. He should leave him there to die. However, Rickman knew that it was no way for a man to die, suffering and alone. He weighed up the options while standing over them both, not once offering him any assistance.

Conrad remained in the doorway, utterly transfixed by the horror and love in equal measure. He felt guilt and regret. He thought of Liza and rubbed his hand as he looked at the old man and unpicked his insanity to find a simple grain of rationality inside him. The old man wanted to be with his lover. Nothing more, nothing less. Conrad realised this and felt a crushing guilt descend upon him. He wanted to die, as death was the only way he could be forgiven. He walked over to the sleeping man and pulled a pillow from under his head.

The old man opened an eye and looked up at Conrad. The eyes asked him to do what was necessary before they closed again. Conrad placed the pillow over the man's face and pressed down, smothering the life out of him. When he struggled no more, Conrad lifted the pillow and replaced it under his head. He then placed two coins over his eyes and draped the old man's arm over his lover's skeleton. He went into the front yard of the house, where he dug a grave big enough for two. He did not once look up to the sky or even notice that the storm had ended.

Chapter Sixteen
A Memory of Murder

Maria sat for an hour by the dying fire and contemplated her nightmare. Her hands trembled the entire time and the muscles in her shoulders ached as if she truly had been swinging the axe into Stanley Spring. The murder, in her mind, was powerful and complete, and she felt all the emotions before, during and after that she imagined she would have associated with actually committing the act. Did that make her a murderer in reality? There was no body, but she could have buried it. She could not be completely sure that what she had imagined was not a pantomime of unearthed anxieties, but in fact the surfacing of a long-buried memory. Perhaps she had killed Stanley Spring and that act of madness had finally driven The Devil to leave her and ride out alone. She wracked her memories, trying to locate proof, but for every shred she came across, a counter argument of an infection sprang up to taint the memory and cloud her reason.

After an hour's contemplation, Maria decided to search for proof. Her head throbbed with the possibility of her crime and she felt dizzy at the splintering of her mind. Her belly felt larger, and the child was moving awkwardly, kicking up tides of nausea inside her. Did the child know?

Was it even a child? Could it be an illness? An evil tumour wrought upon her by God as punishment for murder? She knew that idea was ludicrous, but the nature of her turmoil prevented her from discarding it completely.

She braced the handles of the chair and stood up, cradling her belly, and began to walk with a wider gait than usual. Azazel stood in the doorway looking up at her. She smiled at him and he cautiously trotted over to her side, still frightened by the shadowplay that had terrorised him during the night storm.

Maria entered the kitchen and walked over to the spot where, in her dream or possible memory, Stanley Spring lay dead. She bent down as best she could, steadying herself on the edge of the table, and with her other hand she stroked the flagstones and closed her eyes. No conclusive proof was revealed to her. She opened her eyes and sighed as she stood up. She looked around the kitchen and saw Azazel standing next to the axe and clipping his hoof against the floor. Maria smiled, walked over and ran her fingers over the handle. Nothing. Azazel moved out of the way to let Maria pick up the axe. She did so and repositioned herself into the spot where she had swung it down into Stanley Spring's chest. She swung. The muscles did not sing any notes to convince her of anything. She dumped the axe unceremoniously onto the table and walked out of the house into the fresh, morning air.

⧜

It was still early in the morning when Conrad finished digging the graves for Fraser and the old man. As soon as he climbed out of the hole and dropped the shovel onto the ground, the fatigue stuck him and he bent double, coughing heavily and trying to steady his knees. Inside, Rickman had spent the few hours it had taken Conrad to dig the graves walking around the house and inspecting every room and every article therein. Fraser's body had been wrapped in a dirty sheet and laid out next to the grave. His boots had been removed and tied to a horse for future use, as had his coat, guns, knives and bullets. Everything of use had been salvaged. The dead had no use for weapons or practical equipment, but Rickman and Conrad did.

Hobson had been laid on a makeshift stretcher that was tied to the back of Conrad's horse. Rickman did not want him to be left to die alone and so had ordered it, even though they both knew that the man had little time left.

Conrad entered the house to see Rickman in the kitchen writing in a small diary, his feet up on the table. Conrad stood in the doorway.

"Get the bodies. Put them in the graves," said Rickman.

"Take your feet off the table, Boss," replied Conrad.

Rickman obliged without looking up. Conrad started to explain the reason for his sudden sense of respect for the household but could not quite find the right words. He left the kitchen and went to the living room where he readjusted the rocking chair he had stayed up all night in, and rearranged the tools around the grate. As he backed away from the room, he concluded that the room bore no evidence that they had ever been there. It was a perfectly preserved shrine to the old man and his lover. He dusted his hands clean on his jacket and went upstairs to wrap the skeleton in a bed sheet, lest he pick her up and she fall to dust in his arms.

Rickman looked up from his diary as Conrad walked back passed the kitchen and understood implicitly the change that had occurred inside the young man. He knew that Conrad had begun to reconcile a great doubt within him and that the conclusion it led to was not beneficial to their mission. Conrad was, rightly, beginning to blame himself for what he had done to Liza. Rickman Chill closed the diary and pocketed it. He watched Conrad ascend the stairs and concluded that the once fearless man had gone soft. And that presented a conflict of interests.

Conrad had decided to perform the easy task first and heaved Tobias's fresh body up, over the skeletal wife, and dumped him onto the floor. He picked up the coins that he had carelessly forgotten to remove first and stood above the body, coins in hand, thinking about pocketing them for himself, until the thought of their souls wandering restless through the afterlife for all eternity, like his wife, made him replace them.

He stepped over to the head of the bed and looked down. Conrad rehearsed how he would attempt to move her then stopped. He rethought, rehearsed again and stopped.

Rickman stepped into the room and grabbed the valance and sheet, his face inches from the body. He held his breath and counted to three. On the third he pulled the valance and sheet up and over the body in a quick motion. He fell over the bed and held the sheet fast over her body. Both men froze. After a few seconds, Rickman let go of the sheet and stepped backwards. Conrad moved to the wall and Rickman moved around to the foot of the bed and together they shifted the bed two feet out from the wall so that they could get around to the sheet and valance on the other side. They spread the other half of the sheet over the body and left her there while they carried Tobias out of the house and into the open grave. Next came the skeleton and, after a long and careful operation, they managed to transport her delicate remains more or less intact and laid her down next to her husband.

Once Rickman had administered the last rites, Conrad finished his solitary duties as gravedigger and filled the earth back in. He made sure that Rickman Chill neither saw nor heard that he was crying as he did so.

Maria managed to walk out from the porch and into the compound where she stood, enriched by the light air, refreshing after the calamitous storm. She looked all around the treeline. Perhaps she had buried Stanley

Spring? With every passing moment in the sun and air Maria felt braver and braver, and began to convince herself that it was only a maddening dream and she had not committed a terrible act, but merely personified her anger at being abandoned. In comparison to murder, it felt better to have been deserted. She breathed a sigh of relief and the weight of guilt lifted from her. The child within stopped fidgeting and rested. The breeze flicked up her hair and stroked her neck, and she looked out towards the ridge. As she did so, the ghosts of two horses appeared next to her. Stanley Spring on one, and The Devil on the other. She did not turn to them. Stanley cantered off towards the ridge. The Devil dismounted Cinereous and turned to her.

"I'm leaving, but I will come back," said the ghost, "I always do, I always will. But I cannot stay. It isn't in my nature. Be free, Maria. Be free to wait, to leave, be free to cry or laugh. Be free to live."

The ghost leaned into her and the breeze sharpened to a point and simulated the shape of his lips as they gently kissed her neck and shoulders. "But don't forget me," he whispered, and he mounted Cinereous. Maria watched as The Devil and his horse trotted slowly towards the ridge, where he stopped and turned to face her. The Devil raised a hand and waved a final goodbye before turning and riding off behind the ridge.

Rickman and Conrad mounted their horses and looked back at the old man's house, now totally abandoned and left to the nature of Montana and her ever-changing seasons to do with as she pleased. Together the men turned their horses from the house, and looked out towards the plains and to the mountains beyond which stood the town of Bel. They had strayed off mission for eight days and it was time to get back to business. Rickman's heart beat slowly as he thought of the mission and the bloodbath that awaited them all. He didn't particularly care if his men didn't make it, but he prayed that he would. Not through a wish for self-preservation, but through the desire to see his mission through to the end.

"Well," said Conrad, affecting a weathered gravitas sounding similar to Rickman's voice, "looks like we are riding to our deaths."

He flexed and massaged his hands and put on his thick leather gloves, pulled the rim of his hat down over his eyes and cantered off, dragging the still gurgling Hobson behind him.

Rickman looked at Conrad and, for the first time that he could remember, felt a sting of concern for the man. He felt nothing for Fraser or Hobson, but for Conrad who constantly displayed great potential, he felt concern. Rickman stuffed tobacco in his mouth and began to chew, realising that the more a man thinks about what he has done, the farther from his mission he will fall. Rickman concluded that perhaps Conrad had ridden enough and should be put to rest shortly.

Before riding out, Rickman had turned back to the empty house and the grave of the lovers, buried together and finally resting in everlasting peace after a lifetime of strife and togetherness. He thought of the woman of his memories lying in the snow, bleeding from her exposed neck, and then he purposefully replaced that image with the one of her getting to her feet, the blood rising back up into her body and the wound sealing itself.

"We're riding to our deaths," he whispered to the wind. He kicked his horse into life and headed for Bel.

Maria, still standing outside in the warm breeze and looking towards the ridge, stroked her belly and felt an immense and unshakable love for the child inside her. She wondered whether The Devil would have stayed if she had told him that she was pregnant. She brought forth the image of The Devil upon the ridge, waving to her before disappearing behind it a final time, and concluded that it didn't matter. It was a long time ago and there were long times ahead. She stroked her belly and turned back towards the house with Azazel by her side, and started to think of names for the child.

PART TWO
Arrival

CHAPTER SEVENTEEN
Maria in the Future

aria had not recalled her precious time with
The Devil for three days. That is to say, she
had not dismissed or forgotten him, but had
instead given her mind wholly to the arrival of their child.
It was with a mixture of giddy excitement and a sense of
responsibility that she set about ordering her house. The
logs were moved from the nursery into the living room;
this was a painfully slow task as Maria could bend down
only so far, and so had to kick and shuffle the logs across
the floor with her feet. To make space in the living room
for the logs, Maria moved out The Devil's chair and his
guitar. She placed the chair on the porch, and the guitar
in the cupboard with his poncho and hat.

The chickens were relocated, surprisingly easily, into
the kitchen where Maria managed to tether their feet with
twine to the kitchen table leg. The noise of their squawking
at first was loud and incessant, but they soon settled down
and quietened. Maria then swept the nursery and opened
the windows to aerate the room. She also showed Azazel
the door; he dutifully returned to the outside, slightly
relieved to be away from the room that had terrified him
with its evil shadow theatre a few nights previously. Maria
watched as the goat bucked and kicked and stretched his

legs as soon as he was off the porch and out into the fresh air. She smiled and turned back to the empty nursery, and her smiled dropped away.

Frequently in the last fortnight, Maria cursed herself for not at least attempting to construct a cot for the child, but instead viewed the pregnancy with alternating feelings of denial and ambivalence. As a result, the baby had nowhere to sleep. To counter this gross oversight, Maria constructed a rudimentary 'cot' in her bedroom. She moved the side table from beside the rocking chair in the living room and placed it next to her bed. Upon that she placed a small wooden crate she used to store potatoes that she hoped would be large enough for the child. From her cupboard she took a thick cotton winter dress and tore it into strips to line the inside of the cot and protect the child from splinters. She gutted one of her pillows as she determined that it was too soft, and if the baby were to lie on its face in the dead of night, it would suffocate. She laid the thin casing in the base of the crate.

Lastly, Maria found a small pot of blue paint at the back corner of the store cupboard and, using a rudimentary brush constructed from a thin candlestick with a clump of Azazel's hair tied to the end, she attempted to decorate the cot as best she could. Artistically, the results were questionable, but she felt happy in her work; a peculiar sensation swept through her that was quite unlike any she had ever experienced before as it was not attached to feelings of desire or lust, anger or hate, but to a stronger, deeper, more powerful feeling of unshakable maternal love. As she painted difficult to decipher flowers and birds around the rickety cot she even caught herself whistling a sweet and gentle lullaby.

Maria finished, inspected her work and was happy with the results.

She placed the table and 'cot' in the centre of the room where the sunbeams fell for the large part of the day, and from where she could see it best when she installed herself in the rocking chair by the fireplace in the living room. From there, she sat, smoked and rocked and looked upon the illuminated cot, projecting many scenes of happy family life. She sat by it, she sang over it and she slept next to it. Maria imagined standing over it, rocking the baby to sleep, and she imagined a man beside her, holding her close and looking down into the cot. The man was tall and clean shaven and bore no resemblance to any man she had ever met, and certainly bore no resemblance to her lover. The thought troubled her slightly and she quickly recast the play and put The Devil into the scene. Despite her powerful imagination, she could not will the projection of The Devil to look loving or even relaxed around the cot. The thought told her everything she needed to know and she felt stung with hatred. She understood the future happiness of her and her child did not incorporate The Devil. A few months ago such a realisation would have caused her to laugh loudly, but now the thought was met with a bittersweet sigh of what was not to be.

Throughout the week, in the evenings while she smoked and looked at the cot, Maria would also contemplate the small, crumpled piece of paper that she carried around in her apron pocket. Whenever inspiration struck during the day, Maria would retrieve the paper and scrawl her idea down and then pocket it, restraining herself from poring over the other ideas scrawled on the paper, saving the act of revision and contemplation for the evening. She would, come the right time, take the piece of paper out, flatten it over a book for a few moments, then lay it across her lap and intermittently stare at it and then back up to the cot.

Upon the paper, Maria had scrawled over one hundred and thirty possible names for the child, some obscure, some obvious, but each one, as soon as she had conceived of it and made it real by writing it down, would suddenly find herself building an entire personality and future for the child based solely around that name and what it suggested to her. She felt it was a clever and sensible way to not only keep track of the names, but also to keep a record of the people that she had invented. It was a nice little diary of possible children and she felt warm when imagining all the faults and strengths associated with their names.

It came to be, on the evening of the third day after the ghost had ridden out, that Maria moved from her chair in the living room to the chair on the porch in order to say 'hello' to the shadows the moment they emerged from the treeline. The sun was setting; soon it would clip the trees and her friends would arise. She had by her side a small bundle of rags torn from various sheets, dresses, blouses and dishrags, in various colours. She had, on the arm of the chair, drawn with a charred stick from the fire the designs for a rag doll for the child. She had never attempted anything quite so grand, but she could sew and she could visualise the sort of creation that a child would come to love and so she began her work.

She sat and sewed the rags together, attempting to cut into shape the various strips using a combination of carving knife, rusty scissors and her teeth. The work was frustratingly hard as she began to realise just how difficult it is to marry artistic ideals with physical execution. But the child needed a doll and that was final. She persevered and before the shadows from the trees had reached the edge of the porch, she had constructed the basic shape of the head. It was large and shaped more like an almond than a head, but Maria could visualise where the eyes would go and where the hair would sit, taken from her own head so that the baby would be comforted to always smell its mother when they were apart.

She held the ragged head up to the light, turning it around and smiling at her accomplishment. In a similar way to which she had fantasised about happy family life after constructing the cot, Maria brought forth many dramas concerning the baby and the doll and, years into the future, the child with the doll. She saw the child running around the front yard with the doll and she saw the child holding it tightly as the fictitious father figure took them both for a ride around the compound on the back of Azazel. Maria had barely enough time to bask in that vision before another presented itself. The child was now older and riding upon Cinereous. As that vision of heaven threatened to overwhelm her, Maria plunged even farther into the future and saw the child, now seven or eight, handing the ragged doll over to its younger sibling.

Maria, still holding the doll's head up to the light, saw both children on the ridge, waving back as The Devil had done, before disappearing from the home to seek their fortune many, many years hence. She took a hand away from the doll's head and held it up to the sinking sun to inspect it in its own right; she saw, instead of the slender and youthful hand of the present, a gnarled, twisted and liver-spotted hand of her ancient future self. She felt no sadness to have suddenly grown old and she did not feel any of the rage she had felt in her youth whenever thinking about the onslaught of time because she had children, and they had grown up strong. She felt, looking at that vision of her ancient hand, younger and freer than before.

She turned her head to the side and saw, rocking next to her, an old man with a blanket over his lap and a faraway, contented look on his face. This time, however, the old man was The Devil. Maria reached out to him and he reached back, their old hands intertwining and squeezing gently. The old Devil looked at her and smiled. A new stage of their life began and, in the twilight of the day, Maria sat on the porch and realised that she had been wrong to cast The Devil from her future before. He may, indeed, love the child when he returned. He may ride out instantly. But, he may stay. He may look upon the child and feel what Maria expected to feel. As likely as he was to flee, he was equally likely to stay. She had not given him the benefit of the doubt. She loved her unborn child and she loved The Devil too.

The sun fell behind the trees and Maria turned back from the vision of the aged Devil to look out at the ridge. She understood that the heart is easily capable of holding more than one type of love and yet value each one as all-encompassing. She had been so enraptured in her solitude and visions that she had not even smoked her afternoon pipe. She would have preferred smoking it outside, but a thick mist was descending from the mountains in the distance and so Maria decided to retire to the fireside, look at the cot in the other room and smoke her pipe there before bed.

She gripped the handles of her rocking chair and stood up. Maria had taken two steps into the house when she felt a contorting sting ripple through her abdomen and a sudden and urgent desire to urinate overcame her. Maria steadied herself and concentrated. The sting of pain passed, as did the need to relieve herself. She stood up straight, cradled her belly and walked into the living room to sit by the fireside.

CHAPTER EIGHTEEN
Descending Mist

Hobson had been drifting in and out of consciousness for the three days that he had been dragged on the stretcher. The pain in his face had transformed from intense burning waves to a dull ache that had spread from his face down through his entire body. He had been lashed to Conrad's makeshift stretcher, his head raised and his feet dragging. The stretcher was pulled by the horse. His vision, when it sporadically returned, offered him little clues as to what had happened. His mind was a whirlpool as memories of his past, his dreams and his ideas fused with his understanding of reason and logic. Images flashed through his mind and there was no way of differentiating between pain-induced delirium, memory or dream. It was a hopeless collage.

As he saw the house disappear into the distance, he had the vague sensation that he had died and his soul was being pulled into the afterlife, and he was looking back at the earthly realm. This notion was compounded by the descending mist that seemed to move in thick and fast all around him the farther away from the house he was dragged. It was entirely possible and seemed reasonable to Hobson that the chaos in his mind was infiltrating the world as his soul ascended through the clouds, the internal and the external coming together. It was only when he felt a wet sensation around his feet that he realised that he had not died, and was not drifting through the clouds to heaven, but was being dragged through a brook which was soaking his feet. He was earthly bound once again and, as such, the pain in his body ascended to his face and reformed into the burning inferno around his wound.

As is the way with some atheists facing a slow and painful death, he turned to God and began to pray for forgiveness and an end to the pain. He closed his eyes, recounted all his sins, and asked for forgiveness for each one. The effect of recalling and recanting his sins was similar to counting sheep, and before Hobson had begun seeking absolution for his teenage sins, he had fallen into a deep and dark sleep which beat back the pain so that it only manifested itself within his dreamscape as a slight itch upon his cheek that he could not scratch.

The ride from the house and into the wilds of Montana was arduous and fraught with dangers, not least by the addition of the mist. Visibility was less than three metres and Rickman and Conrad, with Hobson being dragged, had to negotiate rocky passes, a large fast flowing brook and dense woodland. As soon as the mist began to descend, Rickman halted their advance and lashed a rope from his saddle bag to Conrad's horse's bridle and then remounted to take the lead. This ensured that as they traversed through the eerie landscape, they would not become separated. The disadvantage was more psychological. Now that they weren't side by side, they had only their minds for company, and no environment to gaze upon. It was a fraught mixture of introspection and acute alertness to the immediate surroundings. The horses moved slowly with a great fear of misplacing a hoof and twisting an ankle or breaking a leg. Each new change in terrain caused great consternation in them; many times they neighed in fear and frustration and tensed up so that their riders had to calm them.

Even the sound of the water did not penetrate the mist and when they came to the brook, the horses suddenly felt water and treacherous wet rocks by their hooves. The lead horse halted and neighed, telling Conrad's to do the same. They refused to move. Rickman turned to look back. He could just make out the shape of the horse and Conrad behind him, though the silhouette could well have belonged to anyone. Indeed, for a few moments, the angle of Conrad's hat, the hunch of his shoulders and the way he rested on the horn of his saddle made Rickman think it was a reflection of himself, that he had walked into the spirit world and was facing a mirror that reflected one's soul. All he saw was an empty shape. Rickman whistled. Conrad's whistle was a reminder that he was still in the waking world.

"Water," he croaked, and turned back to look out at the white wall. Both men dismounted, splashing into the stream. Rickman bent down, cupped some water into his hands and splashed his face, hoping to revive his senses a little further and beat back the mist that was encroaching into his mind. He bent low and could see a little farther as the mist hovered just above the water. He could not make out the bank on the other side, but he could see a few rocks clipping the water's surface. It seemed that the water was traversable. Conrad patted his horse and walked up to Rickman, bending low also and inspecting the small window of visibility.

"Can we make it?" he whispered.

Rickman squinted and inspected further.

"We can," he said finally.

"Hobson?" asked Conrad in an even quieter whisper, lest his voice carry over to the dying man. "Will he make it?"

Rickman stroked his chin.

"Everybody dies," he said, finally, "don't matter where, only how."

He stood up to calm his horse and whisper into its ear.

Conrad looked back at his own horse and could not see the stretcher attached. He walked over to it, bent down to the sleeping Hobson and watched his chest rise and sink. He was alive, just. Conrad looked at his face and carefully lifted the dirty rag that had been draped over the wound. He winced at the sight of the bone and flesh on display. One pair of eyelids had been blasted away, but the eyeball remained. Hobson looked away, but he was sleeping which, Conrad concluded, due to his open eye must have been a bewildering state to be in. He reached backwards to the edge of the stream and ran a hand through the water, collecting some. He dabbed his wet fingers onto Hobson's lips and watched as the droplets fell into his mouth. He patted the dying man's chest, turned back to his horse, and he and Rickman began to lead the horses out across the stream.

Hobson's feet were dry when he awoke from his dream. He could not recall the events that had unfolded as his mind battled against his injuries. All Hobson could recall was a drifting voice that echoed through his dream and repeated over and over: *'Everybody dies, don't matter where, only how.'*

The words faded, but the meaning remained and as his lethargy fell away, his physical faculties returned. His face hurt, but it was not as severe as before. The other side of his face felt warm. He was on his back looking up, but could not see the sky, only dark mist that carried a strange orange glow infiltrating the right side of his vision. He heard a familiar and welcome sound, that of gentle crackling and spitting. They had stopped for the night and he was lying next to a campfire. The thought warmed him more than the heat and he decided to conduct some tests. He flexed and gripped his hands. They still functioned. He moved his legs. He was not paralysed. He craned his neck to the side and looked at the fire. Behind it he saw Conrad and

Rickman sitting next to each other, whispering in hushed tones. His brother was not there and he remembered what had happened. The campfire had beaten back the mist and had brought a focus to his mind. The chaos of memory ordered itself slightly and Hobson was able to differentiate memory from dream. He recalled seeing his brother blasted from the landing of the old man's house and landing on the floor. The gurgling of his brother's final indistinguishable words entered his mind and became intelligible. As in his dream, he decided that his brother had tried to tell him that "Everybody dies, don't matter where, only how." His brother had died for nothing.

Hobson looked through the fire to Rickman Chill and the flames of rage in his heart burned fiercer than those flames that ravaged the nerves around his awful wound. The campfire warmed him no longer; Hobson turned away from Rickman and Conrad and looked out into the darkness. He flexed and gripped his hands and tested his legs again a little more aggressively than before. The darkness seemed less oppressive and more inviting, and a tide of conviction flowed through him. He closed his eye and forged a dreamscape of singular focus.

The campfire waned and the mist still hung heavy when Rickman and Conrad finished talking. With Fraser dead and Hobson perhaps hours away from the grave, their mission looked all but over. Conrad thought it prudent to take time to regroup. Perhaps ride west to Couldwell and recruit some new riders. He knew of at least four guns for hire that often dwelt there. Rickman did not agree. He was of a singular focus and when he flatly told Conrad that Hobson was deadweight and would be left to die in the morning, Conrad felt a chill run up his spine. Conrad knew his leader was cold and determined, and had never questioned him before, but now, encompassed by the mist and alone, he feared that perhaps even two riders were too much for Rickman. He imagined falling asleep and not waking up, having had his throat slit in the night by his leader, his body left to rot, undiscovered. His treacherous thoughts ran deep and when they retired for the night, Conrad barely slept. He lay with his head propped up against a log and his hat pulled down over his eyes so that he appeared to be asleep. In fact, he was awake and had his hands on his pistols.

Rickman smoked a cigarette and watched Conrad pretend to fall asleep. He looked down at his hands and contemplated their future. He looked at his bowie knife on his belt and did think about slitting both their throats. Hobson was deadweight and would be left. Conrad, well, he was growing soft and could prove to be more of a risk to the mission than anything. Rickman Chill had ridden out alone before, most notably in the years when Conrad had settled down with Liza. But the Preacher always returned to hire his most trusted gun. The Devil had taken Conrad's mother, as Rickman had reminded him on any occasion where he felt his belief in the mission was fading, or his concentration faltering. He should have done so doubly when Conrad told him that he had met someone, but Rickman's feelings concerning Conrad ran deep; he had consented to him marrying Liza and had even performed the ceremony. To that day, in the mist, he could not recall just what exactly had made him do it. His mission-mind was dumbfounded that he did not shoot Liza dead for distracting Conrad. He concluded that it was the last faint glimmer of humanity in his black soul that allowed him the good grace to marry the two. It must have been because God had returned the act of charity with another by striking Liza dead and returning Conrad to Rickman more angry and dangerous than ever before. God was fair, and God was on the side of the avenging Rickman. He smiled as he saw Conrad's head nod to the side, his façade of pretending to be asleep crumbling and true lethargy taking over. As if on cue, the mist fell down thicker and the campfire burnt out. Rickman Chill stood up to find a secluded spot far away from the campsite to sleep, as was his way. He packed his tobacco and stepped into the darkness.

CHAPTER NINETEEN

Time of Times – Part One

Barely an hour after sitting down in the chair, the twist in Maria's abdomen returned. She likened the sensation to the pains she suffered during her period, but that was so long ago that it felt even more acute. As it had done an hour before, the pain went away as quickly as it came and Maria returned to her rocking and staring at the cot. The pain in her stomach had strangely eradicated her desire to smoke and the thought made her feel slightly nauseous. However, the hold of tobacco over her was great and she began to rock a little faster and drum her fingers on the arms of the chair. She turned her attention from the cot and to the guitar resting on the wall next to her lover's empty chair, and tried to invent a tune. She began to feel more agitated as her concentration was not focused enough to conjure the image of her lover playing her a soothing melody. A mild sweat broke out over her brow and her fingers drummed harder. She began tapping her left foot and biting the inside of her lip. She reached breaking point and hit her head on the back of the chair in frustration at her agitation. Maria stood up to find something useful to do. She walked over to The Devil's chair and moved it to face the fire. She then picked up the guitar and rested it upon the arms. Another twist in her abdomen contorted her, this time more acute and more sudden than before. Maria winced, gripped the edge of The Devil's chair and bent herself over its back until the cramp fell away.

She left the living room and walked, this time slightly hunched, to the cupboard that stored his clothes. She opened the door, took out his poncho and his hat, and returned to the living room. She had no idea why she was occupying herself in such a way, but the sudden instinct to keep busy was too much to ignore. She threw the poncho over the back of the chair and went back into the hallway to grab the hat stand. Her movements were too sudden and too aggressive and the contorting pains in her abdomen returned, harder, sharper and for a greater length of time.

She dragged the hat stand into the living room and placed it behind The Devil's chair. She had just managed to put the hat on the hook when a fearsome pain stabbed at her belly and shot down towards her groin, causing her sex to feel like it had burst into flames. Maria breathed in sharply in shock, and bent double, clutching her belly.

She knew what was coming and had, perhaps, known since she had sat on the porch and watched the mist come in, but she had tried to ignore it. She was about to give birth and had, up until that point, not thought once about the actual process of delivering the child into the world. She had only dreamt the serene dreams of sleeping babies in cots, and loving parents looking down upon it with doting eyes. She had not thought about the pain, stress and blood yet to come. Another stab. Maria grabbed the edge of her dress and almost fell to her knees. The baby was going to come and she was alone. Far worse than that, she was alone and had no idea what to do.

Maria rallied herself and apportioned a part of her mind to dealing with contractions and another part to thinking practically about what needed to be done. The baby was coming so she would need blankets for the blood. She would need water. She would need a pillow for her head and she would need a knife, perhaps, as she would need to cut the umbilical cord.

Maria was literate, but not educated, and had not spent a great deal of time around other people or books and even less time around pregnant women and children. In fact, as she scanned her memory trying to locate a time, place or conversation which had something to do with delivering a baby, she could not even remember a time before the house and a time before The Devil. She could not remember her parents or her childhood.

She gripped her belly and squeezed as the contractions grew stronger and more frequent. The strength of them seemed to travel through her nerves and into her mind, charging her memories with lightning. She could not hold onto a single image, or give weight enough to any idea so that it became solid and not fleeting. Did she even exist before this house? What was happening? Was she a figment of someone else's imagination? A background character in someone else's dream?

She grabbed the back of The Devil's chair and pressed her forehead onto her hand, gritting her teeth and focusing harder. The galaxy of new and terrifying existential questions was not helping her. She had to think straight and address the problem at hand. She regulated her breathing and reinforced the part of her mind that was dealing with the situation and not the pain. Sheets. Water. Pillow. Knife. Maria stood up and made her way to the bedroom.

As she walked, she felt as if she were on a listing ship. She barrelled from door frame to wall, one arm holding her belly and the other arm outstretched to absorb the impact of her stumbling. Her legs were heavy and her back ached. The sweat on her brow was no longer caused by agitation but now by exertion. She rationally thought that the hardest task needed to be performed first as her strength was depleting and the contractions increasing. She had to get upstairs and get some sheets and a pillow from her bed.

Maria reached the foot of the staircase and gripped the banister rail. She took three deep breaths and was about to take the first step when an almighty contraction hit her. She lost her grip on the banister and fell forward. She managed to protect herself and her child from impacting on the stairs by grabbing onto the edge of the step near her face. She clenched her jaw and slowly, breathing as steadily as she could, began to climb.

She reached the top of the stairs and took a few seconds to catch her breath. She was beginning to understand the pain of the contractions and was able to adapt to them, controlling her breathing to numb the pain as best she could and anticipating their arrival and their departure. Her mind was finally beginning to synchronise with her body.

While resting on the stairs, her arms on the landing floor, her head resting in the crook of her elbow, and her body still on the staircase, she looked across the way to the bedroom. She needed the sheets and the pillow. She thought about the comfort of the bed and the soft mattress and she knew she should give birth there. She realised she had made a mistake in getting the pillows and the sheets first. She should have got the knife and water and ascending the stairs, sought comfort in the bed and delivered her child there.

She thumped the landing with her fist and cursed in her mind at her foolishness. She now had an even more difficult choice: continue with her plan, get the sheets and pillow, descend the staircase somehow, get the water and knife and deliver on the floor downstairs, or she could do all that and then attempt to climb the stairs and deliver on the bed.

Maria thumped the landing harder as her contractions returned and she craned her neck to look down at her body spread out on the stairs, and down further to the floor below. The distance seemed insurmountable but she knew that whatever happened she could not deliver on the staircase without anything at hand to help her. She knew that the longer she debated what to do, the less chance she had to accomplish either. She screamed in frustration and turned onto her back. She had to descend the staircase, get the knife and the water and then summon all her remaining strength to get back up the staircase and onto the bed.

Maria looked down at the stairs. She could see her knees shaking and she could feel the weakness in her arms as she prepared to descend feet first and on her back. She lifted her left foot slowly and transferred her weight. Her right foot instantly slipped off the step and Maria slid down, her back cracking into the edge of the step. She thrust her left arm out and grabbed the banister spindle, and prevented herself from crashing to the floor.

She breathed out in relief, and concluded that all her schemes were ridiculous. She did not have nearly the strength, stamina or indeed control of her body to attempt what she wanted to do. There was no way she could make it into the kitchen and back up the staircase. As she was nearer the ground than the landing, the only way forward was to continue down the stairs and deliver on the cold, hard wooden floor. She would attempt to get the knife and the water, but made no promises to herself.

She also, wisely, concluded that attempting to descend the staircase on her back was not going to be possible. Maria heaved herself up onto her feet, grabbed the banister, leaned over and instantly felt much more secure and stable. She began to walk sideways, crab like, down the staircase, one step at a time in a steady rhythm, breathing in and out through her mouth and rolling with the ever-decreasing timing of the contractions.

Maria reached the foot of the staircase and looked around the room. Now back on her feet on the level ground, and not attempting any stupid feats like climbing the stairs, she felt suddenly more confident and capable. She looked to the kitchen and saw the water jug on the table and the knife on the sideboard. She let go of the banister and staggered to the wall opposite, using her shoulder to take the impact as she cradled her belly with both hands, rubbing it in an attempt to calm the tumultuous sea raging within. She took a deep breath and, employing the same steady rhythm she had used in descending the staircase, she took a few steps towards the kitchen.

Maria grabbed the door frame for support and looked around the room. She considered climbing onto the table and birthing upon it as a substitute for the bed but concluded that it would make little difference. There were no sheets around so she could not make it more comfortable. It was the floor or nothing. She had little time. The stone floor of the kitchen was too cold, the living room too far away. The only option was the hallway as it was narrow enough for Maria to lay on her back, reach out with both arms and easily touch each wall, thereby enabling her to brace and aid her expulsion of the child. She was convinced it was the right thing to do.

Maria staggered into the kitchen, grabbed the knife from the sideboard, turned to the doorway and flung the blade into the hallway, deciding that where it lay would be the spot where she stopped moving around, lay on her back and got on with delivering her child.

The knife skidded down the hall and stopped halfway between the kitchen door and the front door, coming to rest next to the living room and by the foot of the stairs. Maria was pleased. The fateful position would provide her a doorframe and a banister spindle to grip and push against should she need to.

Maria moved from the counter to the kitchen table to grab the jug of water, stopping briefly to plunge her hand inside and splash some water over her face and neck, revitalising herself.

She picked up the jug, looked down at her large carving of Wild Goose Island on the table and decided that it was there, on that perfect night when they had made love, that the child inside her had been conceived. The thought calmed her and happiness swept through her momentarily. She had come full circle from Wild Goose Island and was now about to give birth. She nodded her thanks to the carving and what it represented, grabbed the handle of the jug and stepped out into the hallway.

Chapter Twenty
Time of Times – Part Two

I t seemed as if the child, her body and her mind were as one because as soon as Maria left the kitchen and took her first step into the hallway, her waters broke. Maria felt a new upheaval from her abdomen and a sudden wetness between her legs. She fell against the wall, bent her legs slightly and reached down between them to feel her sex. She did not expect to feel the extent of the dilation and it worried her greatly.

The image of the baby appeared in her mind, followed by her innate understanding of her sexual organs and how narrow it was whenever she used to pleasure herself. Her eyes widened in fear for what was to happen. Her breathing became slightly erratic and the sweat poured from her

She rested her back against the wall, squatted slightly and attempted to close her legs as tightly as she could in a last ditch attempt to push the child back up into her womb.

The pain and pressure were too much. The baby was coming. She looked over to the knife on the floor just two feet away and slid down the wall until she was sitting down. She shuffled along the wall until she reached the knife, whereupon she pushed against the wall and slid herself forward onto her back, and 'walked' up the opposite wall of the hallway so that her feet were flat against it, spread wide and her birth canal ready.

She imagined that, if she were in a hospital, she would be in a similar position. She rested the jug to one side, and pulled the knife closer on the other.

Her mind settled into the understanding that it really was time and, as if to confirm this, her contractions merged and there was no time in between them.

Maria screamed as the respite between the contractions fell away and the pain became indescribable. A primal instinct kicked in and Maria quickly turned over onto all fours. Something told her that it would be more comfortable and it was. The pain increased and the pressure mounted. Maria pressed her palms against the wall and breathed sharply through her pursed lips, the spit mixing with the drops of sweat on the floor. Her position was not correct. It was comfortable, but she knew it was not right. She did not want to move, but the same primal instinct overcame her desire for comfort and she turned back into the correct birthing position and screamed again in pain.

She thumped the floor with one hand, and with the other she gripped the handle of the knife and hit its butt on the floor repeatedly in time with her breath in an attempt to regain some more control. The contractions did not abate and she began to hit the back of her head against the wall in time with her hands. It did not help to ease the pain or the abject feeling of her body controlling itself.

Her sex began to burn and she felt as though it was being stretched paper thin. Her scream became a high pitched wheeze and she clamped her lips together and shut her eyes. The burning increased and she involuntarily thrust her hands down to her groin and bent forward. Her eyes were wild and panicked as she felt the unnaturally large dilation of her delicate sex and, in a flash of abject revulsion, she felt something inside, at the opening: the baby's forehead.

She knew what it was, but fear overcame her; she held her hands over her sex and began to panic, breathing hard and erratically, her eyes wild.

Her hands held fast as she attempted to stop the child coming farther out by pushing it back inside. She began to cry as the panic intensified along with her body's refusal to do as she bid. She looked around the hallway, her nightmare thickening. She looked down at the knife and thought that she could halt the pain and fear very quickly if she took it in her hand and plunged it into her heart.

Her hands began to tighten as she felt her sex stretching farther than she thought possible. It was going to tear wide open, she was sure of it.

Maria released one hand from her groin and went to grab the knife. She picked it up and looked at the blade shaking in her hand; she tried to summon the courage to end the pain and bewildering fear. It was in that most desperate of moments that Maria was saved.

As she looked at the knife, she saw a shadow creep across the blade and fall onto the wall opposite. She dropped the blade instantly and looked at it. The fire in the living room had silhouetted the chair she had placed in front of it, along with the guitar, and hat. The perfect silhouette of The Devil sitting by the fire and playing his guitar for Maria was right in front of her.

The fear inside was beaten back and she released her other hand from her groin. She felt confident and focused once more, and the pain inside her and the pain of her dilation became manageable.

She looked at The Devil's shadow and felt excited about showing him the child he had sired once he returned. She wanted to give birth. She wanted the child out of her; not to end the pain, but to start her life as soon as possible. Her breathing became regulated and steady and she began to push hard, using every muscle she could. She felt a tearing sensation between her legs, but instead of screaming she grunted in exertion, taking in the pain and forcing it back through her towards her muscles to fuel the energy of her pushing.

She bent forward, adding more strength to her pushes. She let go of the floor and moved her hands back to her genitals, not to halt the child's arrival this time, but to aid it. She could feel the head as it forced its way through and she cupped it for support. She pushed again and felt the baby turn of its own accord as it twisted its shoulders out of her.

Maria held the child with both hands now and with one more final push the baby slithered out of her.

Time froze. Maria was holding something in her hands, between her legs but she could not see it. The pain was subsiding and her breathing was slowing. The shadow on the wall did not flicker but remained eerily motionless. The hallway was silent.

Maria fearfully lifted her arms out from between her legs and up over her belly. She was holding her child. It spluttered twice, causing her to gasp in shock as she strangely had not expected the thing that had come out of her to be a living entity.

Then the child, as it took in its first breaths of air unaided, began to scream. Maria's mouth fell open and her eyes were wide. The child was covered in blood and a dark brown amniotic fluid and over all that, a white waxy coating. In shock, Maria held the creature for a few seconds as it screamed, and it was not until she saw its tiny hands grab at the air that she realised it was her child and that beyond everything it must be protected.

Maria began to laugh and cry as the emotion of the birth and realisation of what she was holding became too much. She brought the baby slowly up to her and rested it against her breast; she was astounded to see the child instinctively attempt to suckle. She was still wearing her blouse and so she quickly unbuttoned it and held the baby to her breast. The child began to feed and Maria was overcome.

She reached over to the water, dipped her fingers in and began to clean the baby's head as it suckled. Once the head was clean, she carefully dabbed the corner of her shawl into the jug and began to wipe off the waxy coating, blood and amniotic fluid until the baby was more or less clean.

It was still suckling when she finished, so Maria sat back against the wall and wrapped her shawl around it, closing her eyes as the tides of relief and love washed over her.

She had been asleep for an hour when another contraction awoke her. The baby was asleep next to her breast and she had, instinctively in her sleep, held it close and kept it warm without once dropping it.

The contraction came again and she had the sudden panic that, perhaps, she was about to have another child. However, she felt empty inside and the contraction felt more like an aftershock to the earthquake before. She reached down between her legs and felt around. She felt the cord still attached to the baby that disappeared inside her when another contraction came and she felt a wet, almost formless mass expel itself from her and slop down between her legs.

Maria had not expected this to happen and was unsure what it even was. She prodded it with her finger. It did not move. It was not alive. She noticed that the umbilical cord from the child was attached to it and concluded that it was not a horrific abnormality but probably something natural.

She looked over at the knife and contemplated severing the chord and the strange liver-like extrusion but decided against it. What if it was helping the child live? What if it was extremely important to keep it attached? She decided to leave what was the placenta attached to the baby and trust that in time something would happen to tell her what to do with it.

She picked up the lump and moved it from between her legs to the side of her so that the cord could not get tangled up with her leg. She then dared to inspect her vagina, fearful that she would find it destroyed beyond hope.

She was astounded to find it dilated but intact and not nearly as wide as it had been. Indeed, it was already starting to reform. Maria was amazed at the unique power of the female body and the strength of her resolve.

She shifted herself along the wall slightly so that she was no longer sitting in the pool of blood and amniotic liquid. She had not yet the strength to move to a chair, let alone make it upstairs to bed. The hallway seemed fine for the moment and was not as uncomfortable as she had thought it would be.

The shadow of The Devil remained on the wall and had begun to shimmer again; it appeared as if the silhouette was playing the guitar. Maria smiled and looked out towards the window and then farther out but could not see anything. The white mist was close around the house, but it did not matter at all. She was content, calm and relieved to be sitting there against the wall with her baby. For a few more hours at least.

She was about to close her eyes and fall into a light doze, with the hope of waking to find her strength recovered so that she could show her child around the house. Her eyes closed for a few seconds before she realised something. She had not even checked to see what sex her child was. How could she have forgotten that?

She smiled, opened her eyes and peeled back the shawl and gently lifted the child's tiny leg. She smiled to herself, closed her eyes and as she drifted into a most wonderful and welcome sleep she mentally cut her list of possible names for the child in half and cycled through each name over and over again, until she found the perfect name and matching personality to attribute to her new, wonderful and alive daughter. Maria was a mother.

CHAPTER TWENTY-ONE
The Bite

Rickman had taken himself away from Conrad and Hobson to seek out a place to sleep. He needed to be far enough away so they would not disturb him, yet close enough to be on hand should anything arise. His heart was beating slowly and his breathing shallow. Through the foliage a rattlesnake made its way towards him. It slithered over the log Rickman was using as a makeshift pillow and moved towards his body. The snake could not tell if he were alive or dead.

Rickman always slept alone. It was there, in his solitude, where he felt only the slightest peace of mind. At all other times, his mind was in constant motion; even his dreams were machines built to process thought and order.

When they were fortunate enough to board in a hotel or flophouse, he would always lock himself away in his room, pull the shutters and lock the windows and then barricade the door, finding something with which to cover the peephole and the lock. His privacy when he slept, bathed or changed clothes was second only to his mission to seek and destroy The Devil.

Before bedding down on the flat ground next to a fallen tree, he had removed his Preacher's collar and unbuttoned his shirt. As was his way before falling asleep, he lay on his back looking up at the black mist and rubbed his neck, his slender fingers running over the large and angry abrasion that ran around his throat and neck and caused his voice to crack and hiss in an awful manner. His fingers knew every crease, divot and impression of that scar. The skin around it was stretched and rough and appeared to once have been stretched and then pulled back into shape. Throughout all seasons, the scarring was purple, red and black and ached constantly. The damage was not only skin deep and the twisted voice was not the only consequence of such a terrible long-ago wound. Eating was painful and he rarely indulged; when he did, he would cut the pieces of food so small they hardly seemed worth bothering with. After every mouthful he would wince and clench his jaw. In the summer, when his throat was dry, it became agonisingly painful, and during daylight hours he had to wear a handkerchief over his mouth at all times to limit the amount of pollen that could be ingested. He was prone to colds and coughs, and their effects were magnified within his ravaged throat. It was a constant, never-ending torture for Rickman Chill but he used it to his advantage. It was another barrel of oil to fuel his engines of revenge.

And so, as always, Rickman lay on his back, fingering his neck abrasion, thinking about his past and how it informed his future. On this night, just before falling into his deep sleep, he concluded that, if he were to ride into Bel, he would need all the gunhands he could get. He understood Conrad's concern, but he could not acquiesce.

The diversion to Couldwell would take too long and, once in that villainous town, there would be no guarantee that they could even hire some guns. Added to that, Couldwell was just as dangerous as Bel. He concluded that they would ride on to Bel and assault the town as an army of two. Presently, he closed his eyes and fell asleep.

The rattlesnake approached Rickman's left boot, coiled underneath it and up around until it was on the roof of his foot. It moved around the boot, over the sole and back up to the ankle, feeling over the cold metal spur, then up the boot and onto his trouser leg. Rickman's breathing was slow and controlled and the snake moved over his groin and found a warm and inviting cave: a gap between his shirt and his belt. The snake entered his shirt and moved up Rickman's torso.

The Preacher did not feel the snake on his skin, so soft and light it was. The snake appeared by his unbuttoned collar and slithered over his neck, passed his ear and moved up onto the trunk of the fallen tree. Once it had left Rickman's body completely and was upon the tree, it turned round and craned its head in close to Rickman's neck. It hissed quietly and inspected the skin before moving up to his face and scanning his nose, cheeks and eyes. The snake turned from Rickman and moved off into the blackness.

Hobson had been awake for an hour or two, as the pain in his face had flared up and destroyed his calm dream. He was still lashed to the stretcher and looked up at the blackness. He had exercised his fingers and legs and felt stronger than he had a few hours previously. He held full control of his physical self, as well as his mental self. He could tell, even in the darkness, what was dream and what was reality. He knew what memories were real, and what were constructed by his subconscious to help combat the pain in his face.

For the first time since catching half of the old man's shotgun blast to his face, Hobson Witney felt confident enough to tell himself that he was going to live. He rolled his head to the side, to see the fire still glowing slightly. He looked at it, the orange pulse hypnotic. His eye grew heavy again when suddenly an abnormal movement caught his attention. He focused a little harder and his eye grew wide in horror as the rattlesnake slithered around the warm remnants of the fire and approached him. He was stricken with fear, and tied to the stretcher so he could not defend himself even if he wanted to. He had but one choice: God. He looked at the serpent and prayed fervently that it would not strike him and that, if it were to strike someone, it would be Conrad, who was just next to him.

He remained deathly still as the snake approached and moved onto his body, sliding up and over his face. His eye was fixed open and his lips clamped tightly shut. He prayed and prayed and held his breath, until eventually the snake moved off his face and back onto the ground towards Conrad.

God was listening to him. God was on his side. God had forgiven him. Hobson smiled broadly in relief and rapture and craned his head back to try and see Conrad. Though his view was obscured by the top of the stretcher, he could see the snake sliding up over Conrad. He could not tell if it was his idea and action, or if God was working through him, but as soon as he saw the snake move up to Conrad's exposed neck he screamed, "Watch out!" as loudly as he could.

The scream instantly yanked Conrad out of his sleep and he sat bolt upright, his guns ready. He had no time to realise the snake was there, let alone react as it hissed and, out of surprise and self-preservation, bit him on the shoulder, discharging all of its venom.

Conrad screamed and rolled to his side, grabbing the snake. Hobson began screaming and thrashing about on the stretcher in fake terror. Conrad grabbed the snake, yanked it off his shoulder and threw it to the ground. He drew his gun and fired three bullets with deadly precision into the poor serpent, cleaving it in half in a split second.

Hobson's scream woke Rickman and before he had time to process what was happening, he was already on his feet and running back to the camp, instinct ruling all his senses.

Though the mist was still thick and the night was extra dark, he managed to leap over the fallen trees and duck the branches as if it were broad daylight. The three gunshots from Conrad spurred him on and he ran into the light spilling from the camp fire. Through the gloom he saw Conrad staggering around for a few moments, clutching the base of his neck by his shoulder before falling onto his knee, then onto his side, and finally rolling onto his back. Rickman skidded across the loose ground, bringing his body down and sliding up next to Conrad.

"Snake! It was a snake!" yelled Hobson, "Goddamn snake!"

Conrad's eyes were panicked and bulging, his breathing fast and erratic. He scrabbled and kicked around, more in shock than in direct response to the venom's effects.

Rickman grabbed Conrad by the legs and put his full weight on them to stop him thrashing about. He reached up and clamped his gloved hand over Conrad's mouth and began to calmly shush him like a mother calming a scared child.

The normal crack and grate of Rickman's voice was absent and a much softer tone managed to not only break through his twisted voice box, but also imbued it with a weight of genuine concern.

"Shhhh, keep calm Conrad, keep calm. Good man, good man."

The strange sound of Rickman's hidden voice battered through Conrad's shock and soothed him almost instantly.

"You have to keep calm, you have to keep calm. Slow your heart, slow your heart down. Good man. Good man."

Conrad's breathing slowed.

"A fucking snake!" shouted Hobson, thrashing around madly. Rickman, not wanting Conrad to be agitated any further, lashed out with his boot and connected with Hobson's head, knocking him out cold.

"It's alright Conrad, it's alright."

He gently released his hand from Conrad's mouth and eased his weight off his legs. Conrad began to regulate his breathing through his mouth, his eyes still panicked.

"I hear... Hobson... is awake," he said, bravely.

Rickman smiled, and made sure Conrad saw the rare gesture. He patted Conrad's chest and climbed off him completely.

"Right," he said, his voice resuming its normal croak, "let me see it."

He turned Conrad's head to face away from the wound before he gently pulled back his collar to reveal the two red pricks from the snake's bite.

The tiny dots already had a white ring around them and an angry red patch was beginning to spread. Rickman clenched his jaw, but silently cursed.

"It's nothing," he lied, "some venom, but not enough to kill you."

"How can you tell?" asked Conrad, the pain burning his shoulder and his vision already beginning to blur.

"Remember Lucky Jake out of Bone City?"

"Yeah."

"How many times did he get bit before he died?"

"Twenty," slurred Conrad.

"Twenty-four, and you only got bit once."

Rickman looked around the meagre campsite, desperately trying to formulate a plan.

"Alright," he said finally, "I'm going to move you."

"No, it hurts… just leave me."

Rickman ignored Conrad, picked up his ankles and rotated him around so that his feet were now by the large log. He backed him up and managed to rest his legs over the tree so that he was resting on his shoulders, upper back and neck.

"What are…"

"I have to keep the bite below the heart. I have to keep you alive."

Conrad looked up at Rickman as his leader adjusted his legs so that the angle of his body was more acute. Conrad could feel the swelling around his shoulder begin to grow and the burning spread. His vision was blurring more rapidly and his breathing became heavy and painful. Lethargy was beginning to consume him. He reached up and held out his hand for Rickman, who took it and knelt down beside him.

"I would have liked," he whispered, fighting off the great sleep, "to have shot The Devil myself to see the look in your eyes. I would have gone into Bel on my own if it meant catching The Devil."

"I know," said Rickman, cupping their handshake with his other hand and squeezing it tightly. Conrad pulled Rickman in close, using his last remaining ounces of strength.

"Promise me," he said, "promise me you will get The Devil."

"I promise," whispered Rickman.

Conrad pulled one of his hands free of Rickman's and slapped him across the face.

"You promise me you'll get the bastard who killed my mother."

Rickman nodded solemnly and Conrad slumped back down.

"I wanna confess…" he whispered in words that barely left his lips. "I killed…"

Sleep finally overpowered him and he could not finish his confession. He breathed out before his eyes closed.

PRUNUS VIRGINIANA
'Choke Cherry'

Found in grassland and sagebrush areas

CHAPTER TWENTY-TWO
Cut and Suck

Rickman, out of desperation, shook Conrad's body vigorously and after the fourth shake he dropped him back to the ground and punched him in the face.

Conrad coughed slightly and moved. He was alive, just. Rickman sat back in relief for only a few seconds before his rational mind snapped into action. He had wasted too much time already. He looked over to the fire. It was still glowing. He leaned over and kicked the pile, knocking off the top few logs to release a bed of hot rocks. He drew his knife and rested it on the edge of the fire so that the top two inches of the blade were resting on a glowing rock.

He patted down Conrad, located his bowie knife and pulled it out of its sheath. He ripped Conrad's shirt open and exposed the large inflamed shoulder. He pulled his glove off with his teeth and gently touched the inflammation. It was scorching hot.

He lit a match off a rock and held it over the infected area, searching for the bite marks. He found them, pushed upwards by the swelling and pulled apart so that each puncture was now the size of a small coin. He looked at Conrad's face and saw he was still breathing slightly.

He counted to three before digging the tip of the bowie knife into the wound and letting the liquid flow freely from it. He drove the blade in further and began to gouge a chunk of flesh out around each fang mark.

Conrad murmured and kicked, his delirium dulling the pain. Rickman then licked his lips, placed them over the wound and began to suck as much blood and venom as he could out of the wound, spitting each mouthful out as he did. He had no idea if he was performing the procedure correctly, or even if it was the right procedure to attempt.

He spat a sixth mouthful of blood and liquid out and sat back. The inflammation had reduced, but he could not tell if he had extracted any venom at all. He had no option but to proceed. He undid Conrad's belt and forced the strap between his teeth. Whilst keeping hold of one end, he reached back over to the fire and retrieved his knife, the tip of which was now glowing red. He counted to three before pressing the blade down on the wound, sealing it.

Conrad's eyes snapped open and he bit down hard on the leather strap as he screamed in agony. He thrashed his legs and kicked wildly. Rickman tried to calm him with his voice as before but this time it did not work. He had no choice but to place the blade onto the second fang mark. Conrad screamed again and passed out from the pain, falling fast into a mad and deep dream world.

Rickman removed the knife and looked down at the wound which now looked ten times worse. Had he gone too far? Had he exacerbated it? Had he sealed the venom inside? He had no idea. He concluded that if there was any chance of Conrad surviving, he had to be taken to the nearest town for treatment.

Rickman calculated that with both of them on one horse, they could make it to Bel in maybe four days. It was hopeless. Conrad would probably be dead within hours. He had at best maybe two days.

Rickman looked around the campfire to see Hobson still unconscious on his stretcher. Rickman stood up, walked over to him, untied his lashings and rolled him off the stretcher. Hobson slumped onto his side, the rag over his wound falling off and presenting Rickman with the full horror of his ruined face. Rickman picked up the stretcher and walked back to Conrad without bothering to replace the rag.

He laid the stretcher down and dragged Conrad onto it, lashing him to it tightly with his feet at the top end and his head at the bottom. Conrad's wound had to be kept below his heart, and that meant he had to be dragged by his feet. He could not be slumped over Rickman's horse as there was no room for both them and their possessions. If they were to come across particularly rocky terrain, or running water, Conrad's head would be totally exposed and they would be undone. It was a desperate plan.

As soon as Conrad was lashed to the stretcher, Rickman stepped back and went to ready his horse to receive the extra weight. As soon as his back was turned he froze. His mind was split. Why was he suddenly going out of the mission's way to drag Conrad around until he died? He was a dead man and the chance of coming across help before Bel was minimal. His mission-mind said over and over, '*leave him, leave him, leave him.*'

Rickman buried his face into the saddle bag and caressed the wound in his neck. He had to save Conrad, or he would have fallen too far from the grace of God. He rallied himself and led the horse over to the stretcher.

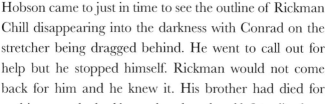

Hobson came to just in time to see the outline of Rickman Chill disappearing into the darkness with Conrad on the stretcher being dragged behind. He went to call out for help but he stopped himself. Rickman would not come back for him and he knew it. His brother had died for nothing; now he had been abandoned and left to die alone in the mist. He closed his eye and fell back to sleep, hoping that when his eyes opened again, they would be looking upon the gates of heaven.

When he awoke, the sight that greeted him was not that of the pearly gates, but that of a pair of large brown eyes staring down at him. It was possibly morning, as the mist was now a light grey. He heard a neighing. Conrad's horse, abandoned as he had been, had walked over to inspect the sleeping Hobson. The horse whinnied quietly and nudged the man.

Hobson furrowed his brow and blinked a few times to prove to himself that he was not in a dream. The horse remained. He reached up and touched his wound. Instead of feeling intense pain, he felt nothing. The cool, damp mist had seemingly numbed the severed nerve endings.

Hobson felt imbued with strength. He reached up and patted the horse's muzzle, which caused it to neigh happily. Hobson was renewed. He tested his hands and feet and felt strong enough to sit up. He did so with only a slight ache and pain which he attributed to having been dragged over the unforgiving Montana lands.

He waited for a few seconds before attempting the next stage. Hobson looked over to the horse for encouragement and he found it in his large eyes. Hobson swung his arm onto the log and heaved himself onto his feet. His knees were weak and his sudden reorientation caused him to sway.

He steadied himself on the log and waited for the nausea to pass. It did so and he stood erect once more. He was alive. He walked carefully to the horse and was amazed to see the saddlebags still attached and still containing some practical items. Rickman had clearly taken what he could, but had left a blanket, a clean shirt and a bottle of whisky.

Hobson almost screamed for joy when he found the drink; he yanked it from the bag, bit off the cork and drank deeply, the power of it returning years to him. He repacked the bottle and adjusted the saddle to his liking. Using the log for a stepping ladder as he did not yet trust the strength of his body, he mounted the horse.

The morning light was slowly dissolving the mist and, though it remained, he could see a little farther than he had been able to over the past few days. He had no compass, he had no map, but he had a horse, his guns and whisky. God had spared him and truly loved him.

Hobson patted the horse and trying his luck one more time as is man's way, he whispered the word 'Bel' into the horse's ear. His heart was enraptured with the love of God when the horse neighed and walked slowly off into the mist. As Hobson sat on the horse, touching his wound, he smiled at the surprise Rickman Chill had waiting for him if and when he finally arrived in that town.

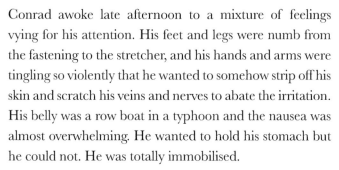

Conrad awoke late afternoon to a mixture of feelings vying for his attention. His feet and legs were numb from the fastening to the stretcher, and his hands and arms were tingling so violently that he wanted to somehow strip off his skin and scratch his veins and nerves to abate the irritation. His belly was a row boat in a typhoon and the nausea was almost overwhelming. He wanted to hold his stomach but he could not. He was totally immobilised.

He could not be sure if his vision was blurry or not as the mist was still all around him. Occasionally a branch swung passed his vision but it moved too quickly for him to focus on it. His hair was soaking wet; not from the dew or the mist but from the never ending flop sweat that was pouring off him, running down his face and into his hair. His mouth was full of saliva and he was stuck in a perpetual cycle of painfully turning his head and spitting out an abnormal amount of liquid, turning his head back and waiting a few seconds before having to repeat the process. He had venom all through his blood. He knew it. He was going to die.

It was getting into the afternoon and Rickman was beginning to think about what they would do in the evening should Conrad make it that far. They crossed through the woods and, just as Rickman judged that the sun was about to set, though he could not see it, they emerged from the treeline onto a rudimentary road.

Rickman stopped the horse, amazed at the strange anomaly that had presented itself. He looked up and down the road, deciding that it was best to join it and pick one direction as it would surely lead to a town. He guided the horse onto the road and turned him left to carry them towards a ridge up ahead.

They had travelled around two hundred yards when they reached the top of the ridge. Rickman halted the horse and looked out. His mouth fell open and for the briefest of moments he actually considered the existence of God. He smiled and patted the neck of his mount. He turned back to look at Conrad, strapped upside down and asleep again. They had made it. Rickman turned back to the view ahead and took a few moments to stow away his relief and scan the environment for dangers, as was his way.

After a few moments, he kicked the horse into action and they descended the ridge, approaching the small farmhouse ahead. As they grew closer, the mist parted around the compound and Rickman saw that there was light inside. He dismounted and led the horse into the compound. To the side of the house he saw a goat staring at them.

CHAPTER TWENTY-THREE
"... I've come home"

Rickman halted in the middle of the compound. The house seemed pleasant and well kept. Apart from a few leaves that needed to be swept away, the porch was relatively clean. There were no cobwebs or signs of neglect. The barn and stable to the side of the house had a sturdy door, closed shut and bolted. The fence line too was well constructed and not fallen to decay. He looked up at the roof and saw no holes or broken shingles. Rickman, his hand still on his gun, stepped back to the stretcher. He looked down to find Conrad awake, his eyes circling, his pupils dilated.

Rickman unclasped the stretcher and gently lowered Conrad onto the ground, leaning in close and removing his glove so that he could check Conrad's temperature. He was burning up, but not as badly as before and he had less sweat upon his brow while his lips were not so white. Rickman removed Conrad's shirt and looked at his swollen shoulder. It was still engorged with blood.

Rickman pulled his knife and showed it to Conrad, who nodded. The Preacher placed his fingers over his lips to signal for silence. Conrad breathed out and braced himself as Rickman dug the tip of his blade into his skin, draining the blood and fluid and relieving the burning. Rickman did not have any hot implements at hand to seal the wound, and so reached into his pocket and pulled out his hipflask. He gave a sip to Conrad who took it thirstily before taking a swig himself, and then poured the rest of its contents onto the inflamed wound. Conrad's eyes bulged but he did not scream, and soon the burning in his shoulder eased slightly.

Rickman untied Conrad from the stretcher and slid his arm under his neck. On the count of three he hoisted Conrad up onto his feet. Conrad's legs were near numb and Rickman had to take the full weight of the man on his shoulder. Conrad felt dizzy and nauseous, and the vision of the house in front of him moved away into the distance before crashing back towards him at a twisting and dizzying speed. He could not feel the ground or feel the breeze on his skin. None of his senses seemed to be working properly.

Rickman took a step forward and Conrad slumped with him. Rickman knew the injured man could not be on his feet for too long as this placed the wound above the heart, which would make the venom pump more vigorously around his system.

They took another step before they heard a fierce bleating sound. A clonk of what seemed like wood on wood came. Rickman looked over to the house to see the mountain goat standing by the doorway, its hoof stamping on the porch and its head lowered in readiness to charge. Rickman did not want to shoot the animal. It could be a beloved pet of whoever owned the house. He could not risk angering the residents he needed so badly to be their saviours.

He leaned Conrad against the horse and hooked his arm through the saddle strap so that if he slumped down, he would not fall completely to the floor.

Rickman quietly pulled some rope from his saddle bag and with no sudden movements stepped towards the porch, fixing a loop in the rope. He squatted low, spreading his arms wide and fixing the goat with a piercing stare. The goat stamped its hoof and huffed more angrily. Rickman took another step towards the house and the goat kicked backwards donkey-like, hitting open the door to the house before charging forward.

Rickman charged to meet the animal and pitched to the side just in time to grab the beast around the neck and wrestle it to the ground. He fell onto his own back, the beast landing on his chest and its legs thrashing wildly but safely away from him.

The animal was strong and fought fiercely, but Rickman was stronger and more stubborn, and in a few seconds he had put the animal into submission by rolling it onto its side and pinning it down by its neck with his knee.

Rickman quickly tied the rope around the animal's neck and tied the other end to the large post at the steps of the porch. He counted to three and stepped backwards. The animal got to its feet and tried to lunge once more but was halted by the shortness of the leash.

Rickman was about to turn back to fetch Conrad when he halted. He looked to the porch and through the doorway and saw a strange shape inside the house, resting in the gloom against the hallway wall.

———⟞∞∞⟝———

Maria's body was so exhausted and her emotions so wrought that her sleep was too deep to hear Azazel's warning.

Her dreamscape was as serene as the night over St Mary's lake where she lay, naked and younger than she was now. Next to her lay her lover with their daughter in his arms. They were young, strong and free. The night was clear and the stars were bright. It did not feel at all like a dream. Nothing was ominous or prophetic. Nothing was surreal or strange. It was simply real. She sighed and turned to her lover, who sighed and turned back to her. She opened her lips to speak when she jolted awake.

Maria looked, firstly at her baby who was still asleep, and she was instantly relieved. She blinked and rubbed her eyes before looking up at the wall to see that the silhouette of The Devil had vanished. The fire had almost gone out and Maria concluded that it must be late afternoon. She looked down the hallway to the kitchen, through the room and passed the window. She could see the grey of the mist darkening.

Maria looked down at the jug of water and dipped her fingers in before dabbing them across her lips. As soon as the water fell into her mouth a most powerful hunger erupted within her. She had to get up. She tested her legs; they worked. She held the baby tightly to her breast and attempted to stand up.

Maria got no further for as soon as she turned her weight to the side and threw a cursory look to the front door she froze. There was a man standing there, silhouetted by the darkening mist outside. Maria could not believe her eyes. She tried to speak, but no words came to mind and no sound came out. Her blood ran cold and her legs became heavy.

Had he come home? Was God really watching her and did he really love her that much to return him after all that time? She raised her hand slightly and waved; her face still pale, her mouth still open and her eyes still wide.

Rickman Chill stood in the doorway with an expression similar to Maria's. He had no words. He stood there in the dark doorway for what felt like hours, and when he saw the woman raise her hand to wave, he could not stop himself from raising his own to wave back. The woman in the house slowly pulled back the shawl to reveal the baby's face. Rickman stepped into the hallway.

Maria did not see the man's face until he knelt down beside her and pulled the shawl back further. A sudden burst of flame from the dying living room fire threw light upon him and Maria saw not The Devil, but a strange man with delicate features and dead, hollow eyes.

Maria recoiled in horror and attempted to slide away from the stranger, the shock of the intrusion and the need to protect her daughter fierce. The stranger held up his hands in a supplicating gesture.

"It's alright ma'am," came his sickly, twisted voice that did nothing to assuage Maria's fear.

Maria backed up further, her hand scrabbling around for the knife by her side. She managed to grab it and was about to bring the blade up to bury it into the stranger when, without even looking, his hand effortlessly grabbed her wrist and applied just the tiniest pressure into a certain spot, causing her to involuntarily drop the blade.

"It's alright ma'am," came his voice again, this time less cracked, and less evil. "I can help, it's alright."

Rickman looked down to see that the baby still had its umbilical cord attached and, at the end of that, the placenta. Rickman removed his hat to let his blonde hair fall down to his shoulders. He pulled it back over his face to reveal his full features and tried to smile, keeping his dead eyes wide in an attempt to appear more pleasant and trustworthy.

"Ma'am, I mean no harm, I promise," he whispered before tapping his Preacher's collar. "Ma'am, I'm just passing through. I have a sick man outside, we just need some assistance. Ma'am… , your child."

Maria moved back and held the baby even closer. Rickman held up his hands and pointed to the placenta that was being dragged back with her.

"Ma'am, please, we need to remove that. Do you know what that is?"

Maria shook her head.

"That's the placenta ma'am. That's the afterbirth. It's what kept your… ."

Maria pulled the shawl back timidly to reveal the child's sex. Rickman smiled.

"… it's what kept your daughter alive inside you. But now she is out in the world she has you to keep her alive, don't she?"

Maria nodded. Rickman smiled. "We have to cut it loose. I've done it before. I had a child. I've done it before. Do you trust me?"

Maria held the baby even tighter.

"Alright, alright… you don't have to let go of her, I promise. We can do it together, understand?"

Maria nodded. Rickman pulled out one of his guns. Maria gasped.

"It's alright, look," and Rickman emptied the bullets from the gun, "I just need something to clamp the cord ma'am," and he drew his other gun and handed it to her. Maria took it.

"You take that, and keep it on me. If you think I'm doing something to hurt you, you can shoot me. Understand?"

Maria cocked the pistol.

"I take that as a 'yes'. My name is Rickman. What's yours?"

Maria pointed the gun closer to Rickman, who smiled and nodded.

"Alright, what I'm going to do now is place the barrel of my gun over the cord and press down on it, stopping any blood and air from moving through it, then I'm going to cut the cord. It will not hurt the baby one bit. I promise you."

Maria moved away from the wall and carefully placed her daughter down on the ground. Rickman nodded and stretched the cord until it was free before resting his gun barrel upon it and kneeling down on the weapon, pinning the cord to the ground.

Maria brought her gun up to Rickman's temple. Rickman grabbed Maria's knife and in one simple slice, severed the cord and stepped backwards. As soon as the cord was cut, the baby awoke and began to cry. Maria kissed the child's head and looked up at the man as he reloaded the bullets into his gun. He held out his hand for Maria to hand back the other, and she was just about to when a shadow from the doorway fell into the room. She gasped and pointed the gun towards the door.

Rickman shouted and cocked his gun, pointing it straight at the baby. In the doorway slumped Conrad, staring at them.

"That's my man," said Rickman, "you don't want to shoot him ma'am. You really don't. I will shoot your daughter and leave you here alone. You do not want to shoot my man."

Maria made safe the pistol and handed it back up to Rickman.

"Thank you," he said as he took the gun and holstered it.

Conrad, in a delirium, looked down the hallway at the sight of the woman lying next to a pool of drying blood and afterbirth, holding a baby. He knew that he had died and been sent to heaven. A heaven where his wife was alive, as was their child, and a heaven where he had been absolved from killing her.

"Liza… ," he whispered, "I've come home." Conrad smiled and he closed his eyes.

CHAPTER TWENTY-FOUR
Hell of a Day

Maria, seeing the ailing man slumped in her doorway, was suddenly imbued with a sense of duty and concern. She had a new life in the house and she had a feeling that the child's first day on earth should not bear witness to death, so she tucked the baby in close to her breast and held up her hand to Rickman so that he might help her to her feet.

Rickman pulled her up and she fell into him, the exertion of the child's delivery having taken more of a toll on her than she realised.

Rickman caught the woman and baby and pulled them into his chest for support. Her head rested under his chin and the baby was pressed between them. The smell of her hair filtered through his body and he relaxed. Maria pressed against his chest, also relaxed. For a few brief moments, both of them shared an intoxicating connection that neither had expected.

Rickman's hand moved up to Maria's head and stroked her hair and Maria, beyond her control, found herself closing her eyes. The air hung still and nothing moved in those moments. Rickman's mind was no longer angered and boiling, but now a calm lake. His heart slowed and

Maria felt in each beat a welcome and hypnotic rhythm that said only one word: "Home."

Conrad gurgled in his sleep and slumped over from his side and onto his front, expelling air in a long, sad and painful sigh. The movement and noise snapped Maria and Rickman back to their senses and they stepped back from each other, unsure of what had just happened and both slightly embarrassed to have dropped their defences in such a way.

Maria pulled her shawl tightly around herself and the baby, and looked over at the sick man in the doorway. Rickman walked over and looked down at Conrad, lying like a dead man, the back of his neck crimson and engorged. Maria bent over the body, holding her baby with one hand and gently shaking Conrad's back with the other. She looked up at Rickman and nodded to the side room where the cot was. She stepped over the body and walked over to it.

Maria held the baby up to her face, kissed her softly on her forehead, and laid her down to rest in her little homemade cot. She picked the cot up and left the room, crossed the hallway, stepped over Conrad's body in the doorway, went into the living room and rested the cot on her rocking chair by the warm fire.

When she returned to the hallway, Rickman was dragging Conrad unceremoniously into the side room by his wrists. As soon he was fully in the room, Rickman stepped over Conrad, twisting his arms over so the man was now lying on his back. He turned to Maria.

"Water," he croaked, "sheets, and a pillow."

He turned back to Conrad and began to unbutton his shirt. Maria disappeared to fetch the items, not once thinking of taking offence at being ordered around in her own home by these two strangers.

Since going into labour, giving birth and seeing the strangers arrive Maria had felt a strange detachment from the world, not quite as if she was in a dream, but more as if she was not a part of her own mind. She felt as if in a waking sleep.

As she stepped out of the room, turning her back on Rickman and the sick man, she noticed in the living room The Devil's hat and poncho assembled over the chair. Maria felt compelled to grab the poncho and hat and hide it away, lest they discover it and... and she didn't know what, she just needed to hide the articles.

She darted into the living room, replaced the guitar against the wall, grabbed the poncho and hat and went to the staircase, which she ascended slowly, the muscles in her lower abdomen screaming out for respite. Still, she climbed and entered her bedroom, taking a few minutes to sit upon the bed and collect her thoughts.

She held the poncho to her nose and inhaled. The light in the room dimmed as the smell of her lover fell into her. She looked around the room and saw the shadows move around the walls, over the ceilings and converge around the cupboard where the poncho and hat belonged. The cupboard door creaked ajar of its own accord.

Maria fully opened the cupboard and replaced the articles. She was about to close the door when an afternoon sunbeam, breaking through the tops of the trees, fell into the room, illuminating the inside the cupboard and reflecting off a metal object propped against the back. The reflection dazzled Maria. The Devil's huge rifle, hidden away after all those months and now discovered, gleaming as new. She reached in to touch the polished nickel body of Leviathan when she heard a cough and splutter from downstairs. She quickly smelt the poncho one last time before closing the cupboard and fetching some clean sheets and a pillow from the bed.

———— ⌖ ————

With Maria out of sight, Rickman's state of mind returned to normal. He stepped over Conrad and went to the window. There was something altogether unsettling about the house that Rickman had begun to sense the moment he had seen it appear, out of nowhere, from behind the ridge. Although his immediate thoughts had been to get Conrad inside and dealt with, the sight of the recently delivered baby, the impromptu surgery and then the otherworldly embrace he had shared with her had compounded his unease.

He scanned the outside world but could not see much; the mist was low and thick, covering the land. However the sky appeared to be clear and the sun was setting and clipping the tops of the trees. The band of mist around the house gave an oppressive sense to the environment, as if the compound was sinking and the sky above was the free world being left behind.

He looked around, his eyes trying to penetrate the mist. He could just make out the trees along the treeline, their thick trunks dark and firm. But the shadows. The shadows seemed to move and twist around, creeping across the ground, merging and re-forming as the sun disappeared behind the trees.

Rickman felt a coldness creep into his soul. Where was this house? Had they passed through the mist and into the spirit world? He let his thoughts blend with the eerie solitude for a few moments before he heard Conrad splutter once more. Rickman was jolted back into reality. He was about to turn from the window when he caught sight of the goat outside. He double-took as he saw the beast standing motionless by the porch, staring straight at him. The shadows and mist enveloped it and as it disappeared into the mist, Rickman could have sworn he saw the animal stand up on its hind legs, rising to the height of a man, eyes still burning into him.

Conrad coughed again and Rickman dismissed the sight as a mere trick of the light. He turned back to his sick man.

———⚬⚬⚬———

Rickman unbuttoned Conrad's shirt and opened it wide, exposing his inflamed wound and burning red chest. It was clear that the venom was coursing through Conrad and Rickman feared that the man was doomed.

Rickman untied Conrad's boots and tossed them to the side of the room before removing the man's trousers. Conrad stirred out of consciousness and grabbed at the air, as if trying to catch butterflies. He mentioned Liza's name before gurgling and choking. Rickman reached over and turned Conrad's head so that he could spit over the floor and not swallow his tongue. Conrad's eyes were vacant and his pupils large.

"This room," he spluttered. "This room is... The Devil is here... .I can... ." And he spat some more bile and saliva across the floor.

———⚬⚬⚬———

Maria turned from the hallway and froze in the doorway to the side room, gasping and holding her mouth in shock. She had not expected to see a naked man, and a hot flush rocketed through her. Rickman turned to look at her and Maria looked away in embarrassment.

"The pillow," said Rickman, holding his hand out and not thinking twice about notions of propriety.

Maria stepped into the room and handed the pillow to him. He snatched it from her and placed it under Conrad's head. Maria held out the sheets and as Rickman took them, she could not help but look upon the young man's body, taut as the muscles contracted to brace against the venom's assault.

Rickman threw the sheets over the man, covering his modesty and returning Maria to her senses. She bent down to Rickman and handed him the bowl of water. Rickman took a rag, and dabbed it around Conrad's mouth and over his brow.

"It was a rattlesnake bite. To the shoulder." he said, removing the sheet to reveal the wound to Maria. She winced in revulsion as she saw the crimson, inflamed shoulder and the bright red tendril like veins under his skin spreading down his torso around his neck. It looked as if a jellyfish was sat upon the man and was attempting to strangle him.

Rickman gently traced his fingers over the young man's neck, following the course of the veins, feeling the texture of his skin and gauging the raging temperature. The man's neck was taut and the veins stood out in relief. Conrad's eyes opened.

"Liza, where's Liza?" whispered Conrad.

"Liza is dead," said Rickman quietly and without compassion. Maria looked at the dying man and saw his eyes grow pale, as if they had lost something.

"No… , she is here. They are all here. I can feel them." He whispered.

Maria stood up and stepped away, frightened at the delirious man's words.

Rickman leaned into Conrad's ear and said: "Who is here?"

Conrad suddenly snapped his neck to the side, fixing his eyes on Rickman, the colour changing from the fading grey to a fierce green and he said, in an exact replication of Rickman's own voice, "All of them. All of the people we killed. The Devil has brought them home." And he snapped his neck back to the side, his eyes returning to their usual colour. The coughing and gurgling returned.

As soon as Conrad's eyes closed, from the next room came the cries of the baby, awake and desperate for her mother. Maria rushed back and picked her up to hold her close, rocking her calmly and kissing her head until the cries passed.

Rickman looked at the sleeping Conrad and placed his hand over his forehead to gauge his fever. It was bad. He stroked the man's cheek tenderly and looked upon his sleeping state, his ominous words concerning the dead falling from Rickman's mind momentarily. The dark rider looked back through the doorway and into the living room, watching Maria as she soothed her daughter. A long forgotten memory returned to him and as he watched Maria, he felt a great affinity with the new parent.

The night had come and Maria and Rickman sat facing each other in the kitchen. Maria had eaten but Rickman had not, instead he sat in front of an empty plate, looking at her.

Maria had placed the baby's makeshift cot by the edge of the table and eaten slowly and quietly, all the while unable to take her eyes from her daughter.

Rickman pulled out a packet of tobacco and rolled two cigarettes. He handed one to Maria who took it thankfully. He struck a match off the table and lit hers before his own.

Maria inhaled the tobacco and was relieved to feel it caused her no nausea or discomfort. She sat back in her chair, folded her arms and looked properly, for the first time, at the face of Rickman Chill. She found it stern, focused and at the same time strangely delicate. Rickman looked at her and sat back, breathing the smoke into the air.

"Hell of a day," he whispered quietly.

Maria nodded in agreement and the pair sat quietly, looking at each other and smoking, the darkness outside shrouding the house in stillness and silence.

CHAPTER TWENTY-FIVE
The Waiting Dead

Quick Bill Reddings came first, walking through Conrad's delirious subconscious from the fog of memory, until he was fully formed. The rear portion of his head still missing, the brain matter still wet and draped over his shoulders. Conrad killed Quick Bill with a shotgun blast to the head when he was fourteen years old. They had laid siege to a bordello on the outskirts of Flanker City, near the Clark Fork River. For three days Quick Bill and his men had dug in and fought fiercely against Rickman and Conrad. The Reddings boys were known associates of The Devil, who had together robbed the Fork Pass Stage Coach and left none alive.

At the end of the third day of the siege, Conrad had grown impatient and stormed the bordello, killing everyone inside starting with Quick Bill.

Quick Bill knelt down next to Conrad and looked him over.

"Well, brother," he said pleasantly, his skin still coloured with life, his eyes still sharp and alive. "We meet again."

"Bill?" said Conrad in his dream. "Am I dead?"

Bill laughed, "I can't say. Difficult to tell but it doesn't matter brother, we're here together now. All of us."

Bill smiled and Conrad looked confused. The dead man stepped aside and then, from the depths of Conrad's blood-soaked past, slowly approached the fresh corpses of everyone he had ever killed. Conrad began to cry in his sleep, desperate to wake up, but at the same time feeling increasingly drawn to them all. They surrounded him and knelt down, each one telling him how happy they were to see him come home.

It was well into the night, and Maria and Rickman Chill were still in the kitchen. Rickman was finishing his last cigarette and Maria had fallen asleep over the table, her head resting on one arm, the other arm resting on the cot. Rickman had spent the time since she had rested her head on the table and fallen asleep inspecting every hair on her head and documenting every nick and divot on the kitchen table, taking in the grand vista of what seemed like a little island in a large lake surrounded by mountains. The carving looked peaceful and lovingly recalled from memory. He dreamt of going there one day and seeing if it was really like that. It was the first time he had ever thought or dreamt about something that existed in a life and future in which The Devil did not inhabit.

He rested his head on his hand and tapped at his temple rhythmically as he dreamt. After the first few hours of standing on the shore of that lake, his imagination began to work correctly and he found, thrillingly, that he could turn from the shore and face away, conjuring a fully realised and exciting new world in which his mind could wander wherever he chose.

He looked at the sleeping Maria and then to the baby, and discovered that not only could he construct a world in which The Devil did not exist, but he could also fictionalise a timeline whereby he could grow old perhaps, or have another family. It was a searing revelation. Was this, now in the dark and oppressive gloom and seclusion of the house, God showing him his heaven, or possibly even his reward on earth, if he fulfilled his destiny and killed The Devil? Could this new imagining be made real? He felt dizzy at the prospect, and as his mind ascended to a higher place he further lost his grip on reality.

It wasn't until he heard Conrad shuffling and gurgling in the other room that his mind fell from his alternate future and back into the kitchen.

His finger stopped tapping on his temple; the faint light in his eyes that had sprung up fell away and the darkness returned.

He looked at Maria and followed her arm to the cot; he watched the baby sleeping soundly and safely, totally unaware of its own existence and blessed with ignorance about how dark and dangerous the world was.

His anger and focus returned tenfold; he remembered The Devil and he remembered his cold and hard existence.

He finished his cigarette, stubbed it out and, instead of gently reaching over to stroke Maria's hair and wake her up, he stood up violently, making his chair scrape harshly over the flagstones.

Maria snapped awake and looked straight to the baby, who remained asleep. She widened her eyes and shook her head, bringing herself back into the room. For a few seconds she didn't know why she was in the kitchen and not her bed. She looked down at the table, sighing at the the carving of Wild Goose Island. She ran her hand through her hair and looked over to the ashtray. The aroma of Rickman's cigarette still hung in the air and Maria remembered that she was not alone. She looked up at Rickman Chill who was standing by the doorway, half in shadow.

"Sleep in your bed," Rickman said, and an undeniable wave of sadness imbued his awful, cracked and twisted voice. He stepped out of the kitchen, crossed the hallway and walked out onto the porch, disappearing into the mist.

Maria watched him leave and sat for a few moments, taking the time to reflect on the events of the day. She looked at the baby before picking up the cot and walking groggily upstairs into her room.

⌇∽⌇

Rickman Chill sat in the warm living room and watched as the timid thirteen year old boy crept down the stairs. He was a slight child with less muscle on him than was desirable in a boy his age.

He stood halfway down the stairs and looked over at Rickman, eyes wide with trepidation. Rickman squinted at the boy and saw through him and into his heart. Though the boy seemed physically meek, it was clear to Rickman that the boy had grit.

"Conrad," Rickman said as he placed his hands palm down on the table. "Please sit down." Conrad remained motionless on the stairs.

His father, Obadiah, had turned away and was standing by the fireplace, shielding his face from his son so the boy could not see his tears.

"Sit down boy," Obadiah said in a severe tone that Conrad had not heard before. He had also never called him 'boy' before.

The turmoil of his recent adolescent angst suddenly turned to stone inside Conrad's gut. He looked back up the staircase to the doorway to his room to see the silhouette of his mother, not looking down at him, but staring out of the window into the black night, her hand over her mouth.

"Please. Sit." Rickman said.

Conrad cautiously approached the stranger at the table. The fire crackled intensely and threw alarming shadows across the room. As he walked towards the man, whose face was still obscured by the rim of his hat, he chanced to look around the walls of the living room at the twisting and swirling shadows that seemed, to his youthful and overactive imagination, to resemble people, places and events. A theatre of shadows cast by the firelight poured over the dark stranger. Conrad pulled out a chair and sat down opposite the man.

"Who are you, sir?" Conrad asked quietly. Rickman removed his hat, allowing the boy to see his face for the first time.

"My name is Rickman Chill," he said quietly, "I've come to talk to you about your true parents, and the man who killed them."

By the fire, unseen, Obadiah hung his arm over the mantelpiece and buried his head into it.

Rickman stepped off of the porch and into the black mist. The dampness clung to his face and he recalled the fateful evening in which he came for Conrad. He remembered every word of his speech that laid upon the boy the details of his parents' demise. Rickman told in brutal honesty how Clara and Daniel Sumner were left to die in the snow while Conrad, their child, lay under a bed, cold, crying and alone.

Rickman recalled how, in his search for The Devil, he had come across the story and tracked down Conrad at an age where he would prove useful.

He told the boy, without glossing over a single detail, how The Devil had taken everything from the child, and that now he was a man he had a choice: ride out with Rickman and seek his vengeance, or live in the warm house with the knowledge that The Devil still walked the earth.

He remembered how the boy did not cry when he heard the news, nor look to his 'parents' for confirmation, but instead kept his eyes fixed on Rickman and showed his rage only by his clenched fists on the table. They had ridden out together in the morning and Conrad had not once looked back.

As Rickman walked around the compound, running his hand over the fence so as not to wander into the wilderness, a single sentence repeated in his mind. It was a statement he had told the boy about his parents and which had appealed to the young man's sense of burgeoning adolescent emotions: "They were lovers who lived only for you until The Devil came and cut them down."

He walked around and around and with every revolution, the sentence fell away until in his heart and mind, he heard only the words, "they were lovers, they were lovers."

Maria sat on her bed, the cot on the bedside table, the unnamed baby fast asleep. Maria looked over to The Devil's wardrobe and was neither shocked nor surprised to see the door open of its own volition. She stood up and opened the door fully. She quietly took The Devil's boots, trousers, shirt, waistcoat, poncho and hat and laid them onto the bed. She ran her fingers over the material. She found, in his breast pocket, a handkerchief which she removed and held close to her nose, taking his scent deep into her heart.

She then carefully placed the handkerchief into the cot so that her daughter would grow to recognise the smell of her father. Maria removed her dress and blouse and put on her lover's clothes.

———✿———

Conrad's victims were all kneeling around him, gently stroking his hair, rubbing his side and smiling. Their eyes were neither happy nor sad, but were frozen, captured in the exact moment of death.

Conrad was gradually falling into his final sleep, into his last dream within a dream, when he whispered for Liza. The stroking and the pawing stopped. Conrad stepped back from the brink of his final moments and looked at the ghosts. At once, they stood up and retreated, waving back as they drifted into whichever afterlife they belonged to.

Conrad woke up, the coldness of the air, the hardness of the floor, the pain and burning in his body a stark reminder that he was truly awake. He rolled onto his back as a shadow was cast over him. He looked up and saw a woman with flame-red hair and deep eyes standing over him. He reached out for the ghost and a great fear overcame him when they touched. Liza was standing over him, and she was real.

"Liza," he whispered, "forgive me. I don't want to die."

Liza looked him over, offering neither love nor forgiveness. She turned away from him and walked to the doorway.

"Don't leave me, don't leave me alone again," Conrad pleaded. Liza froze at the doorway for a few seconds before stepping out into the corridor. Conrad fell asleep.

Maria held onto the doorway as the pleading words of the delirious man reverberated through her and quickly took on her own voice as she recalled what her heart cried almost every moment of the day. She left the sleeping man and walked over to the window to look out at the dark stranger who was walking around and around the compound.

Outside, Rickman did not once look to the window. If he had done so, he would have seen The Devil looking back at him.

CHAPTER TWENTY-SIX
Gathering Medicine

Rickman had slept on the porch, sat on the step and slumped against the post, his hands on his pistols. As he opened his eyes he saw that the mist had lifted slightly. He could see farther into the treeline than before and could just about make out the winding track leading up to the ridge ahead.

The air was still and the dampness on his face revived him. He stretched, yawned and looked around. He saw the goat, standing still and staring at him. They locked eyes for a few seconds. The beast seemed unnaturally still and its unblinking eyes grated with Rickman's early morning state.

He yawned again and pulled the rope tethering the goat to the post assuming the animal wanted to run off, or do whatever it was it liked to do. The rope fell slack but the animal remained, standing there and staring at him. Rickman hissed and hit his boot against the porch step. The animal was undeterred. Rickman spat at the goat and entered the house.

Maria was still asleep and the house was eerily silent. Even the noise of the clock had fallen away. Rickman stepped carefully into the living room and looked at the guitar resting against the wall. He feared to touch it, lest he accidentally pluck a string and disturb the strange solemnity that abounded the room. He peered in close to the neck, inspecting the worn fret board and wondering if it had been Maria's hands that had played it, or if it belonged to someone else. Her father? A lover?

Rickman had not had time to consider Maria and her situation properly since arriving at the home and so took a few minutes, as he liked to do, to walk around the room.

He left the guitar and stood by the chair positioned at the window. He knelt down beside the chair and looked at what the view would have been like had he been sat in it. He could see the fireplace, naturally, as it dominated the room, however, the eyeline of the chair's would-be-occupant was not focused on the fireplace, but on the chair on the other side of the room.

Rickman stood up and walked over to the second chair. This rocking chair was more worn, the cushions threadbare, the armrests deprived of varnish. He picked up the cushion and smelt it. The tobacco odour was deeply set and fresh. He looked across at the eyeline and saw the window ahead, the treeline beyond and of course the other chair.

Rickman felt a slight twinge of sadness as he replaced the cushion, realising that Maria was the only one person living in the house. Clearly, she sat regularly in the same chair and looked at the chair opposite, perhaps to remember happier times when someone would sit in it and look back at her.

He looked up to the window beside the empty chair and understood that, since nobody sat in the chair, Maria must have looked out at the window, to the ridge, perhaps waiting for her lover's return, or perhaps looking even higher to the heavens waiting for her time to be called. Rickman understood that he was standing in a living tomb.

Conrad was awake when Rickman appeared in the doorway. The burning in his shoulder was still severe, but the swelling had reduced remarkably overnight. Conrad was still delirious and his self-perception constantly flitted between placing himself in the waking world and the land of the dead where he knew, without doubt, the souls of all of those he had killed were waiting for him. Every time he closed his eyes, in long laboured blinks, he could hear them calling to him.

"Come home brother, come home," they whispered.

His body seemed to sink into the ground with every blink and suggestion of leaving, but his eyes would always open again and the harsh reality would pull his body back out of the ground. The sight of Rickman in the doorway, obviously not an apparition, did much to restore some balance to Conrad. He even tried to sit up.

Rickman stepped forward and removed the pillow from behind Conrad, cradling his head with one hand, whilst folding the pillow in half and returning it. He handed Conrad a cup of water, which he took thirstily.

"Good morning," wheezed Conrad. "Where's Liza?"

"Sleeping," said Rickman, playing along to the confused man's delirium.

"I've come home," said Conrad as he nudged the cup away with his chin to signify that he was done. Rickman lifted his hand and patted Conrad's knee.

"Will you stay here, brother?" whispered Rickman. Conrad's eyes flickered with unease and they rolled over to meet Rickman's. He held up his hand and Rickman took it, holding it tightly.

"We have to leave. We have a job to do. We have a destiny," Conrad said with as much conviction as he could muster. Rickman smiled back.

"Get some rest. I'll find some medicine. Get some strength back, and then we'll ride out to Bel and finish the game."

"And come back to Liza?"

"And come back to Liza," Rickman confirmed.

"They are waiting for me," whispered Conrad, "the men and women I've killed. They are calling me home."

Rickman smiled.

"Am I going to hell?"

Rickman nodded. "Yes. Yes, you are. For all the things we've done."

Conrad smiled and rested his head on the pillow.

"Then I guess," he said quietly, "when we get there, The Devil will know our names and fear us already."

Rickman patted Conrad on the chest and left him to walk the tightrope between their world and the next.

——— ◦∞◦ ———

Rickman had walked into the surrounding woodland for over two hours before he came to a clearing large enough for the shadows of the trees to not entirely oppress. The mist was high in the mid-morning and the sun was strong enough to penetrate through. He stood on the edge of the woods and looked out, overcome with the expanse of the clearing. It felt like months or years since he had been in open space, having survived within the belly of the dense woodland. The grass was waist high and swayed hypnotically.

He looked around his environment taking in the intoxicating rush of fresh air and openness. Eventually he removed his gloves and stepped out into the clearing, allowing his fingers to brush through the tall grass.

He walked for ten minutes before he came to the first item he was searching for: Prairie Coneflower. Rickman bent down and inspected the base of the large flower, its green stalk a shave under a foot tall and its large brown, bulbous flowerhead bobbing and swaying in the breeze. Rickman looked at the large yellow petals that drooped down from the base of the bulb. This patch, containing maybe three hundred coneflowers, would hopefully make enough to aid Conrad in his recovery.

Rickman opened his knapsack. He took out his knife and began to dig around the plant's base, making sure to gather up as much of its root system as he could. After he had extracted one, he moved onto the next, aiming to harvest at least fifty. If he needed to, he could always come back.

———

"Liza, you're here, I can hear you breathe," whispered Conrad with his eyes still closed. He was partially correct; there was someone else in the room. But it was Maria and not his dead wife, as he thought. Maria was awoken by the sound of the front door closing and, looking out of the window, she had watched as Rickman Chill attended to his horse before leaving him and walking off into the mist.

She did not know where he was going or why, but she knew that he would return. The purpose of his stride and the purpose of its nature dictated that. Maria did not know if she was happy to have him return or not. She didn't even know if she wanted to be left all alone just yet.

She rolled over in her bed and looked at the sleeping baby who had, strangely, not woken a single time during the night. She scooped her up, unbuttoned her nightdress, and the child instinctively began to feed.

Maria sat on the edge of the bed feeding her daughter while she stared at the cupboard that contained her lover's clothes. It did not open. There were no shadows in the room.

She left the bedroom, went out to the porch and introduced Azazel to her daughter. The animal looked over the baby and bleated quietly before nuzzling into Maria's hip. She kissed the goat and returned to the house, letting him jump and buck around the yard.

After she had made herself a little breakfast and ground some coffee to boil, she poured some water into a bowl and decided to see how the sick man in the side-room was doing.

She kept the baby close to her and felt an unusual trepidation while walking down the hallway to the side-room. The other man was not around and she felt all the more alone. If he didn't come back, she would have the child and the sick man to look after.

Maria entered the room and knelt beside him, mopping his brow with the cloth. She removed the sheet and held her hand over his wound. She could feel the heat rising from him. The wound was angry. Conrad moaned slightly in his sleep, his legs twitching involuntarily as he did so. Maria reached out and gently stroked Conrad's hair with a touch so chaste that she could not even be sure that contact had even been made.

"I can hear you breathe," Conrad said once more. Maria did not shirk away from the man and he did not turn to her. "I've loved you from the moment I first saw you. Do you remember?" he whispered. Maria looked forlornly down at the back of his head.

"You were so fierce and happy. Wild and laughing. A devil, not an angel. That's what I thought. I remember walking up the staircase to see you. You turned to look at me and said your name was Liza before I had even spoken. Liza. I remember just the way you said it. I remember the way you were… I remember."

Maria saw Conrad clamp his eyes shut and clench his jaw, burying his face further into the pillow as if he were crying. He began to murmur indistinguishably. Maria had no control over her thoughts or actions at that moment and felt that she was indeed Liza and that those words of love were hers to keep. So she buried her hand into his hair, letting the locks wash over her fingers, and she began to massage his head tenderly hoping he would turn to her renewed with the face of her lover, telling her that he had come home for good. Her fingers struggled to recall the tender touch of a man's hair and scalp and she almost fell into tears.

❧

Rickman had almost finished his work. His knapsack was stuffed with Prairie Coneflower, Giant Goldenrod and Stork's Bill Geranium. He began to walk back to the edge of the clearing and to the treeline when, to his left, the mist eerily parted to reveal a shrub he had not seen before. He looked around, sensing a strange otherworldly trap before stepping over to the shrub. He could not believe it: a Choke Cherry and below that, against all nature, there grew a ring of echinacea, purple Coneflowers which were indigenous to parts of America well beyond Rickman's borders. He had heard stories and seen pictures of the plant, but never dreamt of seeing them. Yet, here it grew.

Rickman looked around once more before bending down and feverishly harvesting as many Coneflowers as he could before standing up and tipping his hat to the Choke Cherry, thanking it for the miracle of the echinacea.

ERODIUM CICUTARIUM
'Storksbill Geranium'

Found in dry plains and low hillsides in
western and central Montana

CHAPTER TWENTY-SEVEN
Thoughts of Family

It was mid-afternoon by the time Rickman returned. Maria had washed and fed herself and her daughter, marvelling at her tiny hands and feet and cooing quietly every time the child gurgled or smiled. It seemed to Maria that she held in her hands a tiny treasure trove of wonders and delights. Her focus was entirely on the child and on their little corner of the world. She tried not to think of Rickman and his terrible voice, or the sick man lying on the floor in her side room with his fevered words of love and his youthful and taut body. Maria tried to think of nothing but herself and the child.

Rickman stepped over the threshold and smelt the aroma of a house alive. There was the dying smell of coffee and tobacco that filtered pleasantly through the air, fanned by the sounds from upstairs.

Maria was awake and walking around. Rickman walked into the kitchen and was imbued with the almost alien and bewildering sensation that he was a hunter returned home to his family and all was right with the world. He went straight into the side room to check on Conrad. His man was asleep, but no longer in the grip of fever. His legs were not twitching, and he was not sweating. Rickman peeled back the sheet and though he instantly felt the heat radiating from Conrad's shoulder, the inflammation had receded greatly. Conrad awoke and turned to him.

"Are we riding out soon?" he whispered.

"Soon," said Rickman.

"Where have you been? How long have we been here?"

"Just a few days."

"A few days?" said Conrad, furrowing his brow and trying to sit up, "It's been years. It must have been."

"Get some rest," replied Rickman. "I have some medicine to prepare."

"Where's Liza?"

"With your daughter."

"Daughter," smiled Conrad as he lay back down. "It's a girl. A little girl."

Rickman's smile fell away and he left the room.

Maria had finished cleaning her daughter and dressing herself when she heard Rickman return and she was calmly surprised to catch herself smiling in the mirror as if she was part of a family, as she had been dreaming to be since she started to love her unborn child. She refused to acknowledge that the man who had come home was the mysterious Rickman with his awful voice and seemingly unstable nature. Instead she pictured the man to be a good husband, father and lover. As her mind constructed him from the boots upwards, she fixed her hair in the mirror and was unable to control her imagination from amalgamating the assets of The Devil and of the sick man in the side room. The man who had come home in her fantasy had The Devil's passion and depth, but also had Conrad's finer features. His sharp nose and strong jaw. His eyes were The Devil's but his mouth was his own.

Maria finished fixing her hair up and looked at herself in the mirror. She turned sideways and smiled at her bump. She ran her hands over her long, thick grey skirt and apron, and was pleased to see that she still retained the bump. As she turned back and forth to inspect herself, she imagined the constructed lover to be standing next to her and smiling. She smiled broadly, happy with the way things were, and went downstairs to the kitchen to face the reality of Rickman Chill.

She found him by the table pulling at what appeared to be weeds and flowers from his knapsack, laying them out and arranging them into little batches.

As soon as he saw Maria he smiled, caught wholly off guard by the feeling of tranquillity compounded by his successful foraging expedition, the pleasant atmosphere in the house, Conrad's recovery and the fact that Maria was smiling like a new parent.

It was a good moment for Rickman and perhaps the first he had managed to hold onto since that fateful day which had set him on his path of revenge and destiny.

He stopped arranging his flora into piles and stepped over to Maria, putting his hands on her shoulders.

"How are you feeling?" he croaked as earnestly as he could. Maria shrugged a little.

"And the baby?"

Maria nodded.

"Good, good."

Rickman and Maria held their pose for a few seconds, each one stepping into the other's eyes for a moment longer than propriety dictated. Rickman saw in her large brown eyes a deep well of sadness, love and hope, but also a strong undercurrent of churning feminine danger that he recognised instantly. He had seen it before, many times.

Maria saw in Rickman an uncontrollable fire licking the inside of his psyche that terrified her, though she hid the fear well. To Maria, in those few moments, she was sure that Satan himself was in her house. Rickman smiled, took her hand and led her over to the table, his grip surprisingly gentle.

Maria looked over the arrangement of plant life and Rickman noted her confusion. He held up a few stalks of Prairie Coneflower and showed them to Maria.

"If we boil this into a tea, we can relieve Conrad's fever greatly. We can also infuse the water we use to clean him with the leaves and stem; if we rub it onto his wound it will draw out the poison."

Maria raised her eyebrow, impressed at the healing properties of the innocuous looking plant.

"I found it in a clearing, a few hours west of here," said Rickman as he placed the flower back onto the pile. He picked off a few of the yellow leaves and handed them to Maria. She took the leaves and inspected them closely.

"She is called Prairie Coneflower," said Rickman, "remember her and remember the petals. When the time comes to wean the child from the breast, you should crush the petals and rub them over the teat. It will help the child greatly."

Maria looked at Rickman and furrowed her brow, wondering how he knew such a thing. Rickman, stung with an unwanted memory, took the leaves from her and dumped them back on the pile of Coneflowers. He then picked up a handful of Giant Goldenrod, a thin stemmed plant with delicate yellow flower heads gathered in pyramidal clusters that ascended the downward curved branches.

"Giant Goldenrod," he said, more matter-of-factly than before, "useful for the inflammation of his wound."

He replaced the Goldenrod and picked up a handful of small stemmed flowers that held five broad pink petals and five bristle tipped sepals.

"Storksbill Geranium," he said, and handed it to Maria.

"Found in the same clearing as the Coneflower. This one is for you," he said. Maria looked at him and smiled, holding it up to her nose and sniffing it.

"I mean, medicinally, it's for you and the baby. Eat the root and leaves and it will increase the flow of breast milk. I have gathered enough to keep you going until you are strong enough to fetch more."

Maria looked at Rickman as he said this not to her, but to the table; she saw in the corner of his eyes the danger she had seen before flicker, and a great sadness momentarily reveal itself. She was about to reach out and stroke his hair, as she had done to Conrad previously, when he moved away and reached over to grab a few large, bulky flowers with thick stems, large, numerous and hairy pink elliptical petals and a heavy looking deep red bulb in the middle. Rickman held it up to her and smiled.

"Echinacea," he whispered, "very, very far from home. It does not belong here. You can make a tincture from it; it will last you years and it will ease infections, cramps and act as an anti-inflammatory. It is a miracle of a plant."

Maria looked ambivalently at the plant. Rickman understood and put the flower down on the ground.

"Her name was Liza and he loved her very much. I have known him since he was thirteen when I took him from his guardians. I told him about his parents; how they were murdered when he was a child. I told him that he could ride with me, and together we could track down the killer."

Maria looked solemnly to the table, fearing to hear the name of the murderer even though a dark voice inside her already knew.

"The boy rode with me, been with me ever since. Except for two years when he lost sight of his destiny. Found a new one."

Maria looked up at Rickman who nodded in compliance.

"Liza," he said. "He met her, fell in love and told me he was staying with her. Told me he was done hunting and the killer was probably dead anyway. I could have shot him on the spot. Sometimes wish I had. But he was fierce. He really did love her. He told me she was pregnant, and so I left them to their happy life. Rode out, left them behind. Didn't see him for two years."

Rickman casually picked up some Coneflowers, moved to the kitchen counter and began to prune the leaves from the flower heads.

"As you can see," he said darkly, "the marriage did not come to a happy ending."

Maria stepped up to the side of Rickman and cupped his chin with her hand, turning his head to hers. He saw that the history he had given her was not the history she sought.

"I had a child and a wife once. Family. Happy family. Future."

He turned back to preparing the petals, but the admission of his past, at least a bastardised version of it, cleaved too close to the truth. He hung his head.

"He took everything. Left me for dead. Thought I was."

Rickman removed his collar to reveal his twisted scarring. Maria gasped in horror.

"It's why I talk so pretty. Left me for dead. Been after him ever since. Done some bad things. Bought my seat in hell ten times over. Done some bad things."

Maria saw his eyes well up and, as he hung his head low and turned it away from her slightly, the tears fell out of his eyes and pattered onto the leaves gently. Rickman controlled his breathing and Maria put her hand on his shoulder.

"Thought I was dead," he whispered to himself. "He was right." Rickman left the kitchen and walked out of the house.

Maria did not rush after him but stayed in the kitchen knowing full well that her lover, The Devil, had been the cause of it. He had never told her about his exploits when he was away, even though she guessed most of it. She had always romanticised the violence and chaos that he had wrought and never once imagined the consequences.

She began to chew on a Storksbill Geranium leaf, as Rickman had instructed her to do so, and felt a great shame at her affiliation with The Devil. Yet her desire to protect her lover began to grow as strong as her desire to protect her child. These men sought to kill him, and had done for years.

She chewed on her leaf, bouncing between anger at the two men who threatened to destroy her dream of reunion with her lover and the chance to introduce him to their daughter, and the sickening guilt of still wanting him in her bed despite coming face-to-face with the consequences of his actions.

Maria dared not consider putting herself in the shoes of Rickman Chill and attempting to empathise with the pain of losing her daughter and her lover. She did not need to. He was the walking embodiment of her worst fears and the representation of a possible future Maria.

The house grew oppressive and dark as the clouds descended and the mist began to encroach upon them all.

ECHINACEA PURPUREA
'Purple Coneflower'

Found in eastern and central North America

CHAPTER TWENTY-EIGHT
Dark Confusion

Rickman had taken one step off the porch when, as if in a nightmare, the sun sank behind the trees, the night came on and the mist fell, all in a matter of seconds.

Rickman turned back to the door of the house but could barely make it out, even though he knew it to stand only two feet from him. He reached out, blinded by the blackness. He could not even feel the posts to the porch beside him. He was blind. He stepped backwards from the house and walked straight into what felt like a couple of barrels, heavy and powerful that struck the backs of his legs, forcing him to fall backwards over them and land on his back.

He heard an angry huff and then felt two powerful feet pressing on his shoulders, pinning him to the ground. He tried to reach for his pistols, but the pressure was too great and his arms were splayed out on the floor. Two more small feet pressed down on his thighs. He heard the huff once more and felt hot breath on his face, then he realised that these were not feet on his chest and legs, but hooves and then, through the blackness, with bright yellow pin-prick eyes, Azazel's face came in close to Rickman's. He could feel and see the animal's breath in the night. The beast brought his eyes in close and Rickman was sure, for a second that they appeared to be almost human.

He gritted his teeth and, with all his might, managed to move his arm and grab his gun. As soon as his fingers touched the grip, the weight upon him vanished. Rickman scrambled to his feet, drew his guns and backed away, searching out the beast. Within moments, he backed against the fence line. He was stunned to suddenly find himself so far from the house when, a few moments ago, he had been standing on the porch.

He trained his eyes and gun on the gloom, searching out the goat until he found the pin-prick yellow eyes, just a few feet away. Rickman looked at the goat's eyes, piercing through the night, and watched as they slowly blinked at him, never moving, always staring. Those eyes burned into him.

"What is this place?" whispered Rickman as he holstered his gun.

He stepped out of the compound and found himself inexplicably walking into the forest. His confession and breakdown in front of Maria had been utterly unexpected and totally out of character for him and he could not fathom just how it had happened. As he walked into the darkness thousands of questions whirled like the gloom and mist in his mind. Perhaps the need to reconcile the past, buried for twenty-one years, was finally spilling out? Where was this house and why did it have such an effect upon him?

He tore at his mind as he walked further into the woods, with no idea of where he was going, or why. The house was a dark spell and he was slowly forgetting the focus on his destiny and diverting it into useless introspection. He pulled at his hair and screamed into the night in frustration at his mind being so out of his control.

⸺∞⸺

Rickman's mental flux was in synchronisation with Maria's. As the moon rose and the darkness befell the house, her mind was split. She, like him, thought that the house was somehow implicitly involved in the drama.

The shadows, once her friends, now seemed menacing and cold; whenever she entered a room, they seemed to back away across the walls, make for the nearest window, seep away under the frame and drift out into the night to enrich the blackness. The fire burned as it always did, but she could see her breath and constantly felt the hairs on her neck rise up, the cold dread of another's unwanted presence occupying her mind constantly.

She did not dare leave her daughter alone, and so carried her around the house, close to her breast, checking on her constantly. She knew that newborn babies were supposed to cry and scream and rage against the harshness of their new world and long for a return to the womb, but this child did not. It never cried, but drifted between wake and sleep in silence.

Maria could not keep still; she moved from bedroom to kitchen to living room and back, spending no longer than thirty minutes in each. She felt tense, desperate and most worryingly of all, she felt unsafe in her own house. She tapped her feet and chewed her lip and occasionally caught herself looking out of the window; for what, she did not know. For Rickman to return? For The Devil to appear on the ridge, dispel the interlopers and her doubts, and restore balance to her heart? She did not know, but still she looked.

⚬⚬⚬

Conrad had been awake for several hours and was fortunate enough to witness the unnatural darkness descend upon the house. Though he was still not in total control of his mind, he had reason enough to understand that day had finished and night had begun.

As he lay there, upon waking, he tested his muscles, flexing his fingers and toes, moving his legs and arms. He had control of his muscles and although the fever was still high and his skin still burned, he felt confident enough in himself to sit up.

He gritted his teeth and rolled onto his side, pushing himself up. The sudden change in his position forced the blood from his head and the room swirled violently, causing in turn the nausea to rise up inside him.

He looked through the open doorway and saw a candleholder on the mantelpiece, illuminated by the warm orange glowing of the fireplace. He fixed his eyes upon it, using its position to anchor and track his other senses and bring his vision back into focus, quelling his nausea. It soon subsided and his heart thumped hard, but his slowed pace made the pain a little more manageable.

Slowly, he placed his palms against the floor, pressed down and slid himself backwards a few inches. The exertion was tremendous and he had to stop to control his breathing and heart rate. He regulated himself and slid backwards again, and again; after ten minutes of hard, and slow work, he felt the welcome hardness of the wall. He relaxed, slumped against it and felt relieved.

He sat there for a few hours, staring at the fireplace in the room opposite and overlaid an image of Obadiah leaning against it, listening to Rickman's speech when he was a thirteen-year old boy.

He looked down at the floor in front of it and conjured a hearth rug, and then constructed visions of himself and Liza making love upon it like the time they did on the night they met in that cheap hotel.

Though the blackness outside was complete, and the oppressiveness of the house unusually obvious, Conrad did not let it penetrate his mind. He felt oddly serene and attributed much of it to the relief of being alive, and being able to move.

He closed his eyes in deliberate long blinks and his relief amplified as the visions of the dead that waited for him grew farther and farther from his mind's eye. Upon the final time of opening his eyes, he found himself looking not at the fireplace, but at a woman standing in the doorway. His fever was abating and he could see now that the woman was not Liza, but a different creature altogether. She had brown hair, large dark brown eyes and a pleasant frame. She looked clearly rattled and was jigging her sleeping baby in her arms.

"Hello," whispered Conrad.

The woman did not answer, but turned from the doorway and walked away. Conrad could not be sure if she was real or not. Moments later, she reappeared holding a bowl of steaming water in her hand and some rags draped over her arm. She stepped into the room and nodded towards Conrad's shoulder.

He understood and peeled back the sheet to reveal his wound. The inflammation was reducing daily. Maria bent down and inspected it, laying her baby down in his lap. She dipped a towel in the hot, murky water that smelt strange and had leaves in it; she moved to dab it on his shoulder.

Conrad blocked her by moving his head in the way and trying to get a better look at the contents of the bowl.

"Wait, what is in that?" he asked.

Maria shushed him quietly and authoritatively, and with her free hand, pushed his head out of the way, exposing his shoulder more. She began to aggressively dab the wound, but Conrad's winces assuaged Maria and her actions became slowly more tender.

Conrad closed his eyes as Maria bathed his inflamed shoulder, and she began to stroke his blonde hair as she had done in his delirium. The touch and tone of her gesture struck a deep chord in Conrad, as if a thought from a long forgotten dream had resurfaced. He absentmindedly brought his hand up and placed it over hers as she caressed the side of his head.

Time had fallen from Rickman. It was so dark and he had been walking for so long without a recognisable marker that he could well have walked into the nether world. He struck himself on low branches, snagged his ankles on rocks and roots, fell down and was knocked about by the malicious dark woodland, and yet he had not stopped trudging.

He turned over in his mind riding out with Conrad for the first time, teaching him to shoot, hunt and kill men. He ordered the events of their lives together into a chronological timeline in an attempt to deconstruct his current dementia, go back to the start and rebuild it, so that he could reacquaint himself with just exactly what had brought him to that house and why he was there.

They had only been there a few days, but each hour felt like a lifetime, each passing moment furrowed his memories and churned up thoughts and contradictions that blighted his focus on The Devil. He had foolishly allowed his heart to open slightly and as a result, feelings of concern for Conrad's well-being and sympathy for

Maria's plight and her baby had come flooding back. As a direct result of that, he had begun to feel remorse for his actions and to question his motives. He was wrong to tell Maria that he was dead. He was not dead, but instead damned. He cursed his existence and all it stood for; his hands reached out for his pistols in order to finish the game when, suddenly, the darkness lifted and moonlight broke through the mist.

Rickman stopped dead in his tracks, eyes wide, taking in as much moonlight as they could. His hands left his pistol grips and his mouth fell open slightly, in awe of the sight that was spread before him. He was standing on the shore of a great lake, the moonlight dancing over the gentle rippling water, the mountains surrounding it calm and sombre, and the mist rising just enough to reveal a small island in the middle of the lake. Rickman recognised it instantly from the giant carving on Maria's table.

"Am I dead?" he whispered to the air. The vista chilled him. He had dared to long for it, and here it was. But he had longed to see it in a future where The Devil did not ride.

"It's not my time," he said, in a whisper that carried a ripple of anger. "It's not my time. Do you hear? It's not my time to see this!" he finally screamed to the air, but no sound came back to answer. Instead, what did greet him was the sight of two pure white geese flying low together across the lake, their wingtips clipping the water. He watched with red and teary eyes as the two mated birds flew up and around the island, weaving in and out of each other's paths before settling down on the island.

"Beautiful," whispered Rickman Chill as he unbuttoned his gun belt and let it drop to the shore. He looked out at the lake, eyes wide, dark and utterly lost. Finally, he knew exactly who he was. He stepped off the shore and began to walk out into the lake, towards the wild geese.

Wild Goose Island, St Mary's Lake

CHAPTER TWENTY-NINE
Martha, Bertha & Annabel

Maria had finished cleansing Conrad's wound and had caressed his hair for a few moments longer than necessary. The strange tonic with which she had washed him had begun to take effect almost immediately and by the time she had finished, the burning in his skin had all but vanished and the aches in his joints dulled considerably.

He opened his eyes, causing her to remove her hand from his hair. He sat up straight against the wall, taking a few seconds to let the feeling of relief wash through him. He cricked his neck and looked over to Maria, who slid back on the floor and sat a foot away from him. He rubbed his shoulder.

"Thank you. That feels… good. I feel good."

Maria smiled and nodded.

"Where is Rickman?"

Maria pointed to the blackness outside.

"Probably sleeping in the woods," concluded Conrad. "He sleeps alone. Always has. Nobody is allowed near him sometimes."

Without thinking, Maria rested the baby upon Conrad's lap. As soon as she had done so, her rational mind rose up and yelled out. Maria had no answers. She had done it.

Conrad looked at the sleeping baby.

"May I?" he asked. Maria looked unsure but eventually nodded her approval. Conrad reached into his lap and ever-so-gently picked up the child and cradled it in his arms, a strange and powerful bond forming between them almost instantly.

"Beautiful," he whispered. Conrad traced his index finger over her forehead and across her body to her hand. Maria smiled at the sight of the sick man connecting with the child, and she allowed herself to take one step further into her fantasy in which she was part of a family. She lay on her side and rested her head upon her hand, watching Conrad smile and inspect the child so carefully that she could have been made of dandelion floss.

Conrad gasped and held his breath as the daughter, still in the twilight of her sleep, reacted to his fingertip as it brushed against her belly. The child gurgled slightly, raised her hand and gripped his finger. Conrad smiled incredulously and looked over to Maria, eyes beaming as if they had just witnessed a momentous event in history. Maria smiled and sighed, happy in the quiet fiction they were sharing. A new happy family.

"How long have you been here, alone like this?" whispered Conrad, breaking the silent magic in the room. Maria sighed sadly and shrugged.

"Where's the baby's father?"

Maria looked at him unblinking.

"I'm sorry, ain't my business ma'am." He went back to rocking the child and dared to intermittently plant tiny kisses upon her forehead, an act which warmed Maria's heart greatly and caused a desirous longing for him to burn within her, though she did not let any emotion show.

Eventually, Conrad could remain silent no longer.

"Ma'am... what is your name? We come here and took over your house and, we're grateful and all... but who are you? What is your name?"

Maria closed her eyes and sat up, evading the question by digging into her apron and retrieving her pipe and tobacco. She began to stuff it.

"Ma'am?" said Conrad, sheepishly, "It's not good for the baby."

Maria furrowed her brow in confusion

"The pipe. The smoke ma'am. She's got little lungs. Smoke will clog them up. Might give her a cough. She's delicate."

Maria thought for a few seconds before putting the pipe and tobacco back into her pouch. Conrad smiled and turned back to the child.

"Do you have a name?" he asked the baby, in a gentle but still adult voice. He looked out of the corner of his eye to Maria who shook her head. He gasped comically and looked at the baby.

"You ain't got no name? You ain't got no name? Well, how will all the boys be able to send you love notes if you don't got no name? What about... Martha?" he looked slyly at Maria who crumpled her face in distaste. Conrad smiled.

"Not Martha… what about Bertha?"

Maria blew a raspberry and playfully shoved Conrad.

"You know," he said to the baby, "your mama talks too much. How about Annabel?"

He looked back to Maria as she contemplated the proposal. She had not considered the name before and so was taking a few moments to match the name to the baby, and to construct a future personality to go along with it. After a few agonising moments, Maria broke into a broad and free smile. She had concluded that the child and the woman Annabel would be bright, clever, funny, creative and beautiful. She grew excited at the prospect of meeting her. Finally, she nodded.

"There you are," said Conrad to the child, "you are little baby Annabel. Pleased to meet you Annabel, my name is Uncle Conrad. I'm a friend of your mama's and she is looking after me while I am sick. When I'm better and big and strong I'll… " he tailed off and the jovial air in the room died down. Maria looked to the floor. Conrad handed the baby back to her. He knew that he was soon to leave her forever, and Maria knew it too. The games were over.

⸗∞⸗

"I think," said Conrad after a few moments' contemplation, "I'm ready to stand up." His words meant more than a declaration of gesture. It was the beginning of the end of his stay there, and the decline of Maria's fantasy.

To stand meant to walk, and to walk meant to leave, and to leave meant to be left alone. She could not deny him and so she held the baby close and stood up to help Conrad.

Before he attempted to stand, he reached for his trousers which lay by the side of Maria. She pushed them towards him with her foot and turned away so as to protect his modesty as he wriggled into them under his sheet. Once the belt was clasped he cleared his throat, signalling to Maria that it was safe to turn around. She did so and looked down at him, ready to offer assistance should he need it.

He rolled onto his side slightly and took his weight on his hands, wincing as he bent his knees. The muscles felt weak and unstable. He pushed down on the floor and slid up the wall until he was standing. The sheet fell off him, revealing his red shoulder and taut, lean and scarred torso. He looked ill and yet, at the same time, fierce.

He focused on the candle on the mantelpiece and took a step forward before wobbling to the side and almost toppling over. Maria stepped forward and threw her arm around him to stop him tumbling. He twisted sideways as he stumbled and, as he locked into Maria's arm they moved together into an accidental embrace, the baby held out to the side.

Conrad regained his balance and motioned to carry on walking when Maria, against her will, pulled him back into the embrace; defying her very existence, she gently kissed him on his red shoulder. As soon as she had committed that transgression, she stepped back from him and brought Annabel in closely to her chest and wrapped the shawl around them both, looking to the floor in shame. Conrad did not want to address the kiss, though it felt real and searing. He could not acknowledge it, because to do so would mean to accept that there was a spark between them that could ignite into a bright future. He had his own destiny and he could not allow himself to deviate from it as he had done with Liza. His path was a dark one, and there was no place for beacons such as Maria and Annabel.

He pulled his concentration back to the present and onto the candle in the other room. He was to walk there, unaided. He stepped forward and the conviction in his heart spread to his legs and feet and he walked, slowly but steadily, out of the side room, across the hallway and into the living room.

Once there, he sat down in the chair by the window, tired but happy to have made the journey. He looked at the fire and began to rock gently in the chair. Maria followed him to the doorway and watched as he rocked in her lover's chair. She did not seem to mind that he had accidentally disturbed the sacrosanct shrine. A few days prior, if someone had done so, she would have cut them down with the axe, but now she felt strangely comfortable with another man in her lover's chair. She kissed Annabel and left Conrad alone while she went to the kitchen to prepare a little food and some tea for him.

Conrad rocked for a few moments, staring into the fire and ascending that nightmare staircase in his memory that led to the landing where Liza sat in a pool of blood, eyes panicked and wide. He reached the top of the stairs and blinked, which sent him back to the bottom again and he ascended once more. Every time he repeated the action, the face of Liza distorted slightly, morphing into a new one; Conrad knew the trick his mind was playing on him and before Maria's face could replace Liza's he snapped out of his daydream and stopped rocking.

He looked around the room, his eyes coming to rest on the guitar leaned against the wall by his side. He picked it up and inspected the neck and worn fretboard and had the same thought as Rickman had when inspecting the instrument. He wondered if Maria played it and if she did not, whether a friend or lover had done so. He rested it across his lap and caressed the neck.

Maria gathered up some scraps on a plate and tried to push the accidental embrace and devastating kiss to the back of her mind. How could she have transgressed so? How could she have betrayed her lover in such a fashion?

The frustration and pain mixed inside her and she had to bite into her lip in order to stop the tears from overcoming her completely. She placed her hand on the edge of the counter and controlled her breathing. As she did so, a hobo spider appeared on the counter by the sink and scuttled across her path. Maria's anger subsided as she watched the spider.

She was about to pick it up and move it to a safer part of the kitchen when the twang of a guitar string echoed through the room. She gasped in horror and turned from the counter, not realising that she had knocked over a bottle and sent it crashing down on the spider, crushing it instantly. She grabbed the plate of food and stormed into the living room.

Conrad was gently plucking the strings when Maria rushed in, a crazed look in her eyes. She snatched the guitar from him and slapped him brutally hard across the face. She froze for a few seconds, as if she had suddenly been returned to herself and given control of her actions once more. Her hand, burning red, remained outstretched.

Conrad looked to the floor, his hand on his cheek. He did not say a word. Maria dropped the plate of food onto his lap and rested the guitar back against the wall.

Conrad looked up at her, cheek red, confused but remarkably calm. Maria stepped forward to touch him, but halted herself before walking out of the room and going upstairs to her bedroom where she sat on the edge of the bed, crying into her baby to muffle the sounds of her sobs.

She remained like that for what seemed like hours until she heard the creak of floorboards from downstairs and the steady yet laboured breathing of Conrad.

She held her hand to her mouth and listened as she tracked his movements. He had gotten up from the chair and slowly made his way from the living room, back across the hallway and had lain back down on the hard floor in the empty, cold side room, to sleep alone. Maria began to sob again.

CHAPTER THIRTY
The Oubliette Town

Bel was a dangerous and unnatural oddity in Montana. It was a boardwalk town comprising a single long and wide high street flanked with tall wooden and brick buildings, and several side streets that spread out into little alleys and backstreets. The population hovered around the two hundred and fifty mark.

Bel had a small bank, a surgery, a town hall with a clock tower at the far end of Main Street and a regulated bordello and hotel that occupied the top three floors of The Devil's Blood saloon bar.

Though the layout and amenities of Bel were similar to many other towns and cities throughout the land, what really made it different were its populace and their strange attitudes to life and the town.

Bel residents, to a man, were indulgent and mad: great sinners of vice and villainy that had purged their souls of virtue the day they stepped into the town or were born into it. They shared no love or loyalty to each other even though they were unified in their vile and debauched lifestyles.

They drank, fought and fornicated openly in the street, and the only church in the town was used more as a public toilet than as a house of worship.

The town was overrun with tricksters and sharps and while fights and raucousness were borne nightly, come dawn enemy was friend again in a perpetual wheel of degradation and redemption.

The reputation for danger and vice was well documented and many young men sought out the town, hoping to find a darkly enriching lifestyle; they found only a never-ending cycle of madness and confusion.

Those who tried to leave always found themselves at the town's borders facing a great plain of tall grass and staring out into the nothingness. Their desires falling away. Nobody passed farther than the border before turning back and, as if sleepwalking, returned into Bel.

The man who controlled that strange town had a real name once, but as memory was transient in Bel, it had been remembered and forgotten more times than the changing of the seasons. His was simply The Nameless.

He was rarely seen, and when he did appear, it was always unannounced and often by surprise. Many people had dared to question his existence, thinking themselves safe in their conspiratorial parley only to find their throats slashed by the man who had stepped out of the shadows from the corner of their locked room. He was everywhere and nowhere.

Rickman Chill had only ventured into Bel once, twenty years previously, alone and barely armed.

He had met with The Nameless, the man Rickman believed to be the blood-soaked right hand of The Devil, and thought he could cut him down. Rickman had been wrong and had barely escaped the town alive, dragging himself through the grassland and using his mission-mind to ward off the powerful hold of the town.

Rickman escaped into the woodlands, the only man ever to leave the town, and left behind the sweet taste of his blood on the lips of The Nameless.

Rickman had never returned, instead adapting his hunt to circumnavigate Bel at all costs.

The Devil was ever present, and as Rickman crawled across the plains away from the town, hiding in the tall grass for two days as the Bel residents combed it looking for him, he vowed to track The Devil down in the open land, praying that Montana would deliver The Devil to him.

That was twenty years ago, and Rickman Chill had exhausted all his leads. So, finally, the only option that remained was to swallow his fear and return to Bel and, if God was on his side, extract the information he sought from that bastard The Nameless via the most pain he could possibly inflict.

But things had not gone to plan; Rickman was not going to ride into the town with three gunmen, each of them armed to the teeth, but instead with only one; if Conrad died from his wound, he would be as he had been before: on his own.

———∞∞∞———

The nighttime revelry was in full swing. The noise and heat from the burning drums made the Chinese lanterns criss-crossing the streets sway under the turbulence. Music poured from every window as did the sounds of screams, cheers and smashing glass.

To a stranger, the scene was akin to the last days of Sodom. Indeed, to the rider approaching, that feeling was not too far off.

The horse stopped two hundred yards from the town. The grass swayed in the night breeze, the noise carrying over the flat land from the town to the rider and far off across the plains, into the woodland and away towards the mountains.

The man sighed and prepared to enter the town. He did not know what would happen, but he had no choice except to go. He had vengeance on his mind. He spurred the horse and it began to approach the town.

Nobody paid any attention to the rider as he entered the town and trotted along Main Street, his head lolling slightly. The madness continued around him unabated; nobody looked up until the man removed his hat and screamed in a loud, twisted voice before pulling out his gun and firing four times into the air.

The music halted, and the fornicating slowed but continued as the partners looked over to the rider and his horse. The rider screamed once more and fired the remaining two bullets before awkwardly trying to reload. He was obviously in some physical distress.

Nobody moved to help him; the band was about to strike up again, the fornicators about to return to their business and forget about the madman, when a presence overcame them all. Everything ceased, including, it seemed, time itself.

The rider turned his horse around to face the opposite end of the street whereupon he saw a man in a dark tanned leather trench coat, broad-brimmed hat casting a shadow over his face, and resting a huge shotgun on his hip.

The horse froze, terrified of the silhouette. The man took a single step forward and the horse reared and threw his rider before turning and bolting out of the town. The mad Bel residents stood up and gathered around the fallen man as he painfully scrambled around on the ground.

The dark man at the end of the street walked forward and bent over the interloper to inspect him. He was wincing in pain from the fall and trying to cover a large, angry and revolting gunshot wound that had flayed the left side of his face clean off. He looked up to see the dark man remove his hat to finally show his face.

He was beautiful, but only partially. From his forehead, across his right eye, down the right side of his face, over his neck and across his throat ran a jagged scar. He had a white eye with a beady black pupil that penetrated deep into every man's heart.

"Nameless? Mr Nameless?" spluttered the man on the floor. "I have a message about someone who is coming for you."

The crowd laughed at the possibility of anyone stupid enough to come for The Nameless. The beady eye was unrelenting in its stare.

"Nobody comes for me," he smirked in a soft whisper.

"My name is Hobson Whitney," coughed the man as he sat up.

"Very well, Mr Whitney, who is coming for me?"

Hobson could not catch his breath and so pointed up to The Nameless' scar and finally managed to splutter, "Rickman Chill. Rickman Chill is coming for you."

The smile dropped slightly from The Nameless' face as the name he hadn't heard but had felt every day for twenty years echoed through his mind.

"Rickman Chill," he whispered finally, "you are mistaken. Rickman Chill died a long time ago."

Hobson shook his head.

"No, you're wrong. Rickman Chill lives and he is coming for you."

The Nameless nodded to a man beside him who then stepped over Hobson, blocking his view. He brought the butt of a shotgun down on Hobson's jaw, knocking him out cold instantly.

Most of the Bel residents drifted back to their nefarious activities and the music started up again. The Nameless remained standing over the unconscious Hobson Whitney. He turned to the man who had knocked him out; a relatively young, weathered man who had a cocky, sly look to him.

"What's your name, son?" asked The Nameless.

"Stanley Spring, sir. 'Ricochet' Stanley Spring out of…"

"Get this man to the bar, prop him up and tip some whisky down his throat till he wakes up," interrupted The Nameless.

"Yes sir," said Stanley Spring dutifully, and he bent down to try and pick up Hobson. He was too heavy. Spring looked up to ask The Nameless for help but, like a ghost, the man was gone. Stanley Spring spat on his hands, picked up Hobson's wrists and dragged him along the dusty main street towards the saloon, where he executed The Nameless' instructions dutifully.

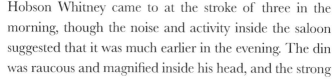

Hobson Whitney came to at the stroke of three in the morning, though the noise and activity inside the saloon suggested that it was much earlier in the evening. The din was raucous and magnified inside his head, and the strong smell of cheap alcohol mixed with tobacco and vomit made him nauseous.

The room swirled and distorted as he struggled to understand his surroundings. He could see two large balconied walkways running around the walls of the building, where semi-naked women draped themselves over the rails. He could see four great chandeliers overhead, and golden garlands stretched across the banisters.

There also seemed to be a never-ending shower of red petals falling all around. He touched his face and was shocked to discover it bandaged with tight gauze. He sat up to see a young man sitting across from him, drinking a large glass of whisky, his hat resting at a jaunty angle.

"You're awake!" he said upon noticing Hobson rubbing his face.

"Where am I?" spluttered Hobson.

"Can't you remember? With an entrance like that, I imagined it would be impossible to forget," said the man as a topless woman sashayed over and draped herself over him.

"I'm in Bel," said Hobson. The young man began to clap.

"Bravo sir, bravo. Welcome to heaven," he said as he shared a passionate kiss with the woman. They groped each other feverishly. Hobson felt as though he was in hell. He looked around for a drink. Stanley noticed, slid him the bottle of whisky and offered him his hand.

"Stanley Spring."

Hobson shook his hand and drank.

"Hobson Whitney."

"So," said Stanley, craning his neck so that the woman would kiss that instead of his mouth. "What brings you here?"

"A message. A warning for him. Rickman Chill is coming to kill him."

"Ain't nobody who can kill The Nameless."

"Chill can."

"Well, who is this character then?" Stanley asked as he put his hands behind his head.

"He's an arrow of vengeance. All he does is ride. And hunt."

"Hunt The Nameless?"

"No, he's just a stepping stone."

"A stepping stone? The Nameless has been called many things but not that. Stepping stone to what?"

"The Devil," said Hobson as he drank. "Rickman Chill rides and hunts The Devil and that's all he does."

Stanley Spring laughed, and lifted his feet off the table to lean forward and slap Hobson on the thigh.

"And if he sent you in to flush out The Nameless and The Devil, shouldn't he be here?"

Hobson shook his head.

"Then why are you here?"

Hobson slammed the bottle down on the table, making the woman squeal in giddy shock. Hobson tore off his bandage to expose his face.

"Because Rickman Chill killed my brother and did this. Because Rickman Chill *is* The Devil, though he don't know it."

Stanley laughed and stood up. The woman fell onto the floor and began beetling around, her drug induced euphoria overwhelming her.

"You know," said Stanley as he turned away, "I used to ride with The Devil."

"If you rode with The Devil, Mr Spring," shouted Hobson, "then Rickman Chill is coming for you too. Arm yourself."

"Drink, fuck, be free," said Stanley Spring as he walked up the stairs and linked arms with two whores before leading them into a room.

CHAPTER THIRTY-ONE
Possessions of the Night

Maria's sleep was light and restless and she tossed, turned and murmured as she struggled in her dreamscape to keep the physical world coherent. The deeper into her dreams she fell, the less stable the ground became and the less protected she felt. She drifted through sensations of falling, drowning and paralysis as everything around her changed to coalesce into an all-encompassing state of fear.

She scrambled at the air and scratched at the ground as her nightmare compounded upon her soul. Inside her room the moonlight had penetrated the thick mist and bathed everything in an eerie silver light, drawing dark and menacing shadows from the furniture that danced, weaved and swooped around the walls and ceiling, tormenting the sleeping woman.

The window was ajar and the warm night breeze flicked the curtains. Annabel, unlike her mother, was awake. She lay in her little wooden cot and stared up at the shadows dancing around the room. She did not cry or scream as she was too young to feel their malevolence. Her eyes were unused to the shifting darkness and struggled to pull definition from anything.

Even though Annabel was only a few days old, she did feel instinctively safe. The room felt as natural to her as her mother's heartbeat and the air was as warm as her mother's skin. Annabel lay, eyes wide open, as a large shadow stopped dancing around the room and turned to her, looming into the cot and covering her in darkness. She felt safe still, and she equated the feeling to the one she experienced while being held and kissed by the other one who wasn't her mother. The one whose finger had tickled her and who had kind blue eyes.

The shadow swept under her little blanket and under her back, shrouding her in a warm, secure darkness; the baby closed her eyes and fell into a dreamless sleep.

Maria, however, did not feel as secure as her daughter. Her nightmares were growing worse and seemingly merging into each other. She felt paralysed, her legs frozen and sinking into a thick, viscous ground, the air gradually being squeezed out of her as she sank lower and lower. The ground rose up, passed her thighs and over her waist. She tried to reach out and grab onto something, but the branches of the nearby trees turned into snakes and recoiled from her. The ground rose up farther, covering her breasts, and she felt her lungs begin to freeze. Soon the soil began to tickle her throat, and she craned her neck back so her nostrils could inhale as much air as possible. The edges of the soil encroached on her vision and suddenly all was black.

Maria gasped reflexively and sat bolt upright in her bed, clutching her throat and sweating profusely. She reached out and felt her legs. One was numb and heavy as she had slept on it, the other taut and still suffering from the trauma of the nightmare.

Maria sat up on her bed and massaged the life back into her legs, regulating her breathing and telling herself in her mind that it was only a dream, only a dream, only a dream.

When her legs recovered their feeling, she sat back against the head board and looked over to Annabel, kissed her finger and gently touched the child's forehead. The silver light in the room seemed now more comforting than menacing. Maria shuffled back into her bed and closed her eyes, preparing to journey back into her dreamscape, confident that her restored mental state could overcome any daemons or devils in her mind that might threaten her sleep once more.

She turned from the room to face the wall and the window when she heard a creak. She opened her eyes. The creak came again. The unmistakable sound of bare feet on floorboards. Maria gripped the edge of the blanket and brought it in close to her face as an icy chill crept up under the bed sheets and licked up her back. She froze, eyes wide in fear.

There was something in the room. Was it Conrad? What did he want? Had she gone too far in kissing him? What if he climbed into her bed? What then?

She heard a sigh – a sad, long, melancholic sigh and the blanket over her billowed. She clamped her eyes shut and began to mouth a prayer to dispel either the force in the room, or convince Conrad to abandon his ideas and return to the side room.

Maria finished her prayer and opened her eyes. The dread was still heavy in the air. She knew that she had to overcome her terror and turn over in bed. If there was malevolence in the bedroom, Maria knew that she had to get Annabel and protect her. The sweat was cold on her forehead and she shrank into a foetal position as she began to pluck up the courage to turn over in bed to face the rest of the room. She turned slowly, leading with her eyes.

She rolled onto her back and looked over to the cot when the door of the wardrobe flung open, hitting the other door and rattling against it.

Maria gasped and scrambled back across the bed, away from the cot, pressing herself up against the wall. Suddenly a gust of moaning wind swept in from under the curtains and whipped around the room. Maria pulled the blanket up to her face in terror, hugging her knees, when the wind pulled The Devil's hat and poncho out of the cupboard and threw them over the bed, covering Maria.

She screamed into the fabric, the sound seemingly absorbed into it, as Annabel did not wake. Maria frantically tried to pull the blanket and poncho off her, but the wind was fierce and the cupboard door was banging against its hinge.

She sank lower into her bed as the blanket sealed itself down, weighted by the heavy poncho on top of it. Maria, in the dark womb of her bed, shrank to breathe. She gasped and clawed her way to the foot of the bed and prised open the sheet, struggling against the unnatural weight upon it. She freed her upper body and slumped over the back of the bed, the wardrobe door still battering and the wind still swirling. She fell out of the bed; as soon as she hit the floor the wardrobe closed quietly and the wind dissipated.

Maria lay there, gasping for breath as everything returned to normal. She had the wonderful, relieving sensation that it had been a nightmare and she had merely fallen out of bed, kicking herself back into reality. She grabbed onto the bedpost, and pulled herself up.

She froze. The poncho and hat were still on the bed. It had been no nightmare. She looked around the room, mistrusting everything she saw and feeling far, far away from any reality she had known before.

Maria did not consider Annabel but instead she backed out of the room, the core of her mind where self-preservation ruled carrying her to a place where she instinctively knew she would feel safe.

Conrad's sleep had been deep and calm. Though the dead that waited for him on the other side were still present in his dreamscapes, they did not threaten or congregate around him but instead remained as background characters that only made eye contact when he looked at them. He had begun to grow accustomed to the realisation that his subconscious and his soul no longer belonged to him exclusively.

His sleep was so deep and so calm, unlike any he had experienced since hunting The Devil, that he did not hear the creak of the floorboards in the hallway. Normally, he would have been up, coiled, and guns trained the moment the noise entered his ears, so attuned had he been. But during his convalescence, and being around Maria, a calm new Conrad had begun to grow inside himself. He was blessed him with a deep sleep.

The second footstep, however, reawakened his old self; his dreamscape fell away and his eyes opened. He was lying on his side, his guns in reach just beside him. He waited for the third creak and, when it came he grabbed his pistol, sat up and pointed at the doorway, pulling the hammer back and training it dead bang on the space where the victim's forehead would emerge the moment they rounded the doorway. He waited, unmoving for a few seconds, before Maria's face appeared before him, pale and beautiful in the silver cross light of the moonbeams flooding in from the front door.

Conrad lifted the pistol up and looked, wide-eyed, at the ghostly looking woman in the doorway.

"Ma'am," he whispered, resting his gun on the ground, "Is that you?"

Maria stepped into the room without looking at him, and with barely a sound lay down on the floor, lifted his bed sheet up and slid in next to him.

Conrad, bewildered at the woman's actions and unsure of her motives, lay back down and turned to face her. He went to speak, but saw that her eyes were closed and she had fallen back to sleep the moment her body had rested upon the floor.

Conrad gently cupped her head and slid his arm underneath her. In her drowsy sleep, Maria wriggled closer to him and slumped her other arm over his chest. Conrad lay on his back with Maria asleep in his arms, and closed his eyes, a faint smile across his face. His dreamscape this time was not populated by the dead that waited, but by strangers his pure subconscious had created. They seemed happy folk, smiling and laughing as he passed through a strange and bright town. His dream revolved around himself, Maria and a young and happy girl called Annabel who had her father's eyes and her mother's smile. It was the perfect dream.

Azazel huffed and stamped his feet as the black mist descended down in the darkest part of the night. His eyes burned an almost luminescent yellow as he circled his hitching post and kicked the ground, anger and agitation rising inside him.

A great storm was coming, he could feel it, and he could also feel a great treachery being wrought upon his world. He yearned for his master and his dear friend Cinereous. He felt rage against the interlopers who had entered the house and the way in which they had cast a spell over Maria.

Azazel felt the need to protect her and the child and his muscles grew stronger. He bit on his rope and yanked it. The hitching post rattled, but held fast in its post. He stamped and kicked the ground, bucking wildly as the rage grew. He was bleating loudly, his cries masked by the wind that had begun to howl around the compound. His burning yellow eyes were fixed on the dark windows and the evil that was inside. He kicked backwards and struck the post hard in its centre, splitting it in two. He bit the rope again and pulled it free. Azazel stretched and cried, finally free of his hitching post, and he clomped slowly and purposefully towards the house.

The wind led the way, opening the door for Azazel in a quick gust that blew through the house, billowing the curtains in every room and dropping the temperature so that the breath of the sleeping Maria and Conrad became visible. They both awoke at the same time, eyes locked on each other, the sudden freezing air forcing them closer as their lungs grew cold from drawing in the icy air.

Conrad turned over and reached for his guns when an awful, demonic shadow entered the room, loomed over the wall and across the ceiling, and appeared to be the shape of The Devil himself. Maria and Conrad looked in shock at the horned beast above them. Conrad slowly grabbed his gun, unsure it would be of any use at all.

The shadow remained and the ominous sound of clomping hooves on wood entered the house, echoing around the room. Maria moved in closer to Conrad as he trained his gun on the doorway. The awful clomps came once more and Azazel stalked into the doorway and stared at them, eyes as yellow flames.

Conrad laughed and lowered his gun, relieved and a little ashamed that the animal had startled them so. He lowered the gun before Azazel shrieked a piercing scream and reared up onto his back legs, his front two kicking and thrashing at the pair. The goat, still screeching, lifted his back leg, showing unnatural strength, and began to walk forward. His scream rattled the windows in every room and terrified Maria and Conrad to the core.

Conrad raised his gun and was about to fire when Maria grabbed his arm to stop. She pushed his gun aside just as Conrad pulled the trigger, the sound deafening in the house, and sending the bullet through the window, shattering it. The wind outside sent a thousand shards into the room. Conrad shielded Maria from the glass and rolled onto his side.

Azazel's possession left him; he fell back onto all fours, and ran out of the room and into the yard to his hitching post.

Conrad and Maria sat up, shocked and breathing hard. Conrad went to put his arm around her when the sound of Annabel's cries emanated from the bedroom. Maria, suddenly realising that she had abandoned her daughter, leapt to her feet. She ignored the shards of glass on the floor, and raced out of the room and up to her daughter, leaving Conrad alone, shocked, frightened and confused.

SOLIDAGO GIGANTEA
'Giant Golden Rod'

Found in open places in the valleys and plains

CHAPTER THIRTY-TWO
A Good Day

The restorative powers of the dawn sunlight vanquished the terror that the night had wrought upon Maria and Conrad. After Maria had soothed Annabel and laid her back down to sleep, she herself had managed to rest for the remainder of the night.

Conrad too managed to sleep, after sweeping the shards of glass into the corner of the room and sleeping underneath the window, where he looked out at the black night, waiting for the first hint of light. When it came, he knew that they were not in hell and that the world still turned, and so was able to get just a couple of hours' rest.

He awoke to a mist-free morning and a bright, clear sky. The smell of coffee was fresh and strong and welcomed him out of his slumber. He rolled over onto his side, away from the window, and smiled when he saw that Maria had placed the cup by his side just moments before. He lay there for a few seconds and considered the ebbs of steam, winding their way up from the black coffee, and he felt a calming sense of peace. He sat up and looked around the room as he drank. The nightmare of the previous hours seemed now to be exactly that: a nightmare; an anxious construct of his subconscious. Only the broken window and pile of glass in the corner of the room told him differently.

He finished his coffee and inspected his shoulder. The swelling had gone completely, the redness now just a small patch around the two pinprick fang marks. He prodded the wound. It stung slightly but felt no worse than a bad nettle sting. He rotated his shoulder and wiggled his toes. The aching fever had passed and his muscles felt strong again and ready to resume their duties. He stood up easily and without losing his sense of balance. It felt wonderful to be upright and in control once more. He stood by the open window and let the morning sunlight warm his torso and restore even more strength to him. Though the dread of the night before had vanished, Conrad could still recall the events. What was the cause of the madness? Simply tricks of the light and wind? Something more? And why had the woman come to him in the night?

He drank his coffee as he turned the questions over in his head. He did not once think of Rickman Chill or where he could be.

———

Maria, like Conrad, had arisen surprisingly rejuvenated and also attributed much of it to the sunshine. She lifted Annabel out of her cot and sat on the bed, shaking her gently until she woke up, whereupon she held the baby up to the window and let the sunlight warm her. It was her first clear sunrise and they sat there for several minutes in perfect togetherness.

After they had enjoyed the sunshine, Maria had taken Annabel down to the kitchen where, while the coffee brewed, she fed her and looked over the Wild Goose Island carving on the kitchen table. She felt torn between her past with The Devil and her possible future with Conrad and Annabel.

The more she dwelt on the fantasy of a happy life, the more the amalgamation of The Devil and Conrad fell apart and the man became less of one and more of the other. She was slowly making a choice and, against all she knew, she found herself beginning to turn from the lover of her past and toward Conrad and to what he could become to her.

The coffee was brewed and so she poured two cups and took one to him. He was asleep when she arrived at the doorway to the side room, lying on his side, facing the window with sunbeams falling through onto his head. Maria smiled at the sleeping man before walking into the room, laying the cup down and then attending to his belongings. She quietly placed his boots together by the doorway and took his coat, waistcoat, shirt and jacket and crept out of the house.

Maria stood on the porch and looked over to Azazel who bleated and stamped his feet merrily, seemingly completely unaware of his nighttime madness. Maria thought that he, like them, had merely been scared by the fierce wind and had only wanted to come inside, the poor beast. Conrad's gunshot must have scared the life out of him, she concluded as she draped the coat over the porch rail. Still carrying the rest of his clothes and Annabel, she made her way to the goat to stroke his back and chin. As she walked, she noticed Annabel reach out and grab the collar of Conrad's shirt. His smell had imprinted into her heart and Maria felt touched by the grace of God; she knew that she was making the right decision to align herself with him.

Azazel was happy to see Maria and her child and bleated sweetly while she rubbed his back – until he caught Conrad's scent on the clothes; he stamped his foot and trotted off to another part of the compound to graze. Maria scrunched her face up at the animal and went to the barn to attend to the horse.

Conrad sat on the porch smoking a cigarette in perfect bliss while across from him Maria sat with her rags and thread sewing together a sweet little doll for Annabel.

They hadn't spoken to each other all day and had not felt the need to. After Conrad had drunk his coffee he had not searched the house for Maria (she was by the stream at the rear of the house, washing his clothes) but had instead swept the glass up and thrown it into the thick bush by the side of the barn. He had swept and scrubbed the flagstones in the kitchen, having felt a desire from his body to do some active work.

Riding with Rickman and taking refuge in houses as and when they could had taught Conrad that there was no differentiation between 'men's work' and 'women's work'; they were simply jobs to be done and duties to be performed.

After the floor was clean, his body was still not tired and so he went back to the barn and heaved some unbroken logs out into the middle of the yard; he went to locate the axe which was not in the barn where he assumed it would be, but inside the house, resting against the wall by Maria's bed. It was a strange place to find it, and he had almost not bothered to look in that room, (partially out of disbelief that it could be in there, but also out of a sense of impropriety at being in her private room without her present).

He compromised by quickly peeking into the room, whereupon he saw the clean blade glinting by the door. And so, he had taken it and chopped the wood into sizable fire logs. Although he had not amassed as much as he had hoped, he was still happy with his achievement. While he had chopped the wood, Maria had returned from the stream and had draped his clean clothes over the porch banister to dry before installing herself in her rocking chair to smoke, making sure that the fumes blew away from Annabel.

After his work with the axe was done, Conrad went and sat down next to Maria on the porch, communicating with her only via a few looks, smiles and nods. And so they sat, she sewed and he smoked until the afternoon turned into the evening whereupon they went silently into the house to open a bottle of whisky and share a drink, their first together.

The sun was setting and Conrad had his feet on the kitchen table. He sat opposite Maria, laughing happily, two plates with only crumbs on them pushed to the side. Annabel was sitting on Maria's lap and her new doll, which Conrad had named 'Miss Kiss' after he had given it to her and kissed her on the forehead which made the child reflexively reach up for his face.

Conrad had not laughed in years. He had ridden, hunted and killed, ridden, hunted and killed. Occasionally, along the way, over a campfire or on a particularly arduous ride, he and whoever he was riding with might share anecdotes to keep their spirits up, and though they shared illicit laughter, it was laughter weighted with the anchors of dread and futility. It was never true laughter, always an approximation tinged with a sad desperation. On that evening, however, half drunk on whisky and totally relaxed, he laughed freely and loudly. Indeed, the sound of his laughter was so surprising to him that it generated further laughs and a few giggles.

Maria also laughed, but it was a silent laugh. She smiled broadly and her shoulders jiggled, but no sound came out. It did not bother Conrad though. She was happy, it was obvious, and that was more than enough for him.

The whisky was affecting Maria gloriously. She had not drunk for months and doing so with company was revelatory for her. She felt totally relaxed, and smoked as much as she wanted, and looked at Conrad longer than she should have with eyes more suggestively than was appropriate, but she did not care. Annabel sat with Miss Kiss wedged under her arm. Annabel did not react to her new dolly, which was natural given that she was barely a week old, but Maria knew that she would grow to love her, as she had fantasised, and in time she would happily pass Miss Kiss onto a baby brother or sister when he or she came into the world. Maria held Annabel and Miss Kiss closely to her as she leaned on her hand and drank wantonly.

Their laughter fell away in unison as the joke faded and they sat there, chortling to each other and catching their breath. Conrad took his feet off the table and rested his head on his hand. Maria did the same, so that their hands and heads met in the middle and rested against each other. Maria placed Annabel and Miss Kiss on the table and Conrad poured two extra-large glasses, draining the bottle dry. He held it upside down, shaking the last drops out and frowning. Maria lifted her leg and shoved open the door of a nearby cupboard to reveal three more bottles stored away. Conrad smiled and they picked up the glasses and clinked them.

Conrad was about to reach across the table and rub Annabel's cheek when the front door to the house opened and a figure stepped into the doorway. Maria and Conrad sat back up from their position straight away. Maria grabbed Annabel and pulled her close. Conrad's hand reached for his pistol which was lying unattended on the counter beside him. He halted when the figure stepped into the hall light.

"Rickman? Where have you been? I was just… we were… "

"I have brought food" he croaked from the hallway.

Conrad and Maria looked at each other.

"Great," said Conrad, unsure of Rickman and his sudden reappearance.

Rickman walked into the kitchen, his eyes dark, lost, and back to how they had been every waking moment since he walked into Conrad's house and recruited him to his cause.

He had returned, more galvanized than ever. He swung his heavy knapsack off his shoulder and onto the table with a great thud, reached in and pulled out two bright white geese, their necks snapped, their heads lolling. He took his bag away and left the bodies of the wild geese on the table, a trickle of blood falling from their mouths and finding their way into the grooves of Maria's table carving of their old home.

Maria put her hand to her mouth in horror. Conrad did not understand the significance of the birds. He stood up.

Rickman looked at him deeply, eyes boring into his soul. He squinted and bit his lip as he uncovered easily the secret that Conrad was trying to suppress.

"Cook them," he said, "we leave in the morning." and he turned and left the kitchen.

Maria's horror overcame her and the tears broke out and spilt over her hands. She got up from the table and left the kitchen via the rear door to cry into the night at the back of the house. Conrad was left alone in the kitchen, looking down at the dead geese and assuming, wrongly, that Maria's tears were for him and his imminent departure.

CHAPTER THIRTY-THREE

Lullaby

Maria came back into the house when the night arrived fully and the whisky began to lose its potency. It was nine o'clock. She could not deny it, the smell of the roasting goose in her stove was almost overwhelming and she resisted as long as she could, not wanting to admit that her stomach forgave Rickman for his awful act. Conrad stepped outside and approached her. She turned from him. He stopped, sensing that she was a coiled snake.

"Ma'am. There is food inside, would you come in?"

Maria stepped farther away from him, pretending to take interest in something by the treeline. Conrad hung his head, turned and left her. Maria turned around and watched him walk inside. The cold became too much and she waited for a further two minutes to make it appear as if she had returned under her own volition before entering the house.

The kitchen was wonderfully warm and the steam from the stove had fogged up the windows. The table was set and Rickman was standing in the doorway, looking out of the kitchen, down the hall and towards the front door. He turned to look over his shoulder and regarded Maria as she stood in the rear doorway. Maria looked at him with stubborn eyes and she held her baby close to her. Rickman tipped his hat and turned back to contemplate the front door and the land beyond.

Conrad opened the stove and, using a rag, pulled out the goose and showed it to Maria. She looked down at it and regarded him with the same eyes as she had given Rickman. Conrad did not feel anger, which surprised him, but instead felt happy forgiveness that Maria's stubborn nature was simply one of her ways.

He tutted and shook his head before placing the tray on the table. Though Rickman did not witness it, his stomach turned in revulsion at Conrad's pathetic display of attempted happy home-making. He needed to eat, that was clear, but to do so it seemed he would have to sit through the charade of familial courtesies that had long since been forgotten by him, but not by Conrad it seemed. His best rider and gunman was too far into some happy delirium or spell to be of use now. Rickman decided to try and coax some fire out of the man in a last ditch attempt to pull him from Maria and the mysterious household and back onto his path, or forget him forever. He turned and sat down to eat.

They ate in silence. Conrad wolfed down his food greedily, his appetite now returned to him. Rickman ate daintily as was his way, turning from the table slightly so that they could not see him eat. Maria picked at her food and pushed it around the plate. Annabel slept in her little wooden cot which was placed on the table next to her mother. Though Maria's taste buds told her the food was wonderful, her stomach refuted the claim and she felt nauseous throughout.

Rickman finished his meal, pushed the plate away and turned to face the other two. Maria, seated across from Conrad, could not help but look up at him every once in a while. Conrad, too, looked up at her, catching her eye before pretending that he hadn't. It was a pathetic display of barely hidden attraction that infuriated Rickman; he did not react but sat and rolled his cigarette.

He lit it and blew smoke over the table, deliberately letting it waft over Annabel's wooden cot. Maria looked over to Rickman who fixed her with his dead eyes. She dragged the cot towards herself and wafted the smoke away from the child. The scraping noise of the cot across the table attracted Conrad's attention and he looked up to see Maria shoot him a look of frustration. He looked over to Rickman who was now looking at him smoking, blowing smoke over the child once more.

"You shouldn't smoke, Boss," he said quietly.

"Really?" said Rickman, curling a side smile.

Conrad felt resilient conviction suddenly swell inside himself.

"Bad for Annabel."

Rickman raised an eyebrow and looked at Maria.

"Annabel?" he said, "That's a nice name. Did you think of it?"

Maria looked to the table. Rickman raised his other eyebrow and turned back to Conrad and folded his arms.

"How interesting," he said with a broad, yet awful smile, "the husband, the wife and the baby."

Rickman took a long, deep draw of his cigarette. "One big happy family," he said, exhaling a great plume of smoke over the three. "I guess second time is the charm, Conrad."

Conrad stood up suddenly, his chair scraping backwards across the floor. Maria was startled by the noise and sat up. Conrad was faster than Rickman and had the drop on him, his eyes burning with rage. Rickman smiled.

"Ah, so you are still you," he said, taking his hand from his pistols and raising them up. "You see ma'am," continued Rickman, addressing Maria but still looking at Conrad. "He is a killer. Oh he is sweet and kind, and loves the idea of a family. But underneath – underneath he is a murderer of men. Murderer of women."

Rickman lowered his hands and looked at Maria, "… and children. Make no mistake, ma'am. He is a killer."

Rickman was right. Maria looked at Conrad, who was staring blankly at the doorway of the kitchen that led out to the porch and the land beyond. Maria wanted Conrad to refute the claims but he did not. Conrad stood and let Rickman's words sink in. He had lost himself to the magic of Maria and the house, and Rickman had pulled back the veil to reveal the falsity. Conrad was a killer and did not deserve to stay. He had a job to do. He holstered his pistol and Rickman smiled, knowing that he had pulled his man back from the brink. Conrad walked out of the kitchen.

Rickman followed him, leaving Maria and Annabel alone in the kitchen.

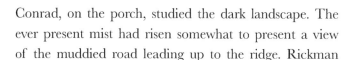

Conrad, on the porch, studied the dark landscape. The ever present mist had risen somewhat to present a view of the muddied road leading up to the ridge. Rickman opened the front door and stood next to him.

"I'm sorry," Rickman said in a soft and genuine tone that at once struck Conrad as sincere, and also strange as Rickman had never apologised for anything before.

"We have to leave, and it would not be fair to leave her with any hope that you would come back. Or any regrets of what life might have been. She needs to know what you are, and to be happy that you are out of her life. She needed to see the truth. And you did too."

"What's happened to us?" asked Conrad more to the air than to Rickman.

"We got side-tracked. We have a mission and nothing should get in the way. Do you really think you can stay here and make her happy? Do you really think you can give up The Devil, and give me up and be happy?"

"I would have tried," replied Conrad, desperately trying to convince himself that it would have been so.

"You would have failed. You have fire inside you. Fire and thirst to find our man and cut him down. If you give it up, and stay here, well… "

"Don't mention her."

"I'm not going to."

"She's not Liza, this is different."

"You have to face facts Conrad, you ain't a man with roots. You are a killer. A murderer and a huntsman. If you stay here and bury that part of you, it will rise again."

Conrad hung his head, knowing that Rickman was right.

"But, if we ride into Bel, find The Devil and kill him, then… "

"… then?"

Rickman shrugged, "then that will be an interesting day."

"What time do we leave?"

"Dawn."

"I should say goodbye."

"Get some sleep."

Rickman patted him on the shoulder and went inside.

"It's what's best," he called back as he disappeared back into the house. Conrad hung his head. A life with Maria was an impossible dream. He sat down on the porch and began to roll a cigarette.

Maria had left the table and gone straight to her room where she rested Annabel down before lying on the bed, burying her face into the pillow and sobbing, all the while thumping the mattress. She pulled at her hair in abject frustration at just how weak she was being. Her tears fell upon other tears, and she had no idea which tears were for which pain. Pain that she had forsaken her lover for Conrad, pain that he was leaving? Pain that he was a killer? Pain that she would be left alone again? Pain that she felt the need to have anyone around at all? The questions compounded and she could not recall a time before when she had felt so desperately mad and so out of grasp with reality. Just what had happened to her?

As she expelled all her anguish, a great tiredness washed over her and she soon fell into a heavy sleep, fully clothed and atop the sheets, totally unaware that Rickman Chill was standing in the doorway watching her.

When he was sure that she was asleep, he stepped into the room and sat on the edge of the bed looking at her. He lifted her hair to the side and contemplated her sad, tear-stained face. He mouthed a frustrated obscenity and looked over to the cot to see Annabel sleeping sweetly. The moonbeams broke through the window and illuminated her in silver light. Rickman lowered his head, slowly resigning himself to what needed to be done. He stood up from the bed, gently picked up the sleeping child, held her close to his chest and turned to look out of the window.

Annabel, in her sleep, huddled in close to Rickman's chest, his warmth and steady heartbeat welcoming to her.

Rickman looked down at the child and whispered the only nursery rhyme he knew. He repeated the rhyme four times over, and when he finished the fifth repetition he realised that he had been crying and the tears had fallen onto Annabel.

He wiped his eyes and laid her back into her cot, wrapping her blanket over her and placing Miss Kiss beside her. A sea change had occurred inside him. He knew what needed to be done. If he was to fulfil his destiny he would not only have to kill The Devil, but he would also have to rectify one other injustice, for what use is a world without a Devil that still has sadness in it?

Rickman crept downstairs and into the living room. Through the window, he could see Conrad, asleep on the rocking chair. Rickman pulled his journal out of his pocket, scribbled some words down, tore out the page and placed the note on the mantelpiece. He went to the kitchen, packed up some leftover roasted goose, and stole out of the house via the back door.

Rickman circled the compound to the barn, saddled the horse and rode out of the barn into the dark night. He stopped at the ridge and looked back. The house stood in the darkness, alone but protected by the woods. He tipped his hat to Conrad and to the sleeping mother and child inside, and vowed that they would live out their lives in peace. He turned away from them and rode off towards

Bel where he intended to ride in alone, as before, with fewer guns but more grit. He felt that God was finally on his side and that The Devil was finally within his grasp. The only thing that stood in his path was The Nameless, the only man Rickman truly feared. But even their history did not slow down Rickman's heart and he rode hard and fast towards the town.

PART THREE
Tegenaria Agrestis

CHAPTER THIRTY-FOUR
Apart & Alone

Hobson Whitney stroked his face as he looked at himself in the mirror. He had taken residence in The Devil's Blood Hotel after Stanley Spring's instructions to drink, fuck and be free. He had performed two of the three suggestions.

After Stanley Spring had disappeared into the side room with the two whores, Hobson had sat for a few moments and finished the bottle of whisky left on the table, taking in the environment.

Thoughts of vengeance upon Rickman Chill had fallen away and a new sense of lust and life had overcome him. The place was an intoxicating spell and the thick smell of tobacco and opiates lulled him. He had started to feel slightly woozy and increasingly amorous, so he picked up the mad prostitute from the floor and took her upstairs to a vacant room.

Nobody stopped him and nobody paid any attention to his awful wound. They all simply moved out of his way as he ascended the staircase, too preoccupied with their own lustful urges to pay any attention to him.

He carried her into the room and dumped her onto the bed before falling on top of her. Hobson felt detached throughout as if somehow separated from the duty and clinically orchestrating a necessary task.

He finished and rolled off her, the thick air causing a delirium to rise inside him. Was he dead? Had he died on the way to Bel, now being caught in some purgatory where pleasure is offered and then denied?

He looked over to the woman and regarded her scarred and bruised leg that was draped over his midriff, disfigured and brutalised by innumerable clients. He felt sick. He had been with women before, but he had never encountered one who seemed so virulent and, at the same time, so lost.

He looked around the room at the rich, deep red walls and gold painted furniture. There were animal skins littering every chair, stool and chaise longue and, in the corner, a large dress mirror where presumably the whore would make herself presentable when she wasn't deep in a lost opiate dream.

She murmured and rubbed her leg over him again, leaving a smear of blood. Hobson, shocked, flung her leg off of him, causing her to roll onto her back, splaying herself and revealing a large, bloody pool in between them.

Frantically, Hobson checked himself and at first relief washed over him, before revulsion set in that she had been menstruating when they were together. He gagged and got out of bed to sit in front of the mirror.

Nothing seemed real, least of all himself. He looked at the red boa draped over the mirror and then at himself, staring deep into his own eyes. He reached up and touched his wound which did not hurt, despite its rugged openness.

"Are you in hell?" he whispered.

"Not yet," came a whisper from the far corner of the room.

Hobson spun around on the chair, his hands reaching for the pistols that weren't there.

"Who's that?" he asked, sternly. No sound came, but a mere shadow in the corner flickered and disappeared under the window frame. Hobson turned white with fear and his eyes grew panicked when he realised that he was, most certainly, damned and in hell. He turned back to look upon his grotesque face in the mirror, not noticing the hobo spider that crawled along the frame and disappeared into the boa.

―――――∞∞∞―――――

A few rooms down, Stanley Spring was sleeping contentedly underneath acres of naked flesh. Across from his large bed snored three naked men and seven naked women. The candlelight flickered as the breeze licked under the windows and kissed their bodies.

Stanley Spring's dream was not a construct of his subconscious, but a firm memory recalled and displayed for him to walk through. He dreamt of his time in the great thunderstorm when he had come to Maria's house and recruited The Devil. He recalled how, when they had ridden out and disappeared over the ridge leaving the house and the woman behind, The Devil had grown sad and quiet. He remembered in flashes of light and brilliance, their year of riding together that had seen them cut a swathe of chaos across Montana.

Stanley had killed, maimed, robbed and scorched all he had seen. The Devil, always in the background, had shown Stanley Spring many, many wondrous things, and Stanley had always ridden headlong into them until, one day, when riding away from a burning farmhouse, The Devil had grown sad and forlorn once more. The morning after, Stanley had awoken to find The Devil had ridden out and left him alive and with three saddle bags of money.

Stanley Spring had gathered his wealth and ridden out, heading back to his wife and home in the far east of Montana and, after two weeks journeying alone through a dense fog he came across the great plain within which Bel was situated.

He cantered into the town, intending to rest and to head out in the morning. It was here that Stan Spring's dream descended into nightmare as he recalled that, whenever he rode out of Bel to seek home, he always seemed to ride in a great circle and end up back where he started. Whichever mountain pass or prairie trail he took and no matter how tightly he plotted his travelling to the stars he always came back.

The last time he had arrived in the town was some months ago, and the dream he'd had the night Hobson Whitney had ridden in with news of the avenging Rickman

Chill was the first time Stanley Spring had thought about his past, and about where he was going.

He awoke under the whores to a tickling on his cheek. He brushed his face groggily and saw a hobo spider scamper off him and over a thigh, disappearing from view.

He sat up in shock at seeing the spider and looked around the room. The recollected dream was still clinging to him and refused to clear. He felt as though he had been in a waking sleep for months and was suddenly awaking from it. Stanley Spring looked on the decadence around him and winced at the sight. He scratched his head as the memories of his life before The Nameless returned and a panic set in. Why could he not leave? Why could he not find his way home?

"Am I in hell?" he whispered to the air.

One of the sleeping whores, lost in her dream, laughed loudly in her sleep before rolling onto her back and lolling her head over the edge of the bed. Stanley Spring felt a cold chill rush over him at the eerie laugh which seemed to answer his question.

A hobo spider appeared on the edge of the bed and crawled up over a body into the whore's mouth and she reflexively swallowed it without waking. Stanley Spring felt his eyes well up in self-pity at his soul's plight when he saw the horror.

—◦◦◦◦—

Conrad, asleep on the porch, had descended into a dream
of pure bright, summer light and still lake water, which was
too searing and too powerful for him to break away from.
The tranquillity and divinity his subconscious had created
made his spirit uneasy. It was too perfect a concoction and,
though he was too deeply asleep to wake up, he remained
by the lake unsure of his surroundings. He wanted the
waiting dead to appear, perhaps upon the lake, to usher
him, but they did not. The waiting dead left him alone.

Conrad shuffled uneasily in his chair and he did not
feel the hobo spider crawl across his face, through his hair,
down his back and into the house.

The arachnid made its way across the flat, smooth
hallway until it came to the stairs, whereupon it climbed
the banister spindle and up onto the banister rail. It
crawled quickly up the incline and halted at the top. Up
ahead it saw the open doorway to the moonlit bedroom.
The spider climbed off the banister rail and scuttled over
to the bedroom. It halted in the doorway and sensed its
surroundings.

It went first to the bed and climbed its way up the edge
of the hanging sheet until it found Maria's sleeping body,
whereupon it crawled up her foot and disappeared under
the hem of her dress.

Maria murmured and squirmed in her sleep as the
spider moved over her warm skin, up her leg, across her
sex, over her belly and up her chest until it came to her
neck where it rested to sense its surroundings once more.

Maria's breathing was laboured and slow as her dream was deep and calming. The spider crawled up her neck until it rested upon her cheek. The weight of it tickled her senses and she murmured again, clumsily brushed her hair and turned over onto her other side.

The spider, in a sudden rush of chaos, found itself propelled off her face, momentarily caught in the tangle of her hair before finding itself alive and safe on the pillow. Maria's face was millimetres from it.

The spider backed away from her, turned and continued on its journey. It crossed the pillow and climbed up onto the bedside table. It scurried along the surface and came to an edge. The spider climbed down the other side of the table until it felt another obstacle made of roach wood.

It climbed up over the top of Annabel's cot and ran along the edge until it had completed a circuit. Upon returning to its original position, the spider began to climb down the outside until it found itself upside down climbing through the cutaway handle and emerging on the inside of the cot.

Annabel was sleeping soundly when the hobo spider began to slowly explore the bedding of the cot. It crawled to her feet, reached out and felt them. Annabel squirmed in her sleep. The surface was soft and warm and the spider climbed up her foot where it rested, looking around. Annabel kicked her leg slightly and the spider hurried up to her belly before resting again. Annabel settled for a few moments. The spider moved up her chest and over her shoulder and onto the little pillow underneath her head where it came to rest. Annabel sighed and gurgled, turning over onto her side and crushing the arachnid with the side of her head.

———◦◦◦◦———

Rickman Chill did not stop riding until he knew that the horse could not continue. He had journeyed off the muddied road and descended deep into the woodland.

Rickman halted his steed and dismounted. He made camp and ate some of the leftover goose he had stored. The forest canopy was dense and the mist blocked out the night sky so he could not see the skies. He did not know what time of night it was and so decided to bed down and recover some energy.

He lay down and, confident that he was truly alone, he unbuckled his trousers, awkwardly placing his hand in his crotch; he clenched his jaw and retrieved a small rag. He opened and inspected it. It was stained with blood. He tutted, reached into his pocket and pulled out a rag of similar dimensions, folded it over and placed it between his legs, wincing slightly in discomfort as he did so. He threw the dirty rag on the campfire and watched it burn.

He rolled a cigarette, lit it and let the infusion of tobacco and its sedative effects wash through him. He was totally alone. Conrad was not sleeping nearby. Hobson and Fraser were dead and The Devil still roamed the lands. It was exactly how it had been before the day he decided to ride back to Mary and Obadiah's house and recruit Conrad.

The cigarette smoke arced into the air and his eyes fogged over with the nostalgic pain that his solitude always brought on. He didn't flinch when the hobo spider crawled over his legs and off into the dark woodland.

CHAPTER THIRTY-FIVE
The Forlorn Horse

Maria woke from her deep sleep moments before dawn. Her head ached slightly and she felt drained. It took her a few moments to remember why she felt so exhausted. She gently brushed the pillow and felt the slight dampness where her tears had not yet dried. The dawn had eased her pain somewhat and she felt a different person.

She rolled over, picked up Annabel's cot and placed it on her lap so that she could gaze upon her daughter while she mentally prepared for the day ahead. She knew the two men were leaving her and that her dream of a bright future was exactly that: a dream. She resigned herself to a life of solitude, growing old while her daughter grew up into a young woman who would no doubt leave her as everyone else had done and ride off to seek her fortune.

She tickled her daughter's cheek as she considered her bleak future. Annabel rolled onto her side, reaching out in her sleep to grab Maria's finger, which pleased her greatly. Her heart told her that, while she would be alone, she would not be unloved; the solitude of her oncoming old age would not be without the bright years her daughter would give her.

She noticed the remains of the spider, crushed by Annabel in her sleep and Maria carefully lifted the baby out of the cot, so that she could wash the lining. She took Annabel in her arms and went downstairs, determined to make it through the remaining hours that she had company in the house with a strong will and a good heart.

Maria relined the cot with a clean rag she found in a kitchen drawer and, while the pot of coffee was brewing, she went to the living room to begin preparing each room for the day. She stopped in the doorway to the side room first and looked upon the sleeping Conrad. She did not enter to open the curtains and wake him, as she intended to sugar that pill with a fresh mug of coffee. Instead she leaned against the doorframe and watched him for a few moments, sleeping peacefully with one hand behind his head, the other across his chest. His clothes and hat were folded neatly in the corner of the room next to his boots. He had not cleaned the floor and his footprints were still visible from where he had awoken on the porch a few hours earlier and groggily moved into the warmer house.

Maria had only a few hours left with him in the house and so she blew him a kiss, as she might have done every time she saw him, if he were to stay with her.

She turned from the doorway and went to the living room where she expected to see Rickman, asleep in the rocking chair, fully clothed. He was not there. Maria frowned, went in and opened the curtains thinking that the man might be out in the yard. He was not. Only Azazel roamed around grazing and bleating a good morning when he saw her at the window. Maria waved and waved Annabel's little hand also.

She was turning from the window when she noticed the small piece of paper on the mantelpiece. She knew every inch of the house so even the slightest change in the environment was a warning bell.

She picked up the paper and saw that it was addressed to Conrad. She looked through the doorway to him still sleeping, opened the letter and read it. Despite the letter's revelations, Maria looked upon them with a detached, academic eye. Upon completion, she quickly folded the letter, pocketed it, and rushed to the kitchen to take the kettle off the boil and prepare the coffee for the sleeping man.

Rickman Chill was already riding when the dawn sun broke through the canopy of trees. The woodland was dense and treacherous, yet Rickman pushed his horse forward with a tenacious zeal. He had slept remarkably soundly for one about to ride into certain death. Rickman feared The Nameless greatly and had made excuses not to return until there were none left to make. He was heading back to face *him* and was less well armed than the one and only time he had done so before.

He knew that there was little hope of survival, but what little hope there was, he held onto and nurtured until it blossomed into another hope: perhaps The Devil himself would be in Bel too. That eventuality was even more unlikely as The Devil, it seemed, never returned to the same place twice. Still, Rickman knew if he could hold hope that he could survive Bel, then he could hold hope that The Devil was there too. The power of his belief and the taste of his destiny forced him to drive the horse onward.

It was late morning when, suddenly, the treeline broke into a solemn, mist-covered clearing. The grass was tall and swayed gently. Rickman wanted to halt at the edge so that he could survey the sudden and eerie change of scenery. The fog within the clearing was thick and hung low.

The horse, however, did not want to wait, and cantered straight into the mist as if it had sensed something, or had suddenly lost all sense of self preservation. Rickman leaned in close to the horse's ear and whispered for him to stop, patting his neck and trying to soothe him, thinking that the horse had gone mad. It did not work and the horse walked on until the mist had fallen all around them both and Rickman could not even see his glove when he stretched out his hand.

Suddenly, the horse stopped, neighed and began to circle around on the spot. Rickman drew his pistol ready for whatever leapt out of the fog. He squinted and focused as the horse walked around and around.

Just ahead, the shape appeared. The horse stopped moving and Rickman drew on the shape. It was a large, black mass that lacked a definite form and was moving towards them. Rickman cocked the gun, aiming it on the middle of shape.

As it slowly approached, its shape began to form into something more recognisable; a horse. Rickman lifted the gun from the direction of the horse and to the position he knew the rider's body to be. His own horse did not panic. It stood motionless, breathing steadily. The other horse came closer through the mist and Rickman was about to call a warning to the rider when the horse appeared fully and sidled up to them. There was no rider. Rickman made safe his pistol and holstered it as the two animals reacquainted themselves. He looked over and recognised the saddle and saddle bags. It was Conrad's horse.

Rickman dismounted and, cautiously as the uneasy air in the clearing was still present, walked around the horse until he came to the saddle bags. He opened them and reached inside.

Everything he had left behind was still there. He pulled out some tobacco, some bullets and rudimentary medical supplies which appeared to have diminished, and some whisky. He loaded the appropriated goods into his own saddle bags before turning back to Conrad's horse and regarding its face. The animal's eyes looked sad and lost, as if it had been somewhere and was struggling to recall it. Rickman knew instantly that the animal had made its way to Bel, quite by chance, and then wandered through it.

He stroked the animal and rested his head against its muzzle, told it that he was sorry and that the strangeness of Bel would always be inside him. He told the horse that it had seen too much and to be free and not to the think of its past.

He stood back from the sad horse and mounted his own. The other horse stood where he was. Rickman shouted for it to leave and he stretched out with his boot to spur the animal. It had no effect. Rickman turned his own horse to face the direction the wandering beast had come from, thinking the path would lead straight to Bel. He tipped his hat to the other horse and rode on. He turned back after a few yards, hoping to see the animal wandering off. Instead, he heard it neigh forlornly before it slowly lay down on its side, probably for the last time.

The contents of Rickman's letter had rattled Maria and she stood in the kitchen, leaning against the counter reading it and re-reading it, trying to understand if her eyes or her mind were playing tricks on her. The implications were great.

Finally, she pocketed the letter in her apron and took a mug to Conrad's room where she found him just waking up. She did not lean on the post and blow him a kiss and, when he yawned and stretched and smiled upon seeing her she did not smile back. Instead she walked into the room, placed the mug on the floor next to him and flung the curtains open, blasting the bright light into the room and causing him to shield his eyes. He took the coffee and stood up to stretch again.

"Thank you ma'am," he said, trying to gauge her mood. Maria gave nothing away, and looked out of the window. Conrad stood beside her to take in the view.

"We ride out in a few hours ma'am," he said, looking out of the corner of his eye to see if it meant anything to her. Maria shrugged.

"Sure will miss this place."

Nothing. Conrad hung his head.

"Sure will miss you, ma'am." He went to put his hand on her shoulder but Maria, sensing the incoming contact, stepped out of his reach and went to the doorway.

"Well then ma'am," said Conrad, taking the hint and adapting his tone accordingly. He picked up his shirt and hat.

"You have been kind," he said as if she were a waitress and had served him a serviceable meal. Maria turned from the doorway and nodded her acceptance of his thanks, still with blank eyes. Conrad walked passed her.

"Won't bother you much longer ma'am. Goodbye."

And he walked out of the house, onto the porch where he expected to find Rickman waiting. He was not there.

"Boss?" he called out, loudly. "Let's go."

There was no answer. Conrad looked around. Azazel was happily grazing by the fence and paid him no mind. Conrad stepped off the porch and went to the barn where he saw no horse and no saddle. He looked to the floor and saw the tracks leading out of the barn, towards the ridge and beyond.

"Son of a bitch," he whispered incredulously. He stepped out of the barn and stood in the yard. Maria was on the porch looking at Conrad who seemed suddenly so lost in confusion and abandonment. She looked down at Annabel and smiled, daring to think that now, perhaps, he was not going to leave them. She dared to believe that she had rescued her fantasy from the clutches of oblivion.

She stepped off the porch and walked over to him, letting the warm sun filter into her and imbue her walk with a touch of happiness.

Conrad turned to her and stepped up. Maria smiled and looked at him, preparing herself to fall into his arms and start their life.

Conrad cricked his neck, leaned forward and kissed Annabel on the forehead.

"Goodbye," he whispered. Maria's smile fell away. Conrad stood up to face her, his eyes blank and distant. He tipped his hat.

"Ma'am," he said. Conrad walked out of the compound, intending to follow Rickman Chill on foot. Maria stood in shock and despair as her chance of a future walked away, stopping at the ridge in an all too familiar pose before disappearing behind it and leaving her all alone.

CHAPTER THIRTY-SIX
The Return

Conrad had lost the trail of Rickman's horse after trudging throughout the day and into the evening. He was exhausted, his strength depleting faster than normal due to the stress his body had endured over the past week.

However, two strange and unwelcome feelings had been brewing inside him since he had left Maria's house: doubt and guilt.

At first he attributed his doubt in actually finding Rickman to the oppressive nature of the woods. The foliage was thick, the air heavy and the ground wet and slippery. He had many times fallen down ditches and into pot holes as he pressed onwards. After a few hours, the doubt began to switch its attack to his morale and started targeting his motivation. The farther away from Maria he walked, the more he started to realise that he should not have left, and the less painful the idea of abandoning Rickman became. Every step forward seemed to cast him more and more into a wilderness of doubt. Still, he pressed on.

It wasn't until the sun began to set and the darkness started to envelop the woodlands that the danger became apparent. He was far, far from Maria's, and about to start stumbling blindly in the dark hoping to catch some luck and find something to point him towards Rickman. By the time the sun had set completely, Conrad was hopelessly lost. The trail had gone cold and he was faced with the harsh reality a foolhardy one faces when the bare truth finally becomes clear.

He looked around. He could see nothing. He reached out and felt nothing. The panic began to settle in and he reached into his pocket for his match book. He struck a match and held it out. The shadows lurched at him and he instinctively ducked, shocked at the sudden proximity of the twisted and grasping branches. He turned around, holding the match out to desperately try and latch onto a location that would offer some hope. Endless trees, branches and ferns. The match burnt down to his finger and he dropped it in pain, plunging himself back into the utter darkness. He scooted down and felt around the ground. It was soft and mossy. He sat down for a few moments to gather his thoughts.

Hobson Whitney walked out of the saloon and stood in the main street. The fug of opiates and tobacco had ransacked his senses and he could no longer perceive any sense of cohesion between mind, and reality. The drunken and mad residents of Bel danced and whirled around him, content and delirious in their never-ending spirals of madness. He smiled at them, thinking that he was dreaming and they were his own constructs, but none smiled back. They just cackled and laughed to themselves as they danced on. He waved at them, his arm flapping like a child's and his eyes lost. He touched the wound on his face and it tingled.

The air in the street was fresh, and as he stood there, his senses began to reorder themselves somewhat. He could not remember how he came to be in the street, let alone in the town, but he could remember why. He looked down the street and out towards the dark plain from whence he had ridden in.

"Rickman is coming," he said to himself, suddenly flushed with fear of the whirlwind the man would bring, and guilt at having betrayed him. The madness of the town was fogging his mind completely. He needed more air. He needed to leave the town and, suddenly flushed with mortal fear and dread, he revitalised his senses and made his way towards the edge of town.

———∞———

From the window of the bordello, Stanley Spring watched the mad Hobson Whitney firstly stumble out into the street and then turn and dash towards the end of Main Street. He knew what was coming next, as it had happened to him many times. Hobson reached the end of the road and his powerful stride slowed down to a walk to and finally to a slow shuffle.

Stanley Spring rested against the window frame and smoked while he watched Hobson stop walking and look around, like a man confused or a man who had forgotten an event or article. Hobson patted himself down and looked at a pocket watch that wasn't there. Slowly, he turned around and shuffled back along Main Street.

Stanley Spring watched the man as he wove through the crowds of Bel residents who also once had intended to only pass through the town and had, like him and Hobson Whitney, become unable to leave.

The lost man wove through the crowd and re-entered the hotel. Stanley Spring stubbed his cigarette out on the ledge and turned back to the room full of naked, sleeping people. Though they were totally lost, Stanley Spring still held onto the fading glimmer of memory that assured him of where he was, and reminded him of the futility of the place. Bel was a place in which memory was cast aside and as such, there was no escape. He left the window ledge and climbed back into the pile of bodies to sleep.

Conrad walked towards the house, the moonlight guiding him, the wind easing his tension. He was home. He entered the compound and the goat bounded up to him, finally accepting him into the fold and nuzzling him affectionately. Conrad reached down and stroked the goat before walking on to the porch where he could make out the shape of Maria, rocking gently and holding her daughter. His heart was calm and his mind at peace. She smiled when she saw him, but she did not get up from her chair; she simply lilted her head to the side to rest it on the back of the chair and just looked at him. He stepped onto the porch.

"I'm home," he said, smiling at her.

Maria smiled and went to speak but instead of words, a torrent of hobo spiders fell from her mouth, tumbling over her baby and lap and scurrying madly over the porch.

Conrad was rooted in fear. Her eyes were black and he could see her hair moving in waves as a thousand more spiders crawled through it. Her hands fell to the side, revealing a large nest of spiders where Annabel should have been. It broke apart, sending its inhabitants in every direction. Conrad opened his mouth to scream.

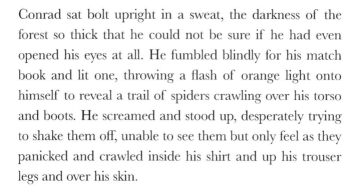

Conrad sat bolt upright in a sweat, the darkness of the forest so thick that he could not be sure if he had even opened his eyes at all. He fumbled blindly for his match book and lit one, throwing a flash of orange light onto himself to reveal a trail of spiders crawling over his torso and boots. He screamed and stood up, desperately trying to shake them off, unable to see them but only feel as they panicked and crawled inside his shirt and up his trouser legs and over his skin.

Conrad woke up from his dream within a dream in an even madder panic, his fear alone dragging him up from the depths of his nightmares.

The night was passing and a blue hue had fallen. He could see a few metres all around him, and the relief was glorious.

He got to his feet and dusted himself off. The nightmare had terrified him and so, upon waking, he knew in the depths of his heart that he could not ignore its meaning. He put his hat on, tightened his belt, and began to walk back the way he came, desperate to find the road that lead back to Maria's: the road that led to the way home.

The morning did not halt the debauchery in Bel. Stanley Spring left his room and walked across the middle landing, looking down to the saloon below where whores still hustled and card players still cheated. Through the murky windows, he could see that the dancers had at least calmed their mania and were now just pleasantly waltzing.

He walked down the staircase, stepping over the bodies of those who had gone too far and had fallen into comatose slumbers. He walked up to the bar and picked up a bottle of whisky; the barman, with a lost look in his eyes, barely noticed. Stanley Spring looked around and saw Hobson Whitney standing by the window, staring out of it, his eyes squinting, clearly in deep thought. Stanley Spring knew what was going through his mind. He knew that Hobson was trying to come to terms with the enthralling power of Bel. He walked over and stood beside him, offering a drink. Hobson took it.

"Where am I? Is this hell?" he asked quietly.

"Somewhere in between," replied Stanley, "a place where you forget if you don't want to, and remember when you try and forget."

"How do you get out of here?"

"I know of one way… , but, do you really want to leave?" said Stanley. "Look around you."

Hobson looked around at the bodies and carnal delights readily on offer. He turned back to the window, his mind split with indecision.

"I don't know. I'm just so tired," he said, resting his head on the glass. "I want to see my brother again."

"This Rickman, is he one to forget?"

Hobson sniggered. "He's been tracking The Devil for twenty one years. He don't forget."

"Then," said Stanley, patting him on the shoulder, "you'll see your brother very soon. Hell, might see if I can meet him myself."

Hobson watched Stanley as he smiled and sauntered off across the bar to the staircase. He turned back and held his arms out, smiling.

"It's the only way I know to get out of here," and he walked back upstairs and into the side room. Hobson sat in the chair by the window and looked out into the street, waiting to see the dark rider appear on the horizon with his avenging whirlwind in his wake.

Maria slept like the dead, which is exactly how she felt. When Annabel was feeding, Maria held little love nor warmth. The fireside did not comfort her and whenever she looked at the empty chair in the living room with the guitar resting next to it, she felt nothing.

After Conrad had left, Maria had returned to the automated routine of life that she had not enjoyed since Annabel had been born.

Maria drank her coffee and ate alone, setting a place opposite her for the partner who was not there. She enjoyed her afternoon smoke and didn't bother to waft the fumes away from Annabel. She cleared away the sheets from the side room and swept the floor; she had washed her bed sheets with barely a thought to anything at all.

And it was late afternoon when she installed herself in the rocking chair on the porch to stuff her pipe for her wildcard smoke, and to await the shadows from the trees to arrive and cast their welcome and missed impressions over the house.

She placed Annabel beside the chair, lit her pipe, rested her head against the rail, and closed her eyes to let the flavour of the tobacco and its sedative effects do their work.

She exhaled and opened her eyes. She stopped rocking when she looked to the ridge. Her heart skipped a beat and, slowly, she stood up.

There was a man on the ridge, silhouetted in the twilight. She stepped off the porch, feeling as if she were in a dream. She stepped out into the yard and walked to the gate, stopping only there as she did not want to step out of the bounds of her home. The silhouette began walking towards her.

Maria cupped her hand over her brow to shield her eyes from the sunbeams and she could not stop herself from thinking, '*He has come home, he has come home, he has come home.*'

What surprised her most, and made her heart beat so fast was that, when the silhouette was revealed to be Conrad and not her lover of old, she felt even more renewed.

Conrad walked towards the gate, removed his hat and let the sunlight fall against his face. He could see Maria and she was smiling at him. Conrad walked up to Maria and, flecked with the twilight sunbeams, they did not greet each other by any other means than that of a deep and longing embrace. Conrad had come home. Maria's fantasy was alive and it was no dream.

CHAPTER THIRTY-SEVEN
Back to Bel

Rickman's horse had begun to slow even though the terrain was more manageable than it had been throughout the day. There were fewer bogs and ditches, fewer slippery boulders and rocks, and the branches appeared to have risen up their trunks so that Rickman did not have to bend low to pass under them.

Indeed, even the width between the trees had stretched slightly so his horse could easily navigate his way. It seemed as if everything was stretching thin: the trees and foliage, the air, and even the sense of youthful energy that Montana exuded had fallen back.

What had replaced it was an overwhelming sense of sadness in everything. The leaves wilted and appeared ashen. The bark was cracked and peeling and the trees moaned and sighed in the wind. It was the melancholy of nostalgia, or more accurately, it was the melancholy of fading nostalgia. As if he was riding to the edge of the world and was forgetting who he was. He knew he was close to Bel.

As the horse slowed, he knew he would have to dismount and lead it as far as he could. It was obvious that he could not lead it all the way into the town, and he had no desire to. Bel was a prison and if one, man or beast, were to make it out alive, they would be forever changed more often than not lost in a fog of memory, unable to grasp where they were going or why. He had seen it in Conrad's horse and he had seen it in himself, twenty years previously when he had escaped the clutches of the town but at great cost.

He attributed his recollection of it, although buried and turned into fuel for his mission, to his fearsome determination to track and cut down The Devil. Only the most focused of men break out of Bel and retain their grasp of things. Rickman Chill was one such man. Heading back into Bel after such an achievement? Rickman Chill was the only one. All others had been pulled back in by its power; Rickman went back of his own volition and with blood on his mind.

He pushed a fern leaf aside and was presented with a sting of remembrance. There was a bent and sad tree ahead, quite like the multitudes around. But this one had a connection with Chill that forked through him like lightning when he saw its twisted trunk. He patted his horse's head and whispered for it to stop a moment and catch its breath. It neighed, and Rickman cautiously walked towards the tree, ever keen for possible traps. He took his glove off and ran his fingers over the base of the trunk and closed his eyes.

He had lain against that tree, twenty years earlier, gasping for air and holding onto the last embers of fire in his spirit. He remembered how his naked body had glistened red in the moonlight as he lay there, clutching himself. He remembered the exhaustion and the need to sleep, and as he lifted his hands up over the place where his head had once rested, he counted two sections of missing bark, recalling the bullets that had thundered into them, banishing his need to sleep and awakening his need to live.

Rickman looked around and saw the direction the bullets had come from. From his pursuers chasing him deep into the forest.

He stood back from the tree and marvelled that it still stood and still bore its scars. He was getting close.

He whistled to his horse to follow him and walked past the tree, retracing the staggers and scrambles from his desperate escape from Bel twenty years earlier.

He came to a rock he knew. It was smooth and half buried in the ground, rising up to his knees and round enough for him to reach around and touch his fingers. He looked at its surface and found a sharp, upward scrape. He stood next to this, took his hat off, pulled his hair up from his neck and fingered a long scar. He remembered the moment the bullet had ricocheted up off the rock and caught the back of his head, knocking him forward and causing him to land on the ground and strike his head on a smaller rock.

He bent down in the space where it had happened and pulled up the moss around him. Sure enough, there was a rock with a jagged edge that mirrored the scar across his forehead perfectly.

He smiled at the miraculous preservation of the event. It felt like the area was a living museum projected straight from his subconscious.

He stood up and walked on for fifty yards, coming across more bullet marks in trees, and more branches and rocks that had struck him in his escape.

After fifty more yards he broke from the treeline and stopped. He was in a clearing, similar to the one in which he had met Conrad's horse, but far, far greater in size. The grass was waist high and stretched out into the gloom, the mist low and blue as the moonlight fell into it, but not penetrating all the way down to the ground. Rickman Chill felt like he was at the very end of the world. He bent down and touched the ground.

The Nameless had beaten and mutilated Rickman's body almost beyond recognition and he was presently lying in a room in the bordello looking up at the ceiling, the pain morphing from intense burning to a dull ache that wooed him to sleep like a lullaby.

Rickman gurgled and tried to talk but the words did not come. He turned his head and looked at the lamp on the floor, its flame golden and flickering, dazzling his eyes like the gates of heaven calling him home. He reached out for the lamp and saw a boot come resting down on his wrists, the pain pulling him back from the brink and into the room.

He turned his head back to the chandelier to see The Nameless standing over him. He was young, handsome, with green eyes that shone brightly. He was holding a large bone-handled knife and it was dripping blood onto Rickman's face. The Nameless knelt down over Rickman and traced the tip of the blade over his face, down his scarred neck, over his body causing him to wince, and down to his genitals. Rickman's eyes began to well up and his fingers worked across the carpet to try and grab the lamp.

"What can I say," whispered The Nameless in a sweet voice. "You have been fun, but you see revenge – revenge is a man's game."

Rickman felt the knife pierce into his inner thigh and his eyes bulged. The knife was about to start slicing its way up his leg when, in a last ditch effort, he managed to grab hold of the lamp and swing it round, shattering it over the left side of The Nameless' face causing him to scream in pain and fall to the side.

Like an enraged animal released from its cage, Rickman leapt and landed on top of The Nameless, their positions reversed.

He screamed like a beast and rammed the base of the lamp into The Nameless' face, twisting and dragging it until the glass had fallen out completely.

The Nameless gurgled and struggled, but Rickman was feral. He threw the lamp to one side and buried his face into The Nameless' wound, tearing at his flesh and muscle with his teeth.

The Nameless had been at the point of death when, from outside the door his men, awoken from their strange internal swirl, opened up their guns and began blasting their way into the room.

Rickman dived off the wounded man, and scrambled across the floor as debris and glass fell everywhere. He got to the window just as the men outside burst through the door to see The Nameless on the floor convulsing and gurgling, and the maimed Rickman Chill by the window. They raised their guns to fire, but Rickman threw himself through the glass and fell the twenty feet onto the ground below. The dancers carried on dancing, as nothing changes in Bel, not even the seasons. The men got to the window and looked out. Rickman was lost underneath the crowd. They raced out of the room to find him.

Rickman Chill, operating on a primal drive for self-preservation, although mutilated and beaten, crawled through the legs of the dancing madmen and women of Bel until he got to the end of Main Street, where he kept on going, losing himself deep in the long grass and headed for the treeline.

The men soon burst out of the saloon and into the street. They pushed through the town, firing in the air to clear people away until they got to the edge of Main Street where they suddenly stopped, forgetting why they were there. They turned back to see The Nameless in the window of the hotel. He motioned them forward and, as if suddenly reminded of their urgent charge, they began to comb the plain that stretched out in every direction from the town.

Rickman crawled on his belly, scratching and tearing even more flesh from him, yet still he kept going until he reached the treeline. As soon as he did, he stood up and began to stagger into the darkness. It was then that they saw him and the bullets came ever nearer to Rickman as he scrambled into the darkness.

That was twenty years ago and much had changed. Not least his appearance. Rickman Chill stood up from the grass and put his gloves back on, the memory of his ordeal burning brightly. He knew where he was.

He turned back and told his horse to stay where it was and that, if he did not come back not to come for him, but to ride back to Conrad and Maria and be with them. The horse neighed in understanding and backed into the dark woodland, relieved to not have to venture out into the grassland.

Rickman tipped his hat to the animal and turned to face the mist. He checked his guns.

As if on cue, the fog rose and cleared, and Rickman was presented with his destination. The plain stretched ahead for many, many miles until it hit a giant horseshoe of unnamed and unchartered mountains.

He ran his hands over the tops of the grass and waited for a few seconds. The mist shimmered slightly and he cocked an assured smile. Bel appeared in the mist. It was lying perhaps a mile ahead. Though no sound carried from it, he could see the lights on and he knew The Nameless was there. The Devil was itinerant but The Nameless was not.

Rickman Chill took a moment to document every injury and violation the The Nameless had wrought upon him, and the twenty subsequent years he had lived in fear of ever returning that had led him to this point. Rickman Chill was ready to bring his whirlwind of vengeance upon the town, and before The Nameless' last breath fell from his body, he knew that his screams would have told The Devil who was coming for him.

Rickman Chill began to walk through the tall grass to the town of Bel, alone and armed for the second time.

CHAPTER THIRTY-EIGHT
Ghosts of the Past

As soon as Conrad had entered the compound and closed the gate behind him, the sun fell behind the horizon and the nighttime was upon them. Maria walked beside Conrad waiting to brush her hand against his so that he might entwine his fingers in hers, but the courage to do so never came to her.

She looked at him as they walked side by side up to the house. She could tell that he was happy to be home, but that he also carried a great sadness that he had abandoned Chill. She knew that their bond was a deep one, stronger than that of mere friends or fellow riders. The two riders were joined in destiny.

They entered the house and Conrad went immediately to the side room, laid his belongings on the floor and removed his boots so that he could feel the welcome touch of the boards upon his tired feet.

Maria looked at him from the doorway, knowing that his room should really be her bedroom but, again, not being able to find the courage just yet to take him by the hand and lead him up there.

He folded and patted his clothes and looked over to Maria. They smiled at each other. Conrad stood up and was about to walk to her when a fierce wind began to rattle the window pane, seep under the frame and billow the curtains.

Maria held Annabel tight and stepped into the room, looking around at the walls as the wind thundered against them all around. The temperature in the room dropped suddenly and their breath became visible. Maria wrapped her shawl around Annabel, stepped out of the side room and went into the kitchen to prepare some food.

The wind outside did not die down and the temperature remained freezing in every room. Maria and Conrad sat at the table and ate the last of the roasted goose, all the time looking at each other and trying to hold onto the glory of their dream despite the all-pervading chill wind.

Conrad finished and pushed his plate to one side. Maria also finished and stacked her plate upon his. She reached into the side cupboard to retrieve a bottle of whisky.

She poured two large glasses, and together they clinked and drank them down in one go, again keeping their eyes upon each other and thinking ahead to the moment they decided to go to bed, and the conundrum that was sure to present.

Who would go where? Would one expect to go with the other? What arrangement would be made? They drank down their whisky at the same time and placed the glasses on the table next to each other.

Maria poured a second glass and, as she handed Conrad's to him, she found the courage to let her finger rub against his and rest its tip upon his knuckle. She maintained eye contact and smiled. He smiled back, and rubbed his finger along the palm of her hand.

He was about to take his drink when an ominous creak filtered down from upstairs. Their smiles dropped slightly as they heard the noise.

Maria removed her finger from Conrad's and sat back against her chair. The creak came again. Directly above them. They looked up to the ceiling. Another creak. Footsteps. Maria made as if to stand up, but Conrad halted her with a silent wave of his hand.

Without taking his eyes from the ceiling, he slowly stood up and drew his pistols. The creaking continued. Maria, suddenly cold with fear, dragged Annabel's cot across the table closer to her.

Conrad, luckily without boots, moved silently across the kitchen. Maria wanted to follow, but his stern eyes told her to stay put. He hung by the doorway, half sunken in shadow, looking up the staircase, his gun leading him. The creaking continued.

He squinted in the darkness, trying to make out any movement in the gloom up ahead. He could see the top of the stairs, and the doorway to Maria's bedroom beyond. The moonlight shone through her bedroom window in one perfect shaft, falling against the wardrobes on the wall opposite.

The creaking came again. He quickly pointed his pistol to the other end of the landing and to the dark doorway of the second bedroom.

Conrad quietly cocked the weapon. He saw a dark mass at the doorway, moving slowly. He started to shout a warning, but no words came out. Only his frozen breath.

He lowered his gun slightly as the dark mass walked into the light on the landing. It seemed to be a woman in a white nightdress, walking slowly and silently, save for the creak of her footsteps.

Conrad watched in astonishment as the figure walked into Maria's bedroom. Just as she did, the wardrobe door opened of its own volition and the figure calmly stepped inside. The air hung deathly still for a few minutes before the wardrobe door slammed itself shut.

Conrad jumped backwards, the colour draining from his face. He turned from the doorway to see Maria, terrified and clutching the baby close to her.

"Stay here," he whispered, before raising his gun and ascending the staircase.

Rickman Chill approached the town purposefully, but not headstrong. His eyes, as ever, were keen and alert, scanning the environment, ready for any surprise. The Nameless was in that town somewhere and there were two ways he could flush him out.

He could walk into the main square and start shooting. The Nameless would then appear almost instantly, however he risked turning the population of mad debauchers into a town-strong posse of armed defenders.

His second option was one of stealth. He could walk amongst the dancers and fornicators, seek a room in the saloon and, from there, take surveillance of the town. Perhaps capture one of the residents and beat The Nameless' location out of them.

He approached the top of Main Street and stepped up onto the boardwalk, hiding close to the walls and blending into the shadows. He waited at the very end of the town for a few moments, inspecting the lively street and boardwalks. The people danced still, and the Chinese lanterns swayed in the breeze.

Slowly, he began to walk up the boardwalk, his guts churning with a mix of fear and rage that were hard to suppress. He needed to calm himself.

He soon came to the saloon. He looked through the murky window and grimaced at the sight. It was as if he had never left. The same people drank and gambled and the same whores draped themselves over drinkers and furniture alike. He looked up at the landings where yet more whores walked up and down, intermittently throwing great handfuls of rose petals from large wooden bowls down onto the revellers below.

Rickman took a moment to calm and repress his memories of the last time he was there. He would have to face them fully soon enough and he knew it was only good to do so if he was facing The Nameless at the same time. He settled himself and stepped into the bar, his entrance not announced or bold, but simply as if he had walked through the saloon doors every day since the town of Bel had existed.

Rickman walked through the throng of people who paid no attention to him whatsoever, but he did not relax. He came to the staircase and stepping over a drunk, he ascended.

In the far corner, almost buried under a whore in a huge dress, Hobson Whitney sensed a change in the room, like the sudden remembrance of a forgotten task or detail.

"Rickman Chill," he whispered as if he had suddenly recalled the name from a long forgotten time in his life.

As soon as the words left his mouth, the candles flickered and a chill wind fell through the interior of the saloon.

From under the window pane, Hobson saw what appeared to be a dark shadow filter into the air. The candles flickered more intensely and the chandeliers rocked, causing the shadow to grow and swill as it circled the room before slipping over the banister of the middle landing and disappearing through the cracks of a door.

Conrad's gun hand was steady, but a cold sweat stood upon his brow. The chill air had sunken into his core and his dread was palpable.

'*What devilry is this? What evil is within?*' he thought over and over again as he slowly walked up the staircase.

He stood at the top, staring into Maria's bedroom bathed in the shaft of silver moonlight. He did not want to enter and it was not through any sense of propriety. Death was in that room, that much was obvious.

He looked back down the stairs. Maria was there, holding Annabel and looking to Conrad for protection and reassurance. It stirred his heart, and his spirit was renewed enough to step into the room.

The wooden floorboards were unnaturally cold and they creaked loudly as he entered. He walked towards the cupboard, turning his back on the window and casting his shadow over the doorway. His breath was icy but steady and he reached out for the handle. The door creaked without him touching it, and slowly it opened, the darkness still clinging to the interior.

At the foot of the stairs, Maria began to feel increasingly unsafe. As Conrad had stepped into the room, he had moved from her sight. She did not want to be downstairs on her own, feeling that her own house was turning against her and giving rise to a great evil. She gripped the banister and slowly walked up the stairs.

Conrad held on to the door and opened it fully, letting the moonlight illuminate the interior. He saw a poncho and a hat, hung up neatly facing him, as if it were the shell of a person.

Maria reached the top of the stairs to see Conrad standing in her room, holding open the door to her cupboard. She froze. He had found the clothes of her lover.

Inside the room, Conrad reached out to touch the poncho. Maria stepped towards the doorway. His finger brushed the fabric and as it did, he saw a pale, fragile hand appear from behind the poncho and pull it to the side.

Conrad gasped and leapt backwards just as a sudden and fierce gust of wind blew the bedroom door shut on Maria.

Conrad stumbled, falling onto his back and scrambling away on his hands and heels until he hit the back of the bed.

Maria grabbed the handle and forced the door open a few inches before a great and unseen force slammed against it from the inside, pushing it closed and nearly sending her tumbling down the staircase.

Conrad looked up at the wardrobe in abject terror as the apparition of Liza stood before him, dressed in her night dress, her flame red hair lank and pulled back over her porcelain skin, her eyes like those of the waiting dead who populated his dreams. Conrad was too terrified to speak

Conrad's eyes flooded with tears as he saw a trickle of blood appear around Liza's ankles.

"My belly hurts, Conrad," she painfully whispered.

Conrad screamed. The wardrobe door slammed shut and the bedroom door flew open, letting Maria tumble into the room. She stood there, frozen in shock to see Conrad, white as the dead, resting against the bed, eyes fixed on the wardrobe.

The chill air fell away. Maria fearfully bent down and touched Conrad on the shoulder. He turned to her slowly.

Maria saw absolute terror in his eyes. She went to touch his hand, but she could not, as he was rubbing the knuckles of his right hand with great force.

CHAPTER THIRTY-NINE
The Absolving Bath

Conrad sat rubbing his hand for what seemed like hours. Although there was moonlight in the room, there were no stars and Maria could not tell the time. Still, she did not leave the man's side. When she had realised that she could not prise his hands apart, she had decided instead to just sit next to him and run her fingers through his hair, not even needing to seek the courage to touch him.

The wind had died down and stillness was returning to the house. She looked over the bed and out of the window in the black night, the moonbeams dissipating into the ever present mist. Time had left the place. Had it even ever been there? Maria did not know.

Eventually, and without warning, Conrad stood up and climbed onto the bed, his eyes fixed forward and unblinking. Maria rested her head on the edge of the bed and ran her hand over his arm. She found his wrist and touched his skin. He was cold. Eventually, Maria stood up and looked at him. He had fallen asleep. She leaned over him and pulled the curtains closed, dulling the light into the room. She kissed her finger and touched his forehead before leaving the room and closing the door behind her.

She walked downstairs and entered the living room, unsure of what she should do. She was tired, but could not bring herself to lie next to him, nor lie on the cold floor in the living room. She was restless and so she sat in her rocking chair, placed Annabel in the wooden cot by her side, pulled her tobacco pouch from her apron and, instead of stuffing her pipe, she began to roll a cigarette in the way that Conrad did. Before lighting it, she reached into Annabel's cot and took Miss Kiss from her, holding her tightly while she lit her cigarette, and looked at the empty chair and the guitar resting against the wall. The tobacco helped greatly in calming her nerves and dispelling the fear she had felt earlier. She rocked and smoked and did not notice that the clock on the mantle had stopped working.

Rickman Chill bolted the door of the hotel bedroom and rested his forehead against it, allowing himself a few moments to reconcile his relief at making it thus far without exploding into fear or rage or both.

He looked through the keyhole. A few people milled about on the landing, but nobody seemed to care about him. Rickman suddenly felt safe. Remarkably so. As if he had finally come home after a long and arduous journey.

He turned from the doorway and looked at the room. Directly opposite the door there was a large double window with heavy velvet curtains that hung all the way from the ceiling and gathered in a pile on the floor. The walls were a matching deep red. There was a dresser with a mirror upon it on the right hand side wall and opposite that, there was a large double bed, freshly made and inviting but the centrepiece of the room was the large slipper shaped copper bathtub. It had a steep back, a wide, lazy brim and was filled with hot water with rose petals floating across the surface. Rickman remembered just exactly how long he had been in the wilderness. He looked over to the mirrors upon the walls. The steam from the bath slowly fogged over everything, including Rickman Chill.

The aroma of vanilla and eucalyptus infusions filled his nostrils. The bath was more than intoxicating.

He stepped towards it, feeling the steam touch his face, warming him then cooling his skin as it turned into perspiration. He ran his fingers over the edge of the bath, losing all sense of himself and of his mission. He was hypnotised by the light glinting off the copper rim and the shimmering water. He touched the surface and smiled as the ripples floated outwards and disturbed the rose petals like row boats caught in a storm. He plunged his hand in deeper, the warm water grabbing hold of his senses.

He pulled his arm from the water and walked over slowly to the window and closed the curtains, turning back to the room. He took off his collar and dropped it absentmindedly onto the bed. He dipped his hand back into the water and rubbed his wet fingers over the scars and abrasions that lined his neck. The water was intoxicating and he plunged his hand back into the bath and scooped out more, splashing it wantonly around his neck. As he rubbed his neck feverishly, manically splashing warm and wonderful water over him, he felt his fingers catch on something around his throat.

He stopped rubbing and felt the little flap by the side of his neck. He thumbed it and teased it. It did not hurt. Rickman walked over to the dresser and looked into the mirror. A section of his neck was peeling. He gripped it with his thumb and forefinger and without feeling any pain at all he peeled away a layer of loose, dead skin and dropped it onto the dresser. He looked down at the wet sliver and prodded it. It did not feel like skin and it did not feel like it even belonged to him.

He looked back into the mirror and inspected the area he had peeled off. Instead of finding raw skin, he saw and felt a patch of tight, youthful and creamy skin. He rubbed the area around his neck. More skin flaked away.

His eyes grew in astonishment and confusion as he began to peel off the layer of scarring from his neck and throat. He gasped a laugh and turned back to the bath, throwing more water over his neck and stripping back the old, painful scarring until his neck was as it used to be: clean, slender and elegant. He rubbed his neck and his eyes welled up. Rickman went back to the dresser and with a few heavy pushes he managed to move it in front of the door, blocking it completely. He turned to the bath and dug deep to find reason in the madness. He found it now. He stepped towards it.

———∞∞∞———

Conrad's dreamscape was identical to his waking world. He was lying on the bed in the house and Maria was not by his side. The air was cool and the curtains were drawn. The only thing that convinced him that he was indeed dreaming was the fact that his hand did not hurt and he was not rubbing it. He sat up in the bed and opened the curtains. As before, the night was in and the mist was thick. He reached out and touched the glass, drawing his finger over the pane but leaving no mark.

Slowly, he turned and placed his feet on the floorboards, finding them to be warm. He looked over to the wardrobe, closed and innocuous. He stood up and opened it.

There was the poncho and the hat. He reached in, feeling compelled to do so, but did not search for the spectre of Liza. Instead, Conrad unhooked The Devil's poncho and hat from their holdings and put them on. He stood and looked at himself in the mirror, finally knowing exactly who lived in that house, who rocked in the other chair and who played the guitar. He knew who loved Maria and who Maria loved back with all her soul: The Devil.

He titled his head, examining the fall of the poncho and the angle of the hat's rim which dipped low over the brow to cast a shadow over the wearer's eyes. Both hat and poncho were a perfect fit.

"Am I The Devil?" he whispered, in a vague rhetorical tone. He shrugged and walked slowly out of the room, stopping in the hallway and turning to the window at the far end where the axe lay.

He walked towards it, inspected the weight and feel of the handle. It felt right. It felt like his. He stood back up and looked out of the window. There, surrounding the house, barely visible by the treeline, stood the waiting dead. From Quick Bill Reddings to Old Man Tobias and every man, woman and child in between. Even Liza, clutching her belly with blood running down her legs stood out there, no longer apart from the great army of souls that waited. Conrad set the axe down and lifted his hand, hailing them. In unison they waved their hands.

"Am I coming home to you, brothers and sisters?" he whispered. They nodded and a choir of whispers appeared in his heart.

"You are coming home. We are waiting for you brother."

Conrad turned away from the window, walked down the hallway and began to slowly descend the staircase.

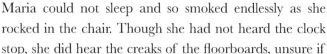

Maria could not sleep and so smoked endlessly as she rocked in the chair. Though she had not heard the clock stop, she did hear the creaks of the floorboards, unsure if it were a spirit or Conrad, now awake. She stopped rocking and sat forward, fixing her eyes on the door. The stairs creaked and she counted them, tracking the movement of the unknown.

Her eyes followed along the wall as whatever was walking passed by on the other side. She gasped in shock when Conrad, eyes closed in a deep sleepwalk, stepped into the doorway dressed as The Devil. He did not turn to face her, but stopped dead in his tracks facing the front door. The cold air returned to Maria's lungs and the fear rose up inside her once more. She stepped forward to Conrad, unsure of who in fact was dreaming. She reached out and touched him. He turned to her, eyes still closed, and smiled.

"They are outside. They are waiting for me."

Maria had to see. She was compelled to do so. Maria opened the front door and jumped back in shock. Azazel was standing on the porch, eyes yellow and staring straight at her. Maria closed the door and turned back to Conrad.

"They are waiting for me, Liza."

Maria stepped forward and slapped Conrad hard in the face. His eyes snapped open, a storm of confusion welling behind them. He had been pulled in two different directions too quickly and he fell to the side, grabbing the doorframe. Maria stepped forward and helped him back onto his feet. His sense of normality returned and he scratched his head.

"What happened?"

He looked down at the clothes he was wearing and, as if discovering he was covered in scorpions, frantically pulled them off and threw them on the floor. Maria held him tight as he sank down to his knees crying in bewilderment.

———⊷∞⊶———

Rickman Chill rolled up his sleeve and splashed the warm bath water over his arm. The self-inflicted scarring, his tally of every soul he had claimed in pursuit of The Devil, peeled away, the flakes falling onto the water and spinning on the surface like translucent petals.

Rickman began to cry in relief at the absolving bath. He took complete leave of his senses and removed his shirt and dropped it to the floor, revealing a lattice of grimy rags tightly bound around his torso. He undid his gunbelt and let it fall to the floor. Then his belt and his trousers, revealing a large, blood stained and filthy rag tied around his waist and between his legs like a makeshift diaper.

He looked into the water, the reflection of the rippling water stripping years of pain, exposure, fear, hate and anger from him and presenting his forgotten, beautiful face.

He unclipped the bandaging from his torso and unravelled it from the waist up. His belly was taut and deeply scarred, showing evidence of numerous burns, gunshots wounds and knife scars. He unravelled the bandage from his ribs and tight skin and then, finally, over a pair of horrifically scarred breasts.

Rickman stroked them, the dampness on his fingers smearing the scar tissue and revealing the pert youth of a previous life time. He dropped the bandages and next unclipped the filthy diaper, allowing it to fall to the floor. Rickman stood in the room completely naked.

Rickman exhaled and cast off the weight of her masculine persona. She smiled at the relief of her nakedness and the promise of the bath's powers; she slowly lifted her legs and stepped into the bath. She sank down into it, submerging herself completely and closing her eyes, felt the history of pain and degradation she had endured dissolve from her.

From the shadows of the room emerged The Nameless. He walked across the room, looked at the discarded articles on the floor. He sat on the edge of the tub and looked at the shape of the woman soaking under the water. He ran his fingers over the surface and smiled.

"Welcome home, Clara Sumner," he whispered.

CHAPTER FORTY

Dirty Tricks and Rope

The warm water rejuvenated Clara Sumner and as the scar tissue began to fade away, so too did the pain and rage she had carried for so long. The Nameless sat on the edge of the bath inspecting the woman, marvelling at her former beauty returning. Through the shimmering water he could see the scars of her legs fade away and the taut muscles disappear under a layer of shapely and healthy fat. Her stomach no longer appeared ravaged but plump, and the awful scarring around her breasts fell away, their womanly shape blossoming. She looked as she had done years before, when she was a happy woman with a bright future burning in her heart.

He smiled as he traced his fingers through the water and fantasised about the times of happiness and warmth she must have known before The Devil rode into her lands. He sighed to himself.

"It was another life, Clara, truly another life," and he plunged his hand into the bath and grabbed her throat. Clara's eyes sprung open in shock as The Nameless stood up, picking her clean out of the bath as if she was a rag in a washing bowl. He held her up by her throat in an unnatural display of strength.

Clara Sumner lurched back from her absolving dream and into reality. The Nameless' beady eye was close to her and she could smell his rancid breath upon her. His trick had worked; she was totally unguarded and unprepared. The vitriol and keenness she had known as Rickman Chill suddenly left her, and the vulnerability of Clara Sumner returned.

The Nameless squeezed her neck, making her eyes bulge. She reached up and, instead of clawing at his face as Rickman would have done, she feebly grabbed his wrists. He relaxed his grip just enough to let her breathe, but not enough for her to wriggle free, nor enough to dull the pain. He pulled her in closer to his beady eye, her feet still dangling from the ground.

"Clara Sumner, it really is you. What a woman you are!" and he threw her down face first onto the floor and pulled her arms over her back in an excruciating restraining hold. Clara screamed in pain as The Nameless knelt on her wrists and grabbed the belt from her trousers, tying it around her and securing her wrists. He stood up. Clara began to push herself along the floor, trying to get to her gun belt, the primal nature of Rickman Chill beginning to resurface.

The Nameless tutted and placed his boot under her ribs, rolling her over onto her back. Clara stared up at him, breathing angrily with a fierceness in her eyes that was at odds with her gentle features.

"I'm sorry about the bath and its trickery. It was most unfair to play so dirty… but you see, I had to know if it was really you, and there was only one way to know for certain. You understand, I'm sure."

The Nameless could see behind her eyes a battle of wills raging between the ferocity of Rickman Chill and the fearful fragility of Clara Sumner. He loomed over her, his beady eye inspecting her panicked expression.

"Have you really come all this way, only to die now?" lamented The Nameless. "Oh dear, that is so tragic."

"I'm going to eat your heart," croaked Clara in her twisted voice, the Rickman Chill within taking charge for a brief moment.

"I see your voice hasn't improved," tutted The Nameless. He bent down and picked her up, threw her over his shoulder and walked to the dresser, dumping her down in the chair. He stood behind her, holding her chin and her head up so that she could see herself in the mirror. Clara's eyes filled with tears. The bath had been an illusion. Her scarring remained. Rickman Chill was still there, but the fragility of Clara Sumner had now been uncovered.

"I feel I should apologise," The Nameless said as he looked over at her awful reflection. He ran his fingers over her neck and across the great scar The Devil had left when he had slit her throat.

"Maybe not for this," he said, running his hands down the remnants of her breasts and tracing them over the gruesome scars, "but for this? Now I really am sorry.

But you know, you were such an animal; I had to defend myself." He rested his head on her shoulder, their faces side by side.

"What a pair we make," he sighed.

Clara tried to struggle out of her bindings.

"Hey, hey, shush now," protested The Nameless, yanking Clara's hair back.

"Where is he?" she snarled.

"Who?"

"You know who."

"The Devil?" The Nameless smiled in disbelief. "Here you are, naked as the day you were born, only a little more... used... in a room with me, and still your concern is about another man. That hurts my feelings. I'm really quite offended. Still, we can't let a little thing like taking offence rule our actions can we, or what kind of world would that be? Come on then, let us do what must be done."

The Nameless stood up, still holding onto Clara's hair, and pulled her back off the chair. She winced in pain and tried to stand. The Nameless threw her to the floor and began to heave the dresser out of the way of the door.

"Truth be told, The Devil is nowhere... and everywhere. He doesn't come round here no more. He never returns to nowhere."

The dresser was finally moved clear of the door. The Nameless unlocked it and bent down to Clara. He stroked her cheek. She struggled to avoid his touch.

"You've been chasing a ghost, my dear Clara," he sighed. "You've been tearing the world apart for so long that you have forgotten the reason you started all this hullabaloo in the first place. My dear, you have become… whatever it was you sought. Justice? Vengeance? The Devil?"

Namless looked at his nails, sighed and shrugged nonchalantly.

"Let me just say now that, finding you here and alive is really something special." The Nameless grabbed her hair, pulled her up and dragged her to the door.

Hobson had been watching the door to Rickman's room carefully since he had witnessed him enter. The dark shadow had swept around the room, unseen to all but him, and followed Rickman in. The wind had then died down and the chandeliers had stopped swaying.

Hobson had sat back down and returned to his drink, placing his pistol on the table and keeping his remaining eye on the door, all the time repeating "Rickman Chill must die, Rickman Chill must die," under his breath in an attempt to stave off the influence of Bel's treacherous air that caused one to forget. He remained focused. He wanted to remain sharp for the moment Rickman Chill emerged and was met by The Nameless and his men, wherever they may be.

He looked around the room, noting each man and woman who looked vaguely sensible, and postulated that they were all armed and under the thrall of Bel. He had no doubt that when Rickman made his move, one hundred guns would be revealed and the bastard would be cut down in a hail of bullets. When it eventually happened, Hobson wanted to be front and centre so that Rickman Chill could see the face of the man he had left for dead, the face of the man whose brother he had led to his death. "Rickman Chill must die," he continued, under his breath.

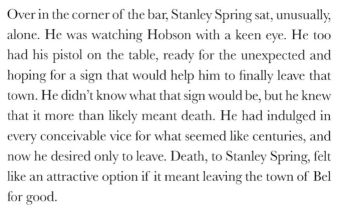

Over in the corner of the bar, Stanley Spring sat, unusually, alone. He was watching Hobson with a keen eye. He too had his pistol on the table, ready for the unexpected and hoping for a sign that would help him to finally leave that town. He didn't know what that sign would be, but he knew that it more than likely meant death. He had indulged in every conceivable vice for what seemed like centuries, and now he desired only to leave. Death, to Stanley Spring, felt like an attractive option if it meant leaving the town of Bel for good.

Hobson stood up the moment he saw the door to Rickman's room fly open. He grabbed his gun, certain that Rickman would storm out of the room, guns blazing and laying waste to everyone.

Upon seeing Hobson stand up and reach for his gun, Stanley Spring spat out the match he was chewing and stood up also. He looked over to Hobson who was staring up at the landing overhead. He saw Hobson's mouth drop open and his gun lower slightly. Stanley Spring stepped out from around the table, hurried across the saloon and sidled up to Hobson to see what had shocked him so. Upon looking up at the landing, Stanley Spring too lowered his pistol.

The Nameless strode across the landing dragging a struggling Rickman Chill by his hair. Only it was not Rickman Chill as Hobson knew him; it was a woman.

Hobson stepped forward towards the staircase, eyes wide, mouth open. The Nameless descended the staircase, Rickman tumbling down after him, his eyes wide with a mixture of fear and fury.

As they reached the bottom of the stairs, The Nameless turned to the door and marched towards it. Rickman was dragged passed a bewildered Hobson, locking eyes with him. Hobson mouthed a silent word. Rickman's eyes, though fierce and mad, offered Hobson the final truth to his identity.

The Nameless dragged him out of the saloon and as he did so the drinkers and whores stood up, as if in a sleepwalking reality, and slowly filtered out after them.

Hobson tried to catch Rickman's eye again as they disappeared behind the bodies. Hobson stood in the saloon, rocked to the core and utterly lost to the madness he had just seen. He turned around to see Stanley Spring standing at the back of the saloon looking at him.

A sudden understanding came over them, clear, bright and focused like a flaming arrow through the night. They nodded to each other. Hobson walked out of the front of the saloon, while Stanley stole out of the rear.

The dancers in Main Street had all halted the moment The Nameless had stepped out onto the boardwalk. They congregated together in the centre of the street and parted to form a gangway down which The Nameless dragged Clara.

As she was pulled, her heels scraping and tearing on the harsh ground, Clara looked up at the residents of Bel all looming over her with dead, expressionless eyes. She knew there was no use calling for help; they would not come to her aid. Nobody would. The further through the crowd she was dragged, the more she realised that she had failed in her mission. And not only failed, she had destroyed many lives along the way, torn up land and scorched the sky in her pursuit of the ghost.

The Nameless halted when he came to a large wooden platform. He threw Clara down onto the ground. She rolled over onto her side and looked up to see him smiling his twisted smile over her and behind him, swaying in the night breeze, a noose. It was time to go.

Hobson tried to push through the crowd, but they had massed too tightly. He could see up ahead the gallows that had seemingly appeared from nowhere. He pushed and shoved his way through the crowd until finally he got to a spot that granted him a view of the lynching that was about to commence.

Stanley Spring had skulked around the back of the saloon and come around its side so that he was behind the gallows. He ducked down behind a barrow and watched. He had a perfect view of the back of Clara as The Nameless, without a word, picked her up, put her on her feet and tied the noose around her neck.

Clara felt the rope pull tightly against her neck and tears filled her eyes as she knew that she was not only about to die and fail her mission, but she was about to do so naked, with her dark secret on display for all to see. Her shame was too much and the tears fell down her face.

Clara tilted her head and looked out at the blank expressionless crowd until she saw a single eye that shone with life. She saw Hobson Whitney looking at her, his hand over his mouth. In those final moments, she did not know if he was a figment of her imagination, or if he was real. It didn't matter to her. She looked at Hobson, the tears rolling down her face, over the rope around her neck and down her ravaged body. She mouthed, "I'm sorry."

The Nameless pulled down on the rope with great force, and Clara Sumner was hoisted five feet into the air, her eyes bulging and her legs twitching.

CHAPTER FORTY-ONE

Clara Sumner Through the Years

C lara Sumner swung in the breeze, desperately trying to cling onto life. As she swayed, her eyes fell upon the twisted and broken church spire at the far end of the street. Darkness fell over her and she drifted into memory.

The Preacher crawled across the floor towards the door of his church trying to get away from his assailant. His fingers, broken and bloodied, tried to grip the edge of the floorboards to pull him forward, but they were useless. The woman with the scar across her throat walked slowly beside the Preacher, her gun pointed at the back of his head. He gave up trying to crawl away and rolled onto his back, blood flowing from a wound on his temple.

"Give me a name," hissed the woman in a painful and wracked voice, holding her throat with one hand. Her hat hung low over her face, shrouding it in darkness. She placed a boot onto his chest and pressed down.

"God forgive me," he said, his eyes looking up to the ceiling.

"It's too late for that, Father," she said. "Where is The Devil? Where did he ride out to after you gave him sanctuary?"

The Preacher pointed feebly behind his head towards the door of the church.

"The Nameless… The Nameless. He rode with him… he knows."

The woman bent down to the Preacher, her face coming into the light. She was young, barely twenty, with fierce eyes.

"Rickman Chill," she said, "my name is Clara Sumner. Do you know who that is?"

Rickman Chill shook his head

"The Devil took my family. Gave me this." and she ran her finger across her angry scar. "Left me for dead. Forgot about me."

She stood up and cocked her gun, aiming it at his head.

"He was right to do one of those things. When you see The Devil in Hell… tell him I sent you."

Clara Sumner shot the Preacher through the temple and the air in the church turned to ice. Clara Sumner slumped onto the pew and covered her head in her hands. She sobbed. The Preacher was the first life she had taken on her path to The Devil.

She looked at him, no longer feeling hatred or rage, but instead pity for the body that lay on the floor, twisted and lifeless. She held her head in her hands and stamped her feet knowing that she had taken a life and had forsaken her soul. She could never now step off that path and would have to see everything through to the bitter end, no matter what. She stamped her foot on the floor and wiped her eyes, regaining some composure. She knelt beside the Preacher, removed his collar and started to unbutton his shirt.

Clara reached across the snow but her fingers could not quite touch the outstretched hand of Daniel. His arm was reaching and his head was craned towards her but his eyes were blank.

"Please," whispered Clara as her own life-force was slowly draining from her, "please reach out."

She dug into the snow and pushed herself along with one final heave until her hand touched his. She closed her eyes and prepared for her final journey.

But she did not die. The sun was setting when her eyes opened once more, a gentle layer of cold fog just above the snow. She flexed her fingers, feeling the cold flesh of Daniel's hand.

Slowly, she drew her hand back to her throat. It had miraculously stopped bleeding. She went to speak, but no words came out, only a painful crack. She rolled onto her back and looked up into the thick mist, fearing that she was in some awful netherworld. Only the cries of her baby drifting from the house told her that she was not in the afterlife yet. She tried to speak again. This time she managed to utter her son's name.

"Conrad."

Clara Sumner rolled onto her side and managed to get to her feet; she stumbled and staggered towards the house.

———❦———

Clara's eyes fell from the church spire and moved down to The Nameless' disfigured face staring back up at her, his beady eye seemingly ambivalent to his actions or her plight.

———❦———

Clara Sumner flew across the room and slammed into the dresser, falling back over it and landing in a heap upon the floor. She scrambled to her feet to face The Nameless who was rushing up on her, knife in one hand and a broken bottle in the other. He swung with the knife and Clara dodged to the side, grabbing a porcelain water jug from the dresser and hurled it at him. It shattered over his face, but did not stop him.

She grabbed his wrist as he swung the knife. He was strong and the knife came down again. Clara just managed to prevent the blade from sticking into her neck. She had to hold it with both hands as he was far, far stronger than she was.

With his other hand he repeatedly jabbed her in the side with the broken bottle, yet still she held onto his wrist, her fierce eyes locked on his. Summoning all her strength she managed to twist his wrist slightly, refocusing the blade towards her shoulder. The Nameless, surprised by her strength, headbutted her square in the nose, shattering it and sending her crashing to the floor, dizzy with tears and blood. He himself staggered backwards clutching his forehead; such was the force of the impact. Regaining his composure and seizing his moment, he kicked Clara square in the ribs and spun her onto her back; the blood from her eyes almost blinded her.

"Rickman Chill was my friend!" he spluttered, as he pinched his temple. "So I am a little annoyed about that."

He stepped over Clara and sat on her waist. "You have shown surprising spirit tracking me down. Finding your way all the way to Bel." He held the knife to her throat. "I want to help you find your man, I really do. If you want to kill The Devil, I can help you... but you won't like it... "

"Fuck you," croaked Clara, the dizziness spinning the room around her.

"Well, that's not likely. Well, not in a few moments anyway. After you killed the Preacher, you assumed his identity, and you did well to get this close to me... but to get close to *him*, you're gonna have to go deeper. It's a man's world, and only a man can get to him... no use just dressing up and pretending."

The Nameless ripped her shirt open. "Don't worry, Clara dear, you can always find another Preacher's outfit."

He traced the blade of his knife down to her breasts. "Like I said, Clara, no use pretending."

He dug the blade into her flesh and clamped his hand over her mouth to stifle her screams.

"No use pretending Clara – or should we now call you Rickman?"

Clara turned her head to the side, the pain overwhelming. Her eyes fixed upon the flame within the glass lamp that stood on the floor across from her. Her hand reached for it, a primal, mad change occurring deep within her.

It was night when Clara finally saw her destination. The little farm house in the clearing was two hundred yards away and the bedroom light was on. She halted the horse and looked around. Everything was calm and everything was still. There was no mist and no stars. The snow was fresh and crisp. Clara pulled her thick animal skin closely around her and looked down at her arms and to the sleeping baby she was holding tight.

"Con… " the pain in her throat was immense and the cold air burned her lungs. She put her hand to the bandage around her wound, damp from continual reopening. She held her throat tightly, easing the pain slightly.

"Conrad… I will come back for you. I promise. I promise."

She bent down and kissed her son before cantering up to the house. She dismounted a few yards away and slowly approached the door. She placed the baby, wrapped in a blanket, on the doorstep.

"When you are strong enough I will come back for you," she said, before knocking on the door and returning to her horse.

The door opened and the silhouette of a man appeared and looked down at the bundle. He picked Conrad up and looked out at the bleak landscape. He did not see the dark rider, hidden in the night. Obadiah closed the door and took the boy inside, thinking it a gift from God.

Clara Sumner kissed her son in her mind once more before finally discarding all sense of love, hope and kindness from her soul. She turned to ride out into the wilds of Montana to seek out The Devil and bring her vengeance down upon him.

Clara's gurgles had become less frequent and panicked, and her legs had stopped thrashing so wildly. Hobson looked at her, slowly dying in the night air, naked and exposed. There was no pity in the crowd and The Nameless looked at the spectacle with no sense of awe or disgust. It was in those moments when a great fog parted in Hobson's mind and the psyche reordered itself.

"I'm in hell," he whispered rhetorically. He knew that there was no hope of seeing Fraser on the other side, because he was already in the afterlife.

He looked up at Rickman swinging there and regarded her awful scars, and he understood the absolute degradation she had put her body through in order to reach her goal.

He understood his love for his brother, and as such he understood Rickman's love for his departed loved ones. He understood that he himself could never have endured so much. Not even for Fraser. He knew that Rickman Chill, or whoever he really was, could not die like that. Hobson drew his gun and aimed it at the hanging woman.

Stanley Spring knew what was coming next and prepared himself. He watched as the woman was hoisted up and dangled until her legs stopped twitching, but he knew she was not dead yet. Her hands were behind her back, still holding the belt that bound them tightly. Stanley knew that when those hands became limp, then the woman would have passed over.

Hobson's gunshot was louder than a cannon and the sound boomed around the street. The shot was true and the bullet passed through the taut rope, sending the woman crashing down to the platform where she immediately rolled off the back and landed on the dirt.

The gunshot startled the crowd and they scattered like sheep. Stanley Spring seized his moment and ran forward to the platform. He grabbed the woman by the ankle, dragging her on her back over the rough ground to the safety of the side alley.

Before Hobson could think to react, The Nameless drew, fired and sent Hobson Whitney truly into the afterlife.

Stanley Spring pulled the noose from Clara's neck, allowing the life to pour back into her and she spluttered frantically. Stanley Spring turned her over roughly and unfastened the belt binding her hands. Clara instantly grabbed her throat, coughing and spluttering back to life.

Stanley looked around the corner. The Nameless was facing them in the middle of the road, flanked by seven gunmen. Stanley leaned back against the wall and chuckled nervously to himself. He looked down at the woman, lying on her back,

He quickly took his coat off and threw it down to her. Clara grabbed it and got to her feet, throwing it on.

"Stanley Spring, ma'am."

"Clara Sumner," she said, offering her hand in thanks. Stanley looked at her hand and smiled.

"Maybe later, perhaps," he said jovially as the corner of the building was suddenly torn apart by a hail of bullets.

CHAPTER FORTY-TWO

Preparations

C onrad stood by the mantelpiece and looked at the carriage clock. It had frozen at ten-to-ten. He retrieved his pocket watch to see that it too had frozen at ten-to-ten. He wound it up fully, but when released, the hands did not move. He looked around the room. Everything was still. The fire was dying and the room was dark. The two rocking chairs sat opposite each other as they had always done.

Conrad knelt down and held his hand over the fire, feeling its warmth and concluding that he was entirely awake. He looked over his shoulder to the doorway, and saw the poncho and hat still piled on the floor where he had cast it off upon being revived from his sleepwalking nightmare. He turned to the window and looked out at the ridge, way in the distance.

The mist had risen and dissipated slightly, though he could not see the stars or the moon. He focused on the treeline, studying the environment. He could see the shadows, moving between the trees, amassing in the woodland. A cold fear began to rise inside him. He pressed himself against the wall and peered back through the window, his hand moving down his side to his pistol.

Maria came to the doorway and looked quizzically at him. He did not turn to her, but scooted down to look through the bottom panes of the window. Maria stepped into the room, her foot creaking on a floorboard. Conrad snapped to the side and drew his pistol. Maria gasped and froze. Conrad breathed out in relief and holstered his pistol before turning back to the window.

"They're coming for us," he whispered. Maria quietly stepped over to the window and pressed herself against the wall, peering out at the treeline. She saw nothing.

"It's them. They found us," Conrad said, pulling his pistol out and checking the chamber. He stood up and rested his back against the wall, assessing the options. He looked over to Maria to see her looking concerned and afraid. He smiled at her.

"Don't worry," he whispered. "I won't let those Bel bastards hurt our family." He stepped away from the window and moved towards the doorway. He stopped and turned to her. "Come on, we have to get ready. They'll come and we need to be ready." He left the doorway and went to the kitchen.

Maria looked back out of the window to see nothing but trees and darkness. She hung her head in despondency at the realisation that Conrad's senses had left him. She fished in her pocket and pulled out the note Rickman had left him. She read it once more before scrunching it up and throwing it onto the fire, the embers catching the paper's edges and burning it slowly. The orange flame centred in the paper and illuminated the room, casting a shadow next to Maria. She regarded its shape but found no recognisable form within it, as she so often had done. Maria, like Conrad, looked at the clock to see it stuck at ten-to-ten. Her shadow friends had abandoned her, and now, so it seemed, had time itself. She left the living room to join Conrad in the kitchen, trying to hide her growing sense of dread that they were alone in the world and that Conrad was not fully beside her.

"Help me with the table," he said, standing at one end and holding its edges. Maria looked fearfully at him, trying to locate Conrad behind his vacant eyes. "There's not much time, my love."

Maria picked up the edge of the table and together they backed out of the kitchen, along the corridor and into the side room.

"Fetch me the axe," he said as they rested the table down. Maria backed out of the room, picking up Annabel's cot that was in the corner as she did so.

"My love," said Conrad firmly, "fetch me the axe. We need to block the windows up! Hurry!"

Maria left the room and rushed up the staircase and into her bedroom where she placed Annabel's little cot on her bed. The child was sleeping peacefully. Maria was lost in confusion. Had Conrad lost his mind completely?

She looked out of the bedroom window expecting to see nothing but trees and darkness. Suddenly, in the gloomy woodland, she caught sight of a shadow moving in a way that she had not seen before. It moved between two trunks, as if a man had walked passed. She pressed herself up against the window and looked harder. The shadow moved again. Maria rested her hand over her mouth. Conrad had not lost his mind. People were out there. She felt relieved to know that he was with her, but also fearful to know that some unknown men were upon them.

"The axe, my love!" shouted Conrad from downstairs.

Maria snapped out of her shock at seeing the encroaching enemy, rushed off the bed and left the bedroom, leaving Annabel unattended on the bed. She did not see the hobo spider making its way across the wooden bed frame.

Maria rushed along the upstairs landing, keeping her back against the wall until she reached the far end. She chanced another look out of the front, upstairs window. She saw a second shadow, just by the treeline, moving slowly and purposefully. Was it a man, kneeling down to take position and dig in? She grabbed the axe that rested against the wall beside the window and hurried downstairs as fast but as quietly as she could.

Maria entered the side room to see Conrad knelt down by the window, staring out. She handed him the axe. He took it with one hand and, with the other, handed her his pistol.

"Take this, keep watch."

Maria took the heavy gun in both hands and stood by the window, looking out at the shadows which were now amassing in greater numbers.

Conrad held the axe up to the table and nodded to the count of three. On three, he stepped out in front of the window, in full view and firing line, and swung the axe down onto the kitchen table, splintering it half way down the centre. He pulled the axe out and stepped back out of view.

Maria breathed out in relief and kept her gun on the shadows once more. After another count to three, Conrad stepped out again and swung the axe down in a hurried, but powerful blow, cleaving the kitchen table in two, straight down the grain. The two halves of the table fell on top of each other with a great crack.

Conrad tossed the axe to the side of the room and took his pistol back from Maria. Together, they upended one half of the table and rested it against the window, before grabbing the second section and taking it to the living room. As they passed through the hallway, Maria kicked The Devil's poncho and hat aside and kept her eyes on Conrad's. They saw in each other the same fear, yet the same conviction to stay together and survive the oncoming siege. They swung the table up over the window and repaired to the kitchen.

Once inside, Conrad closed the kitchen door behind them and, with two almighty kicks, managed to knock it clean off its hinges, sending it battering down the hallway and skidding along the floor, pushing the poncho and hat up against the front door. Maria and Conrad hurried to retrieve it. They picked up the door and carried it back into the kitchen where, with much effort, they managed to lift it up onto the counter and slide it behind the sink, blocking the kitchen window. Conrad then took a chair and wedged it under the handle to the rear door, jamming it closed. The only way in now was the front door. They stood with their backs to the sink staring down the corridor towards it.

"When they come, if we can't hold them in the front rooms, we'll retreat back into the kitchen," he said firmly. "They will be forced through the narrow door and down the hallway. At best they will be only able to come two abreast."

He grabbed her hand and pulled her towards the doorway, positioning her on one side while he took the other. He handed her one of his guns.

"We'll take a knee, lean our shoulders into the wall and fire, and fire, and fire. The bodies will pile up and it will be harder for them to get to us. Understand?"

Maria nodded.

"We won't go backwards from this point. We will move forwards, using their bodies as cover, pushing them back out of the house. Understand?"

Maria nodded. She looked back down the hallway, imagining the onslaught of attackers. Conrad sensed her fear and reached across to put his hand on her knee.

"It's going to be noisy, and there is going to be smoke and madness. You will be scared. I will be scared too. Just look over to me and you'll be alright."

Maria looked at him and smiled. She placed her hand on his.

"It's going to be alright," whispered Conrad, "I'm not going to leave you. We'll stand and protect each other. Won't we?"

Maria's confidence grew and she felt strong and alive.

"Remember," he whispered, "there is nothing so dangerous as lovers."

Maria's smile dropped suddenly and her hand left his. She tossed the pistol down, and rushed out of the kitchen and up the stairs. Conrad followed her.

Maria entered the bedroom and picked up Annabel's cot. Conrad entered the room and went over to the bed.

"Good idea," he said. He grabbed the bed posts and dragged the bed to the side wall, creating a space underneath the window where he could kneel and look out.

The shadows remained at the treeline. He looked up at the sky and still could not see any stars. Maria held the cot in the crook of her arm and brushed Annabel's face with her finger. The baby did not move, but breathed slowly, lost in her sweet dream world.

Conrad looked from the window and up to his lover, cradling the cot in her arm.

"We will need to hide her," he said. Maria looked at him.

"She can't be in your arms when the time comes. It will be too dangerous. We have to hide her."

Conrad stood up and walked over to them, forgetting momentarily that he was standing in plain view in the window. He bent over the cot and kissed Annabel before looking around the room.

"In here" he said, opening the cupboard door. "Trust me my love, she will be safe."

Maria kissed Annabel and laid the cot into the dark cupboard, and pushed it to the back until it struck against an object. A moonbeam broke through the mist outside and found its way into the room. It glinted off the nickel plated rifle resting at the back of the cupboard. Conrad grabbed the gun and pulled it from the cupboard.

"This will come in useful!" he smiled, running his hand over the stock. He reached into the cupboard and felt around for a box of shells. He found them in the corner and pulled them out.

"Perfect," he said. He handed the box to Maria. "Empty the shells into your little pocket my love," he said. Maria complied with his wishes.

"You will be in charge of the shells, understand? When I run out, I will call out to you and you will hand me one at a time. Understand?"

Maria nodded. "Good. It also means that you will have to be close by my side so that you can hand me them. Do you think you can do that?"

Maria smiled and nodded.

"I thought so." He cocked the rifle, "Alright, let's go downstairs and wait for the bastards."

Conrad kissed Maria on the cheek before bending down to push Annabel's cot into the very corner of the cupboard. He closed the door. The two lovers left the baby and the room and went downstairs to await the battle, unaware that the intrusion of Annabel's cot into the dark recesses of the cupboard had disturbed a small nest of hobo spiders.

TEGENARIA AGRESTIS
'The Aggressive Hobo Spider'

CHAPTER FORTY-THREE
Escape

S tanley Spring instinctively bent over Clara, protecting her from the shower of debris. Clara pushed him off, sending him sprawling across the floor and taking his place against the wall. She counted to three and peeked around the corner and back in a flash, taking in her surroundings in the briefest of moments.

The Nameless and his men were spreading out across the street, some moving to the boardwalk on the other side of the street, others stepping onto the boardwalk on Clara's' side. She looked down at Stanley, trying to collect her thoughts and assess her situation.

"Ma'am, this way," whispered Stanley, motioning for her to follow him around the back streets. Clara shook her head.

"What do you mean, 'No' – ma'am let's go."

Clara held out her hand and clicked her fingers. Stanley hung his head and handed her a pistol. Clara checked the chamber. It was fully loaded. She closed her eyes and counted to three. On three, she spun around the corner and fired four shots in quick succession. One flew along the side of the boardwalk and struck an advancing man in the throat; he slumped down in a heap, the arcing jet of blood spraying up the wooden wall and across the floor. The other three bullets went across to the opposite side of the street and connected with three men, advancing around to flank Clara's position. The men fell to the ground, dead.

Stanley got to his feet and peered out. There were still men advancing, but now they were crouching low and looking for cover. The Nameless was nowhere to be seen.

Clara reached into Stanley's belt, retrieved four more shells and reloaded.

"How did you… ," he began, flustered and amazed.

"Four of them didn't fire before. They were the best shots. Waiting for a better target."

She cocked the gun and peered out again. A hail of bullets crashed into the wall. Clara dived onto the floor and rolled to cover behind a barrel. Stanley Spring fell onto his back as debris fell all around.

Clara had been right. Though the bullets had flown, they were shot wildly. Stanley drew his other pistol, held his breath and dashed over to the barrel Clara was hiding behind.

Their cover was semi-exposed on the edge of the boardwalk. From there they could see straight down the wooden boardwalk, and out across the dusty street. Clara leaned on her side and fired another three shots. Only two found their targets and one ricocheted off a post.

"Dammit!" she cursed as she sat back up. Stanley, invigorated by Clara's skill and tenacity, stood up and fired his entire chamber at nothing. He did not duck down quickly enough, and a fast drawing gunman fired from the far end of the street. A single bullet whistled along the street and slammed into Stanley's gut, knocking him onto his back.

Clara grabbed his ankle and dragged him back under cover behind the barrels, propping him up. Stanley gasped, struggling to pull air into his lungs.

"Ma'am, we ain't getting out of this one," he winced.

"Not with shooting like that, no."

The men on the other side of the street slunk along, hidden in the shadows and ducking behind cover until they had a perfect firing line on the barrels.

Clara looked into the gloom, fixing her attention on the hanging Chinese lanterns swinging underneath the covered boardwalk. She looked back to the lantern swinging over her head on her side of the street. The lanterns lined the boardwalk and also crossed over the street in a golden lattice formation.

"Ma'am?" said Stanley. "You starting to think coming here for The Devil was a mistake?"

"A little bit," said Clara, peeking out and seeing the gunmen move in, their numbers seemingly increasing.

"Where is The Nameless?" she asked herself. "Show yourself, you bastard."

Stanley feebly patted her knee.

"A ghost… The Nameless is a ghost… you can't catch him ma'am and The Devil don't come round here. I know him."

Clara fired a few shots across the street, slamming the bullets into some windows and showering the enemy with shards of glass, forcing them to duck down for cover. She'd bought some time and bent down over Stanley, grabbing him by the lapels.

"What do you mean?" she hissed, her rage overcoming her.

"Devil never goes back… 'cept to her."

Clara looked confused. "Who?"

"His woman… he only goes back to his woman."

"What woman?"

Clara turned out from her cover and fired more shots down the boardwalk to buy more time. She turned back to Stanley. His eyes were closed and he had slumped to the side. Clara did not have time to waste. She jammed her thumb into Stanley's bullet hole, twisting it around. He lurched back into life and grabbed her hand, trying to pull it out. Clara was far stronger.

"Who is the woman?" she hissed, her true 'Rickman' voice breaking through.

"Maria… lives in the woods… in a house. She don't ever speak, but he loves her."

Clara's eyes widened. Stanley looked at her.

"You want The Devil, that's where he'll be."

Clara pulled her thumb out of his gut, her mind a flux of confusion. She suddenly felt remarkably helpless, pinned in Bel, far, far from her mission and with her son abandoned in The Devil's lair.

"I gotta go, I gotta go, I gotta go," she started saying over and over, quietly to thin air. Her panic was overcoming her.

"Only one way outta here ma'am," said Stanley, "and I'm halfway there."

Clara hit her head against the barrel in despair.

"I gotta go, I gotta get to my son, gotta come back to my boy. I promised him! I promised I would come back."

Stanley looked at the desperate gunslinger, huddled against the barrel, her legs tucked in and naked, save for his large trench coat around her.

"Ma'am," he wheezed, "where are your guns?"

Clara looked at him. "In my room," she said vacantly.

"Second floor, five to the left?"

Clara nodded, understanding where Stanley Spring was headed.

"Well then," he said, pulling the hammer back on his pistol, "Let's send you on your way." And with that, Stanley Spring got to his feet and ran down the boardwalk, firing his pistol accurately and swiftly.

The men on his side of the street dived over their cover, off the boardwalk and onto the dusty street. Stanley staggered passed them, shooting them as they crawled across the dusty ground. He did not stop to reload, instead dropping his pistol and grabbing a dead man's gun to continue.

Clara stood up from behind the barrel and fired a single shot across the street, hitting the Chinese lantern and sending it crashing down onto a sandbag, the oil and flame licking over the wooden boards and canvas bags, igniting them.

She ran up onto the boardwalk, catching up with the staggering Stanley Spring as he made his way down the street towards the saloon door. The remaining gunslingers fired from their positions, raining glass and splinters over Stanley and Clara.

Stanley finally got to the saloon door and slumped down next to a barrel. Clara reached him and bent down to inspect his wound. He lifted his arm up and held out his hand.

"I'm leaving Bel in a moment," he said, smiling. "I wonder where I'll end up?"

Clara took his hand and went to offer her thanks. Stanley coughed and picked his gun up for one final burst of life.

"Second floor, five to the left," he said, before pushing Clara into the saloon and firing off more shots.

Clara rushed through the saloon as the windows detonated behind her, bullets flying over her as she dived to the floor. She scrambled to her feet, and dashed up the stairs and across the landing to her room as the gunmen finally overcame Stanley's position.

Clara barged through the door, slid across the floor and crashed into the bath. She grabbed her gunbelt and went to gather her clothes when four bullets ricocheted off the copper bath by her head. Clara dropped her clothes, dived over the bath and sought cover on its other side. She looked over the edge and saw no targets, yet still the bullets flew through the doorway and hit the bath.

Clara tried to order her thoughts, but the only words that entered her mind were those of Stanley Spring: "The Nameless is a ghost, you can't catch him, The Nameless is a ghost, you can't catch him."

Clara knew that she had to get out of there. She looked ahead to the window opposite the doorway. The bullets still thundered into the other side of the bathtub. Clara screamed to invigorate herself before getting to her feet, running to the window and diving through it, as she had done years before to escape the madness of Bel.

She landed on her shoulder and rolled onto her back, her guns trained on the window above. Nobody peered over the edge. The pain in her arm told her that she had been shot. She counted to three, got to her feet and staggered towards the edge of town, down the street behind the saloon, clutching her arm.

Up ahead, Clara saw the back street open out and the grassland appear. She was approaching the edge of the town and she could feel the cool air of the plains hitting her face. She imagined the treeline in the distance and her horse there waiting to take her back to Maria and to her son.

As the edge of the town approached, against her will she found herself slowing down. Her feet began to drag and her arm ached. More distressing than this was the fog that was clouding her mind. The edge of the town seemed to appear farther away and the mist on the grassland became thicker and began to approach the town.

Tiredness began to overcome her muscles, her head lolled and her eyelids grew heavy. She reached the end of the road, and her bare feet touched the grassland.

Clara turned back around and faced the dark side street, unsure why she was out in the night and starting to feel a strong need to return to the town.

Up ahead, in the distance, the silhouette of a man walked out into the street and stood facing her. Clara could not tell who it was, but she felt a deep sense of connection with him running through her veins. The silhouette remained motionless.

Clara felt the wind from the plain against the back of her neck, and the tips of the blades of grass brushing against the backs of her legs.

The silhouette began to walk towards her. Clara's tiredness was too much to bear and she felt her knees buckle slightly. She felt pulled in two directions, as if her soul was being vied for by powers beyond her control.

She took a step from the grassland and started to walk back down the street towards the silhouetted man. From behind the buildings, floating over the street, plumes of smoke began to form and the smell of burning wood filled her nostrils. The sky began to turn orange. Clara's feet slowed and the sting of remembrance spiked her memory. She stopped walking down the street and looked up at the smoke and the orange flames. The town was on fire. She looked around, like a child in wonder or an interloper in another's dream, suddenly aware that she did not belong.

She turned back to look at the grassland, sensing that something beyond the mist and darkness was calling her. Then, through the fog, a shape formed. Clara turned fully to see it. A glimmer of recognition entered her mind and a spark of memory fired.

A riderless horse trotted through the mist and stopped at the edge of the grassland, neighing to her. Clara remembered it and started to walk back towards the edge of town, her strength returning with every step. She reached the horse and mounted it, grabbing the reigns and sped off through the grassland.

Before she rode out of the town for the second time she turned back to see The Nameless standing in the dark side street, his town an inferno all around him.

Clara smiled, ran her hand over her scarred throat and pointed to him. The Nameless smiled in return, waved to her and walked back into the burning town.

Clara knew her vengeance on The Nameless would come, but she had to get to Conrad first. She spurred the horse hard and they galloped across the grassland disappearing into the mist, racing back to Maria's house.

CHAPTER FORTY-FOUR
The Confession

Maria and Conrad had stood guard by the boarded up windows for countless hours, perhaps even days. They had peered through the cracks and surveyed the shadows that never encroached, but never left. Their conviction did not wane and they were sure, unequivocally, that they were moments away from impending doom. If the clocks had been working, and if the sun had risen, they would have known that they had been awake, watching, for two days and two nights.

Conrad had stripped and cleaned one pistol, while Maria held the other to the gap between window and upturned table. Once he had cleaned one pistol, they would switch over. Occasionally, Conrad and Maria would walk around the downstairs of the house, checking the fortifications over and over again. She never left his side. They were inseparable: two mad lovers, under siege by unnamed assailants. They had the same conversations over and again, forgetting that they had done so. Conrad would explain the idea of rationing their food supplies and what they would eat and when, and Maria nodded in understanding. In the two days and two nights that they had continued this routine, they did not eat or drink once, their hunger and thirst seemingly purged from their bodies. Their minds were lost.

⚮

The only change in their routine happened in the darkest part of the third night. Conrad was kneeling by the window in the side room and Maria was knelt by his side, holding a pistol in one hand, and fondling her pouch of shotgun shells with the other. Their eyes were wild and bloodshot from the sleep deprivation and their senses were heightened.

Azazel, unaffected by the perpetual night and not sleep deprived like the lovers, had grown tired of wandering around the compound and, sensing a great deal of unease from within the house, had decided to investigate.

Neither Maria nor Conrad saw the goat bite and kick at his tether and hitching post, even though he was in plain sight. Their eyes were locked on the treeline, and they were concentrated on divining menace and movement in the dark recesses of the woodland.

The animal bucked and thrashed until finally he was free. He walked around from the fence over to the porch and stopped, staring at the doorway. He huffed and stamped his hooves, assessing the house that suddenly seemed filled with dread and danger. He stepped up onto the porch.

The sound of the goat's hoof stamp snapped Maria and Conrad out of their dreamlike states.

"They are coming," whispered Conrad, cocking his gun. Maria looked out to see a shadow moving along the porch; she too readied her gun.

The goat's steps were loud and foreboding. Conrad looked out at the trees, trying to locate the sound. He could not. Maria, however, was struck with the primal sense of immediate and close danger. She turned her attention from the window and looked to the doorway of the side room. She heard the front door creak open. Conrad too became aware of the intrusion. They both turned their guns to the doorway. Conrad stood up and Maria remained low by his legs. The clomping hooves entered the house.

Azazel's shadow filtered into the room looming like a horned man filling the air with menace. Conrad put his hand on Maria's shoulder and Maria laid her spare hand on his leg. They could sense each other's terror, but they were together and so found some conjoined strength.

The goat appeared in the doorway. Conrad and Maria both saw a gunman. Conrad screamed and fired a bullet. Maria, in reaction to the scream and the noise of the gunshot, fired too. Conrad, believing himself to be shooting at a man, sent his bullet through the hallway and into the wall at the far end of the living room opposite. Maria's bullet, fired from a low position, found its target. The smoke cleared and silence returned. Nobody spoke. Nobody screamed.

Conrad and Maria both cautiously stepped forward to inspect their joint kill. They saw a man on the floor, stone dead. They sighed in relief and Conrad stepped over him to slam the front door shut.

Azazel lay in the hallway, a bullet hole in the centre of his forehead from Maria's gun, his eyes wide and dead.

Conrad stepped back into the room and Maria grabbed him, pinning him up against the wall and kissing him ferociously, utterly lost to the power of taking a life and to the immense and undeniable needs of sudden lust that it inspired. She felt feral. Conrad too, imbued with the power that desperate lust incites when one is faced with impending death, needed to feel her. Their barriers came crashing down and they tore through each other's clothes, desperate to find each other's bodies and remind their souls that they were alive and what exactly that meant.

As they fell to the floor, pulling at dresses, shirts and trousers, Azazel's corpse looked on, the faintest glint of malice present in the beast's glazed eyes.

Clara had not stopped riding since Bel. She had dressed her gunshot wound by leaning back over the horse, pulling a rag from the saddlebag and tying it around her arm as the horse carried her. She did not eat and she did not drink. The horse, by extension of its rider's intent, did not do so either. They tore through the woodland and over the plains through the eternal night and mist.

Clara thought not of The Nameless and her unfulfilled revenge upon him, deeming it secondary to cutting down

The Devil. As she rode, she galvanised just what it was that had set her on her rampage in the first place: the death of Daniel Sumner and the mutilation of her own body. The Devil had intended them to both die in the snow, therefore leaving Conrad alone to die under the bed in his cot. She recalled how, as he threw back the blankets of the bed to discover the mother and son cowering under it twenty one years before, he had held her up by the throat; while he dragged his knife over her neck, his eyes were always on the child.

The Nameless, despite his evil actions upon her body, was nothing compared to what The Devil had done to her, and that was why he was secondary. '*The Nameless for the flesh*,' she thought while she rode, '*The Devil for the soul.*'

With every stride of the horse and every pound of her heart she recalled each and every action she had undertaken in her journey, from leaving Conrad with the good people who had raised him to the moment she truly did come back for him, which was soon to come about. She did not spare a thought for Maria and what was to become of her.

Maria straddled Conrad and drove her hips onto him, receiving him deep within her. The connection was complete and they were conjoined in flesh and mind. The dangers outside dissipated along with the fog, and the intense focus of their delirious pleasure took control of their instincts. Maria bit her lip so hard it bled, and she dug her nails into Conrad's chest. He in turn dragged his hands into her back and pulled her down upon him with increased vigour.

Soon they both reached the edge and neither had the restraint to stop. They leapt and climaxed together in waves of sea-changing power. Maria arched her back and opened her mouth to scream in relief, but the sensation overcame her and no sound came out. Conrad gritted his teeth and convulsed as he exploded. Maria slumped down over him, both breathing hard, and dizzy from the freefall of pleasure.

She rolled off him and lay on her back by his side, their eyes fixed on the ceiling, both trying to regulate their breathing.

As they did so, the madness that had befallen them over the last few days slowly fell away, and as if waking from a dream they began to come to their senses. They did not move, nor look around the room, but instead tried to reconcile their thoughts with their actions. Finally Conrad spoke in a tone that almost seemed rhetorical.

"You're not Liza", he said.

Maria, without looking at him, lifted her arm, heavy from the exertion she had endured in their madness, and rested it on his thigh.

"Liza is dead... I killed her."

Maria furrowed her brow slightly and turned to look at him. She noticed out of the corner of her eye that he was absentmindedly rubbing his hand.

"I met her and we were lovers," he said to the air. "I loved her so much. So much. I left Rickman to be with her. I told him that I loved her and that we were to be together."

A faint tremor of dread began to seep through Maria's skin.

"I stepped away from the path to be with her. And we were happy. She loved me. But being away from Rickman, it was hard, so hard. I felt torn all the time. Torn in two."

The dread seeped further into Maria.

"Torn in two... I should have been with him. He took me from my bullshit life and showed me the path of light..."

Maria slowly lifted her hand from Conrad's thigh.

"... and I abandoned him for Liza. I started drinking and I fell fast to the demon drink. I lost myself and lost sight. Then she told me one day that she was pregnant."

Maria could see Conrad rubbing the knuckle of his left hand and the dread seeped all the way through her skin to attack her stomach, causing a nausea to rise.

"... I came home... " his voice wavered slightly, the pain of confession almost too much... "I had been drinking for days, maybe weeks... I don't know... .I was so torn. She told me that she was pregnant and I knew I was trapped. That I would never ride with Rickman to find The Devil... I knew I would be with Liza forever... and suddenly, a calmness washed over me and I struck her in the belly. It was so clear. I was sober."

Maria's eyes glazed over as the horror of Conrad's words filtered into her mind. Her mind only said back to her, *'You've known all along, you've known all along.'*

"She miscarried," he said in an awful matter-of-fact way. "I found her sitting against the floor of our house, legs apart and blood everywhere. I remember looking at her and feeling… ." his voice broke, "relieved."

Maria cupped her mouth to prevent herself being sick, her horror almost complete.

"… Three days later she hung herself. Rickman was right, I do kill babies."

A cold realisation hit Maria like an express train. The clock in the living room began ticking. Time returned to the world and Maria knew that she had been lost to madness for more than just a few hours.

Conrad stopped rubbing his hand, turned to Maria and took hers in his, holding them tightly.

"That's why I said 'Liza' when I first saw you in the doorway, lying on the floor. You're my redemption. You're why I am reborn. You are my love."

Maria tried to speak but no words came out. She was stricken with terror. Conrad smiled and his eyes were bright, seemingly weightless after his confession.

"You're my redemption. You're my love. When I saw you there, on the floor and with a baby."

The baby. Maria's stomach turned. Annabel. Conrad smiled again and turned back to stare at the ceiling, feeling wondrously relieved and blissful in his new heaven. He closed his eyes for a second and sighed; the dead were no longer waiting for him.

Maria felt numb. She sat up and saw the body of Azazel on the floor, blood trickling from his forehead. His tongue was lolling over his mouth, causing his jaw to twist. It looked like he was grinning.

Maria had no control over her body. She stood up as if sleepwalking as Conrad had done, days, months or years before, and stepped over the dead goat. She did not turn to look back at Conrad. She stepped into the hallway and looked down at her lover's crumpled poncho and hat by the doorway. She bent down and picked them up. Mechanically she put the poncho on and placed the hat on her head.

She turned from the door and walked to the staircase, the floorboards creaking under her bare feet but she could not hear the sound, nor feel the cold wood upon her skin. Her body was walking to its death, but her soul had already gone.

Conrad opened his eyes and turned his head to see that Maria had gone. He looked down at his semi-naked state and smiled to himself, pulling his trousers on and buckling them. He stood up and went to remove the barricade from the window, sighing at the madness that had overcome them in thinking that they were under siege. He moved the table aside and looked out. There was a rider on the ridge. Waiting.

Conrad ducked down and grabbed his gun. The danger was real. He cocked it and smashed a pane of glass out with the barrel.

The smash of glass alerted Clara. She had halted the horse on the ridge to scan the environment. The house in the compound ahead was different to how she had left it. The window in the living room was boarded up and the goat was nowhere to be seen.

She pulled out her guns and wrapped Stanley Spring's trenchcoat around her. She dismounted her horse and led him into the woodland, where they merged with the shadows intending to use them as cover get closer to the house.

Maria reached the top of the stairs and went into the bedroom. A moonbeam broke through the mist and illuminated the wardrobe. She opened the door, bent down and reached for the edge of Annabel's cot.

A baby hobo spider crawled up her arm but she did not feel it. She pulled the cot into view and stood up. Whatever part of 'Maria' that still lived in her head and heart blew into the night sky. She was empty inside. Maria did not cry or scream. She just looked down at the little body in the cot, hobo spiders crawling all over it. Annabel had been completely forgotten by her mother and protector during the days of delirium. The nest of spiders, however, had not fallen prey to the madness of the oppressive, dark mist. Annabel had disturbed their home and, as instructed by their proud mother, the baby spiders had swarmed over her, biting her soft pink flesh and filling her with their poison. And so, poor Annabel had died, alone, in the dark and far, far from her mother.

Maria turned from the wardrobe and walked out of the bedroom.

CHAPTER FORTY-FIVE
The Two Mothers

Conrad looked at the floor beside him. Maria was not there. Instead, in her place lay Leviathan and his second pistol. He looked out at the treeline and saw the shadow by the ridgeway moving. He cocked his gun and readied himself. He planned to fire his rifle, perhaps draw the attacker out into the open, then press upon him with the pistols, making short work of him.

He whispered as loudly as he could to Maria but she did not answer. He contemplated leaving his post to find her, but the shadow moving in the trees told him to stay where he was.

He reached down for the rifle and kept his fingers on the stock, ready to grab it fully should he need to. A solitary hobo spider walked along the gun, across the stock and up his arm, disappearing under the sleeve of his coat. He did not notice.

Clara looked at each window of the house, assessing the danger. It was barricaded and dark. She knew that it had been prepared for a siege and therefore those inside would be on guard. Slowly she stepped out of the treeline, preparing to advance on the house with her hands in the air, hoping that she would be recognised by Conrad and Maria before they mistakenly opened fire.

She slowly made her way to the compound. Her hands left her sides and made their way above her head when, in the upstairs window, she saw the silhouette of The Devil. She knew the shape of the hat and the outline of the poncho as it had been branded on the inside of her eyes. The Devil had come home.

Clara screamed and gave way to her rush of panic and exhilaration; she drew her pistols and fired wildly on the house.

Conrad ducked down from the window as the muzzle flashes burst in the night. The bullets shattered the window and slammed through the wooden walls. Upstairs, in the hallway, Maria did not flinch as the shards and debris erupted around her.

Conrad, in the panic of the onslaught, abandoned his plan and grabbed the huge rifle first, stood up and fired through the empty window frame. Clara dived onto the floor as the buckshot whistled passed her. Conrad fired again and Clara felt her trench-coat flay as some of the pellets passed through. She rolled onto her side and fired again, the smoke mixing with the fog and obscuring her view totally.

Clara's bullets hit the wall to the side room just above Conrad's head, causing him to fall to the side. He kicked himself along the floor, through the side room and out into the hallway. He was lying on his side and facing the front door. He reached out and prepared to push it open to give himself a full view of the outside and, from his unexpectedly low vantage point, he hoped he would be able to gun down the enemy.

Maria slowly descended the staircase, her eyes blank, her hands by her sides. She could not smell the smoke. Conrad did not hear her walk down the hallway behind him and turn into the side room. He reached for the door, gently nudged it open, and took aim at the shape lying ahead, on the ground at the edge of the compound.

Clara cocked her gun as she saw the door open. She was about to fire when, out of the corner of her eye, she saw movement in the side room to the left of the house. The Devil was in the room. Clara turned her sights to the room and opened fire.

In the house, Conrad slammed the front door shut, assuming that his position had been spotted.

In the side room, the bullets missed Maria completely. She walked over to the corner of the room and looked down at the axe lying on the floor.

The smoke cleared and the dust settled. Conrad trusted that the enemy outside was reloading. He reached to open the door when a shadow was cast over him. He turned on his back to see the source. His face recoiled in horror and he raised his hands up instinctively.

Without expression on her face, Maria raised the axe above her head and swung it back down onto Conrad's chest, striking him across the shoulder.

He inhaled sharply in shock and panic. Maria, operating on a level of vacant automation, placed her foot on his ribs to help her pull the axe head out of his chest, as if she was pulling it out of a chopping block.

Conrad looked up, his vision blurring. He could not see the face of his killer, only the dark outline of The Devil.

Maria raised the axe again, Conrad's words floating through her soul: '*I kill children, I kill children.*'

She brought the axe down again on his belly. His legs buckled up and his body folded up around the axe-head. The suction caused by his organs around the axe head almost pulled the tool out of Maria's hands. She leaned into the handle, sliding her hands down towards the head to gain a stronger grip upon it, and yanked it out again. She raised the axe back up in one motion and brought it down upon him a third and final time.

Conrad saw the moonlight glint off the blade, throwing light up onto the face of The Devil. Before the blade cleaved his face in two, the last image he saw was of Maria, his love looking down upon him with eyes that did not blink.

Maria stepped on his chest once more, her foot sinking into the first strike wound, the muscle and flesh squelching through her toes. She pulled the axe up from his face. It had passed right through and wedged into the floor board. Half of Conrad's head slid slowly from the axe blade and slopped onto the floor. Maria dropped the axe on the floor and walked back upstairs. She entered the bedroom and

Maria & The Devil

removed the poncho and hat, opened the cupboard and neatly hung them back up.

Clara's breathing calmed. The firing had ceased and the smoke had cleared. She did not know if she had killed The Devil, and dared not believe she had. It was no time to lower her guard. Slowly, she got to her feet and approached the house.

Maria picked up Annabel's little cot and walked back out of the bedroom. She walked down the stairs, stepped over the body of Azazel and the remains of Conrad Sumner, and went into the living room. She placed the cot on the floor, picked up Annabel, held her close and sat in her rocking chair to look at the empty chair opposite, and the window next to it.

Clara stepped onto the porch and, as the floorboard creaked, the front door opened slowly of its own volition. She looked down at the porch floor to see a thick tide of glistening blood seep out from the house. Her eyes widened and she slowed her steps, bringing her gun up.

The door opened wider and Clara stopped dead in her tracks. The moonlight fell upon the gruesome remains of her son, Conrad, lying in pieces just inside the doorway.

Clara cupped her mouth, gripped the frame hard and screamed into her gloved hand, her eyes wild and lost in abject despair.

She tried to lift her pistol, but could not find the strength. She stood in the door, looking down at the remains of her son, and a strange accepting calmness came over her. She stepped into the house and picked up the axe.

Maria did not turn from staring at the empty chair opposite her to see Clara enter her house, naked save for a trench-coat.

Clara stepped into the living room, holding the axe with both hands at waist level. She looked at Maria and, recognising the lost look in her eyes to be the same as her own, looked down at the bundle in her arms.

Clara began to feel dizzy as the events and revelations of the last few moments compounded on her heart. She stepped into the room, the floorboard creaking under her bloodied foot, causing Maria to turn and look at her. Slowly, and still cradling Annabel's body, Maria stood up to face Clara. She looked over Clara's body, taking in the scars, ravages and abrasions that had almost obliterated any physical evidence of her femininity.

Clara looked at Annabel's body, puckered in tiny lesions from numerous spider bites. Clara blinked, slowly and lethargically, breathing out and letting the axe fall to her side.

"I should kill you," she whispered in her awful voice, "but I think we're already in hell."

Clara looked down at the axe in her hand, turned from Maria and stepped over the body of her son. She stopped at the front door and looked back at Maria for the last time.

"Bury him in a shallow grave," she said softly, "so that God has a chance to find him before The Devil knows he's dead."

Clara Sumner walked out of the house, taking the axe with her, and disappeared into the mist. Maria sat back down in the rocking chair and mouthed a silent lullaby to Annabel as she rocked back and forth, staring out into the darkness.

Six Months Later

CHAPTER FORTY-SIX

January

The front door creaked open and the walking skeleton stepped, painfully slowly, out onto the porch. Her skin was almost translucent and was pulled tightly over her bones. Her cotton dress hung from her like a sack.

She stood on the porch, her mouth open, eyes blinking slowly. She could barely feel the bitter winter air on her skin. She held onto the banister and stepped off the porch. Her bare foot sunk into the deep snow. She looked over to the treeline and began to walk slowly over towards it. She had walked barely six yards before her strength left her legs and she fell to the ground, half burying herself in the snow. The shock of the freezing ground revitalised her somewhat and she gasped in a large lungful of burning cold air.

Maria reached out and crawled across the snow to the trees. She passed the half buried body of Conrad Sumner, his arms and legs protruding from the shallow grave, blue and twisted. She did not stop to regard it, but carried on crawling towards the trees. The body of Azazel was buried next to Conrad's, the soil scraped aside by Maria's bare hands. The beast lay on his back, his hoofs straight up in the air.

Maria reached the trees and managed to sit upright in the snow, her feet already turning a sickly grey colour from the exposure. Her yellow teeth chattered painfully as she began to scramble around collecting up twigs and sticks that were lying on the ground. She bundled them into her arms and turned back to the house, walking slowly and steadily, her mind lost to the reality of the world, swimming deep and darkly down through her empty internal abyss.

Maria returned to the house and walked into the living room, where she slumped down by the fire and began to break the twigs into small pieces. The fire was barely large enough to warm her hands, let alone thaw her out. The room was in disarray.

Maria had rocked on the chair as Clara rode away, until the next morning when the sun began to rise and dispel the three days of night that had claimed Annabel, Conrad and dispelled the part of Maria that counted.

As soon as the sun broke over the treeline and shone into the house, Maria had awoken from her black dream to find that the nightmare of her mind was also the nightmare of her reality. Annabel was still was dead and Conrad still lay in pieces on the hallway floor.

The sunlight did more than just reveal her crime and Annabel's traggedy; the sunlight also highlighted a simple and dreadful fact. Clara had taken the axe. Maria, when she realised this, stopped rocking in her chair, the realisation washing over her in cold dread. The summer would soon be over and autumn would come and, after that, winter. Without the axe, Maria would not be able to chop wood and keep the fire going. She would not survive the weather. She was doomed to a slow and painful death.

Maria stopped rocking and decided to bury Conrad and Azazel. She walked into the warm sun, feeling its heat on her skin and knowing that she would not see another summer. She scraped the soil away at the side of the house with her bare hands before dragging the bodies out. She did this without feeling fear or regret. It had become a simple, irrefutable fact and she did not care. She did not feel anything. She just buried the dead and went about dying slowly herself.

That was six months ago and the end was approaching. She had barely any food left and could no longer differentiate between night and day, dream and reality. The routine of her life had become similar to the routine of her life what seemed like years before, when she was waiting for The Devil to return. She walked, when she could, from room to room and when she found the strength, she would wear his poncho and hat and pretend he was around. He no longer played the guitar, as Maria had burned it, and he no longer sat opposite her at the kitchen table as Maria had burned what she could of the remnants. Now, there was nothing left to burn.

She sat and broke the twigs and placed them on the fire, the popping and crackling failing to ignite properly. It was pathetic.

She looked around to her rocking chair and thought about smashing it into kindling, but there was no axe and the kitchen knife would be ineffectual. She picked up her twigs and sat in the chair. She looked to the side and into the wooden cot where Annabel's frozen skeleton rested. Maria felt nothing towards it, the numbness of the winter frost overpowering even her grief. She turned her head painfully to the side and looked at the window, the ridge visible in the distance and no rider upon it. There never was.

Maria's thin fingers began to grip and twist the twigs in her hand. She did not look to see what she was doing, her fingers bending and fashioning the twigs seemingly of their own volition.

The sun began to dip behind the treeline and, as it did, the shadows began to move across the ground and approach the house. The hues of the world began to merge and form in front of Maria and she felt her eyes become heavier than they ever had been before. She blinked three more times and, just as they closed on the third, she could have sworn she saw a figure on the ridge waiting for her.

Maria tried to smile and say, "I've waited for you so long, I've waited for you to come back to me, and here you are," but the words never came from her mouth. Her eyes closed and she stopped rocking in her chair.

CHAPTER FORTY-SEVEN
February

Cinereous halted on the ridge and looked down towards the house ahead. The horse neighed sadly and kicked at the ground, eager to move into the compound. The Devil sat upon him and looked at the environment, his icy blue eyes taking in every detail. He could see that the house was not as he had left it. He could see bullet holes in the wall, smashed windows and a strange mound to the left, by the barn.

He took his weathered riding hat off and let it hang around his neck, his three day stubble catching the bitter winter air and pinching his skin.

He patted Cinereous' neck, and slowly the horse walked down the ridge towards the house, stopping to let his master dismount when they came to the gate.

Both rider and horse knew that a great tragedy had befallen the house. The air in the clearing hung still and sad. He let go of Cinereous' reins and they walked side by side over to the mound, unsure just what was wrong.

The Devil stopped and drew his pistol when he managed to recognise a twisted human hand sticking up from the frozen soil, the fingers bony and blue. He and Cinereous walked cautiously over and he inspected the gruesome remains lying unceremoniously buried in a half-hearted grave.

Cinereous was unfazed by the sight until he walked around to the side of the mound and saw the body of Azazel, hooves still sticking up into the air. The horse neighed loudly and forlornly before lowering its head and nudging the dead animal with his muzzle.

The Devil looked over to the horse, sadness evident in his eyes. He looked back to the house, and began to walk over.

The Devil looked at the bullet holes in the wall to the side room, and he ran his gloved hand over the empty frame where the window had been. He looked inside the room and saw that it was empty. He walked along the porch to the front door, which swung gently in the breeze. He pushed it open with the barrel of his gun. An old, large bloodstain had seeped into the wood by the door.

He called out for his lover, but his heart told him that it was hopeless. He stepped into the hallway and turned to the living room. A great gust of wind blew through him and it seemed to sweep his soul away.

He stood in the doorway and looked at the blue body of Maria in the rocking chair, so emaciated that she almost fell through the slats in the back. She had been dead for weeks and her head was twisted to look out of the window towards the ridge. Her eyes were closed and a faint, melancholy smile had been frozen on her lips.

The Devil's eyes filled with tears. He looked around the room and saw the wooden cot, the paint flaking from its sides. Something in his dying heart told him not to look inside the box, but he could not resist. He stepped forward and looked in to see the tiny body of Annabel, the daughter he had never met. Tears rolled and he turned back to Maria. He held out his hand to touch her but could not bring himself to make contact. He looked at her lap. In her hands he saw a little doll, fashioned by her out of broken twigs and bracken and held close to her as if it were a child. He had no words to say. He did not see the new rider appear on the ridge and halt there.

Clara Sumner looked down at the house and saw the riderless horse standing by a mound. She looked at the house and understood what had occurred since she had left it seven months previously.

She looked to the door and saw a man leave the house. As soon as he stepped onto the porch he looked up and saw her. He did not wave or holler, but just stood there regarding her. From the edge of the barn, his horse turned and walked over to him. Together they began to walk out of the compound and up towards the ridge.

As The Devil approached he began to make out the rider. It was a woman, dressed in a white blouse and thick cotton dress, wrapped in a bearskin. Across her lap she held a shotgun that he knew to have once belonged to

The Nameless. As soon as he recognised that, he knew who had finally caught up with him. He smiled to himself and carried on walking.

After countless years of tracking, fighting, murdering and sacrificing, Clara finally came face to face with The Devil. There was no fear or anger, no pain or regret in her eyes.

The Devil mounted Cinereous and trotted the last few yards up to her. He stopped in front of her and smiled.

Clara Sumner looked The Devil in the eye and she did not blink. Clara Sumner did not blink.

THE END

ACKNOWLEDGEMENTS

With grateful and loving thanks to my family for
their encouragement and support. To my friends, in
particular Luke Searle, Craig Coole, Donatella Marena,
Chris Rolfe, Helena Caligari, the Tippler Crew and my
'Daily Person'. To that one teacher, mentor and friend
who set me right – Mr John B Peacock – and, finally,
with love and thanks to the legends of TheNeverPress:
Dave Hollander, Leighton Johns, Bryon Fear,
Sarah Nasar and Mauro Murgia.

I love all of you more than The Cure.

As a wee lad, Graham Thomas wanted to be a pilot, a butler, a film-maker and an author. The only one that really stuck with him was 'author'. So far it seems to have worked out well for him, creatively. He has a slate of 50-odd books queued up for the next decade or so, each one planned and developed and just waiting for the start date to roll around. After which, he intends to retire to the sun to live in a hacienda filled with animals and let the surrounding land do what she desires.

Alongside writing, Graham loves fancy drinks, cooking giant roasts, compiling lists of fictional band names and racehorses, the Prince Charles Cinema and The Cure.

About TheNeverPress

Based in South-East London, TheNeverPress is an independent publishing house specialising in magical realist fiction. Traditionally, our focus has been on producing strange and beguiling novels, short stories and poetry, but we're soon to take our independent spirit and taste for the askew into new territories as we produce graphic novels, audiobooks and children's picture books. We may be a small press at the moment, but that's fine – we're just going our own way.

Visit our socials to see what we're up to, and to check out our previous projects.

@TheNeverPress

www.theneverpress.com

Printed in Great Britain
by Amazon